Graphically Speaking

Graphically Speaking

An illustrated guide to the working language of design and printing

Mark Beach

ELK RIDGE PUBLISHING
PO BOX 633
MANZANITA OR 97130
Imprint of Coast to Coast Books, Inc.

Produced in collaboration with
Graphic Communications Association
Affiliate of Printing Industries of America, Inc.

Distributed to the trade by
North Light Books
1507 Dana Avenue
Cincinnati OH 45207

Library of Congress Cataloging-in-Publication data
Beach, Mark.
Graphically Speaking: an illustrated guide to the working language of design and printing / Mark Beach; Spanish indexing by Marcos and Shana Galindo. – 1st ed.
p.   cm.
Includes index.
ISBN 0-943381-07-X $29.50
1. Printing – Dictionaries – Spanish.
2. Graphic arts – Dictionaries – Spanish.
3. Spanish language – Dictionaries – English.

I. Graphically Speaking
Z118.B4 1992   92-13818
686.2 – dc20   CIP

Printed and bound in the USA using paper made in the USA.

This guide includes many trademarked names identified as 'brand name of....' The author and publisher used the names only for editorial purposes, for the benefit of the trademark owner, and without intent to infringe upon the trademark.

Contents

Acknowledgments

This book would not have happened without the expertise and energy of **Peter Brehm**, Vice President, Print Technologies, Graphic Communications Association. Peter's high standards of accuracy and thorough knowledge of the graphic arts improved my writing beyond measure. I cannot express how deeply I appreciate Peter's commitment nor how often his enthusiasm stimulated my efforts.

Kathleen Ryan and **Elizabeth Collins** add far more to my books than their roles of production manager and editor can reveal. Each brings to every project a sharp eye for detail and, more important, what every author needs most – unhesitating willingness to slash a red pencil through words that seem wrong or confusing.

Bob Shaw, Director of the Graphic Arts Program, Chemeketa Community College in Salem, Oregon, shared his wealth of experience and resources. Bob's good humor and keen sense of business as well as technology often helped me distinguish between the important and the trivial.

Seventeen additional industry experts thoroughly reviewed at least one version of the manuscript. Several reviewed two versions. All gave generously of their time and knowledge, often responding to my phone calls asking for further information. I deeply appreciate the help from **Susan Antal**, Printing consultant, Monroe CT; **Doug Carr**, Trade Litho, Portland OR; **Ken Coburn**, InterPrint, Petaluma CA; **Bryan Constable**, Printing consultant, Arlington VA; **Helene Eckstein**, Spectrum Color Center, Golden CO; **Stephen Haag**, Herlin Press, West Haven CT; **Bruce Lanzerotti**, Hoechst Celanese, Wood Dale IL; **Brian Lawler**, Desktop publishing consultant, San Luis Obispo CA; **Mike Lewis**, Liberty Engraving, Chicago IL; **George Leyda**, 3M Company, St Paul MN; **Charles Seelig**, The Sheridan Press, Hanover PA; **Stephen Terrillion**, *USA Today*, Arlington VA; **Richard Harth, William Rogers, Richard Velter,** and **Charles Young**, Toppan Printing, Clarke NJ; and **Jan White**, Graphic designer, Westport CT.

In addition to those listed previously, many other graphic arts professionals contributed their special expertise. They include Vince Bellini, Holly Derderian, Jack Derderian, Elizabeth Dirkx, Mark Fuller, Alan Kotok, Kathy O'Malley, Harry Przekop, Jr, Marilyn Riggs, William Riley, Bill Strub, William Voglesong, and Cindy Wiley.

The Spanish index required hundreds of hours of careful research and deliberation carried out by Marcos and Shana Galindo. Their painstaking efforts added immensely to this book. Marilyn Fleming proofread the index.

Finally, I wish to thank Graphic Arts Technical Foundation, Macbeth Company, Oregonian Publishing Company, Steve Seeger, and Meisel's ImageCenter for permission to use copyrighted material.

Production

Text by Mark Beach using Microsoft Word. Illustrations and cover by Steve Cowden using Aldus Freehand. Design and production by Kathleen Ryan using QuarkXPress and Aldus Freehand. Prepress by Trade Litho and L-Grafix, Portland OR. Further electronic prepress, printing and binding by Western Computer Press, Tigard OR.

Photography

Mark Beach, pages 81, 226, 232

Kristin Finnegan, pitcher, page 219

Alfred A Monner, farm, page 226

Jerry Robinson, page 162

Arnold Rustin, umbrellas, page 226

Kathleen Ryan, pages 60, 67, 72, 82, 156, 215, 218, 228, 233

Steve Seeger, page 75

About the author

Mark Beach is author of *Getting It Printed, Papers For Printing,* and *Editing Your Newsletter,* guides to design and production used throughout North America for corporate training and as college texts. He holds BS and PhD degrees from the University of Wisconsin in Madison.

Introduction

This book helps you communicate clearly with customers, vendors, and employees so you can produce printed pieces quickly, accurately, and at reasonable cost. Definitions represent a wide range of processes, materials, and fields of interest.

• Processes include offset, gravure, flexography, screen, and letterpress and their related prepress, finishing, and binding operations.

• Materials include films, papers, inks, and proofs.

• Fields of interest include advertising, computers, marketing, photography, postal service, public relations, and publishing as they relate to graphic design and printing.

In addition to technical words, you find business terms such as alteration, estimate, and house sheet.

Please examine the sample entry on the opposite page. Understanding how the entries are arranged helps you gain maximum benefit.

Language of design and printing

Graphic arts professionals use many words, such as flat and format, whose meanings depend on their context. Other words, such as text type and orphan, mean different things to different people. For these reasons, many terms have two, three, or even four definitions.

In contrast to words with different meanings, many items and processes have more than one name. Terms such as knockout, reverse, and drop-out each refer to the same technique. The words final art, pasteup, and mechanical, are synonyms.

As the language of the graphic arts evolves, many old terms, such as kern and stripping, acquire new meanings. In this book, you find the old terms with their original definitions as well as learn their new meanings.

Industry experts urged me to omit imprecise meanings. For example, you find no reference to process blue or process red as alternate terms for cyan or magenta.

To help you take advantage of today's business opportunities, *Graphically Speaking* has Spanish indexes.

If you have a friend or fellow worker who would benefit from this book, please use a form from page 323 to order a copy. If you want to suggest changes or additions, please write your ideas in a letter to me addressed to the publisher.

Thank you for using this copy of *Graphically Speaking*. I hope you find the information you need to make your work pleasant and profitable.

Mark Beach
July 1992

Get the most out of this book

Main entries are
in bold type

References to
related entries are
in italic type

You find the
concept illustrated
on this page

grain 1) In paper, the predominant direction of fibers. Illustrated on page 179. See also *grain direction.*

2) In photographic film, crystals of chemicals that make up the emulsion. Illustrated on page 228. Fast films have larger crystals than slow films. Negatives, prints, or transparencies made from fast films may show these crystals, so appear 'grainy.' Enlarging any photographic image, regardless of the film used to photograph the original, may lead to a grainy appearance.

3) (verb) To roughen the surface of a lithogaphic plate so that it holds moisture better. – 1, fibra; 2, granular; 3, granear

You find the
concept illustrated
on this page

When an entry has
more than one
meaning, a bold
numeral preceeds
each definition

Equivalent Spanish words
follow the definition in English.
When the English word has
more than one meaning, the
Spanish words have
corresponding numerals

A

AA Abbreviation for *author alteration.*

A-board Alternate term for *sandwich board.* Also abbreviation for *artboard.*

abrasion resistance Ability of paper or ink to resist deterioration from rubbing. Also called rub fastness and scuff resistance. – resistencia a la abrasión

abridgement Alternate term for *digest.* – compendio, resumen

absorption 1) Regarding light, the extent to which a substance, such as paper or film, reduces light passing through it or reflecting from it. 2) Regarding fluid, the extent to which a liquid, such as ink, soaks into a substrate instead of drying on the surface. See also *dot gain* and *ink holdout.* – 1 & 2, absorción

abstract Brief summary of an article, book, or report. Also called précis. – resumen, sumario

AC (Author Correction) British term for *author alteration.*

accent marks See *diacritical marks.*

accent tone Light ink coverage over an entire sheet. Used to print patterns such as wood grains. When the light film coverage is not wanted, it's a defect called blush, haze, or scum.

accordian envelope Alternate term for *expansion envelope.*

accordian fold Parallel folds that resemble the bellows of an accordian. Also called concertina fold, fan fold, z-fold, and zig zag fold. Illustrated on page 105. – doblado tipo acordeón

account executive Alternate term for *sales representative.*

acetate Thin sheet of transparent plastic used to make overlays on mechanicals. – acetato

acetate proof British term for *overlay proof.* – prueba de acetato

achromatic color removal Alternate term for *gray component replacement.*

acid-free paper Paper made from pulp containing little or no acid. Acid-free paper resists deterioration from age. Also called alkaline paper, archival paper, neutral pH paper, permanent paper, and thesis paper. In Great Britain called neutral-sized paper. – papel sin ácido

acknowledgment 1) Part of a book expressing thanks to people and organizations that gave the author information and ideas. 2) Memo from a printer to a customer confirming receipt of an order and reviewing specifications. – 2, carta de recibido

acronym Word created from the initial letters or syllables of a phrase. For example, DOS (pronouced "doss") refers to disk operating system. – sigla

across the grain Alternate term for *against the grain.* – contra la fibra

across the gutter Alternate term for *crossover.* – sobre el canal

action card Alternate term for *reader service card.*

action paper Alternate term for *carbonless paper.*

active white space White space that separates and organizes design elements, as compared to passive white space. – espacio en blanco activo

actual basis weight True basis weight of paper, as compared to nominal basis weight.
  Due to variations during manufacturing, actual basis weight may vary from nominal basis weight by as much as 5%. For example, the actual basis weight of a paper advertised as 100# might be any-

where from 95# to 105#. – peso base real

addendum Piece of paper inserted into a book to add information after the book has been printed. – anexo

additive color Color produced by light falling onto a surface, as compared to subtractive color. Additive color could be sunlight on a tree, a transparency viewed on either a light table or a screen, or hues on a computer display. – color aditivo

additive primary colors Red, green, and blue. When all three colors of light overlap, they yield white light. Red and green yield yellow; red and blue yield magenta; blue and green yield cyan. Illustrated on page 78. – colores primarios aditivos

address label Piece of paper on which postal address is printed for sticking to a mailing piece. Illustrated on page 163. See also *Cheshire label* and *peel-off label.* – etiqueta de dirección postal

address panel Portion of a self-mailer or publication left blank and reserved for the address of the recipient. Illustrated on page 163. – panel para la dirección postal

adhesive bind Alternate term for *perfect bind.* – encuadernación perfecta

advance copies A few copies of a publication sent from the bindery to the customer as soon as possible, before the bindery finishes and ships the total order. Advance copies may also be sent to reviewers or used in press kits. – copias por adelantado

advanced bar code US Postal Service 11-digit bar code composed of the ZIP + 4 plus the last two numerals of the street address. Allows machine sorting into delivery sequences used by mail carriers. – código de barras avanzado

advance sheet Press sheet pulled during production run for use by the customer before receiving the final product. Some printers ask customers to approve advance sheets before binding begins. In Great Britain called out-turn sheet. – pliego por adelantado

advertising printer Printer that specializes in products such as free-standing inserts and direct mailers. – impresor de anuncios

advertising specialties Items such as calendars, coffee cups, hats, match-books, or pencils printed with advertising. Also called premiums. – artículos publicitarios

advertising units Portions of pages sold by a periodical to advertisers. – unidades de anuncios

aerograph British term for *airbrush.*

A4 paper ISO paper size 210 x 297 mm (8.27 x 11.69 inches) used for letterhead. Illustrated on page 178.
     In countries that use ISO paper sizes, envelopes, file folders, photocopy machines, and other office products conform to the A4 sheet just as they conform to the 8½ x 11-inch sheet in the US and Canada. – papel A4

against the grain At right angles to the grain direction of the paper being used, as compared to with the grain. Also called across the grain and cross grain. In Great Britain called cross direction, cross fold. See also *grain direction.* – contra la fibra

agate Unit of typographic measure equaling 5.5 Anglo-American points, the height of type normally used in newspaper classified ads. There are 14 agate lines in one column inch. – ágata

agate copy General term for copy set in very small type. – texto ágata

agenda List of items for discussion at a meeting. Also called calendar. – agenda

agent Person who handles marketing and business matters for freelance professionals such as authors, designers, photographers and illustrators. – agente

airbrush 1) (noun) Pen-shaped tool that sprays a fine mist of ink or paint. Airbrushes are used to retouch photographs and create continuous-tone illustrations. In Great Britain called aerograph. 2) (verb) To retouch using an airbrush, or electronically using a computer, to produce effects similar to mechanical airbrushing. – 1, aerógrafo

airmail paper Paper with a basis weight of 30# (40 gsm) or lighter and usually light blue. – papel aéreo

albertype Alternate term for *collotype.* – albertipia

album Book containing blank pages used to protect and display items such as photographs and postage stamps. – álbum

album cover Square envelope made of paperboard and open at one end. Album covers enclose and protect phonograph records. Also called jacket. – cubierta de un álbum

album format Alternate term for *horizontal format.*

aliasing Alternate term for *jaggies.*

alignment 1) Orientation of type with regard to edges of the column or paper, such as aligned right (flush right), aligned left (flush left), and aligned on center (centered). Illustrated on page 270. Also called range. 2) General term describing the visual relationship of elements to each other. For example, a caption whose baseline does not parallel the graph below it is out of alignment.

Correct alignment depends on the design of the printed piece, not on a rule or formula. – 1, alineación; 2, proporción

alkaline paper Alternate term for *acid-free paper.*

alley Vertical space between images or columns of type on a page, as compared to gutter. Illustrated on pages 23 and 164. – callejón

allocation Quantity of a product, such as a brand of paper, that its manufacturer can supply to distributors and customers before a specified date. Paper on allocation means that supply is rationed and customers may not receive more than they are alloted. – asignación

all-rag paper Paper made using only fibers from cotton or linen, as compared to paper made using some wood fibers. – papel de trapos

almanac Book or booklet containing data about tides, sunrises, weather, and other natural phenomena. – almanaque

alphabet length Width of a line of type containing all lowercase letters of a given typeface and size, with no spaces, numerals, or punctuation. Typesetters and designers use alphabet length as one way to compare typefaces and estimate how much space copy will require. – longitude de alfabeto

alphabet sheet Alternate term for *dry transfer lettering.*

alphanumeric set Complete collection of upper and lower case letters plus numerals, symbols, and punctuation marks in one typeface. – juego alfanumérico

alpha test Test of computer software or other product within the organization that developed it, as compared to beta test. – prueba alfa

alteration Any change made by the customer after copy or artwork has been given to the service bureau, separator, or printer. The change could be in copy, specifications, or both. Also called AA, author alteration, CA, and customer alteration. In Great Britain called Author Correction or AC.

Alterations are invoiced to the customer, as compared to errors by a service bureau or printer which are not billed. – alteración

amalgamate To combine two or more orders into one order for the purpose of achieving higher quantities and lower unit prices. Orders for paper and other supplies are often amalgamated. Also called consolidate. – consolidar

Amberlith Brand name for yellow masking film.

ambient light Light coming from all directions, as compared to light coming from only one direction, such as back light. – luz ambiental

American National Standards Institute Organization that coordinates development of standards for measurement, terminology, and safety, for many industries. Headquarters in New York City. Abbreviated ANSI. Pronounced "an-zee."

Examples of ANSI standards affecting printing are conventions for proper viewing conditions, norms for the interchange of electronic data, and guidelines for calibrating instruments.

American Standard Code for Information Interchange Uniform system of representing alphanumeric information. Abbreviated ASCII. Pronounced "ask-ey."

Information in ASCII enables interfacing of digital equipment. Computer files in ASCII may also be called print files. ASCII files contain only text and formatting commands, not graphics.

ampersand Type character '&' used instead of 'and.'

Anglo-American type system System of using points to express leading and the height of type, ems and ens to express the width of spaces, and picas to express column measures.

aniline ink Fast-drying ink often used in flexography. – tinta de anilina

aniline printing Alternate term for *flexography.*

anilox roll Metal or ceramic roller used to transfer ink on a flexography press. Illustrated on page 101. – rodillo anilino

announcement 1) Card or small folder with news of an event such as the birth of a child or a change of address. 2) Plain or folded sheet of high-quality paper, often text, used for products such as announcements, greeting cards, and invitations. The most common announcement is known as the panel card, a one-fold card with a frame embossed around one panel. – 1 & 2, carta informativa

announcement envelope Envelope designed for announcements, invitations, and greeting cards. Some have deckle edge flaps. Illustrated on page 209. – sobre para carta informativa

annual 1) Periodical published yearly. 2) Alternate term for *yearbook.* – 1, anuario

annual report Report published by a company or organization to describe the previous year's financial results and business highlights. Annual reports are required of all publicly-held corporations in the US. – reporte anual

ANSI Abbreviation for *American National Standards Institute.*

anthology Book containing works by several authors or several works by one author. Also called omnibus in Great Britain. – antología

anti-aliasing Computerized technique of making jaggies less visible by adding half-value pixels along the stairsteps. – antiperfil dentado

anti-offset powder Cornstarch or other fine powder lightly sprayed over the printed surface of coated paper as sheets leave a press. The powder prevents offsetting (setoff) and blocking by holding sheets slightly apart as they accumulate in the delivery pile, allowing the ink to dry. Also called dust, offset powder, powder, and spray powder. – polvo secador

antique paper 1) Regarding surface, the roughest finish offered on offset paper. Illustrated on page 31. 2) Regarding color, alternate term for *natural color.* – papel rugoso

A paper sizes One of five categories of ISO paper sizes. Illustrated on page 178. – tamaños de papel A

aperture 1) Opening in a camera that regulates the amount of light reaching the film. See also *f/stop.* 2) Open space between the threads of a screen used for screen printing. – 1, diafragma; 2, abertura

aperture percentage Percent of a screen used for screen printing that is not blocked by threads, thus open for ink to pass through. Also called mesh opening area and open area. – porcentaje de abertura

appendix Portion of a book or report, appearing at the back, containing information supplementing the main text. – apéndice

application Computer software for a specific purpose, such as word processing or accounting, as compared to an operating system. – aplicación

approval slip Small form, attached to a proof, showing the customer's reaction to the proof. Most printers require a signed approval slip before making plates. – etiqueta de aprobación

approval tag Alternate term for *approval slip.* – etiqueta de aprobación

aqueous coating Coating in a water base and applied like ink by a printing press to protect and enhance the printing underneath.
  Aqueous coatings are available in finishes such as gloss and matte. They dry quickly and, as compared to coatings with petroleum bases, accept ink-jet printing well and may be better for the environment. – baño acuoso

arabic numerals Numerals 0, 1, 2, 3, 4, 5, 6, 7, 8, and 9. – números arábigos

archival paper Alternate term for *acid-free paper,* referring to its ability to resist deterioration for many years. – papel archivo

archive Collection of seldom-used, old, or especially valuable information in long-term storage.

Archives may include hard copy, such as manuscripts or photos, or soft copy, such as data stored on hard disks or magnetic tapes. An archive is sometimes called a morgue by publishers of newspapers and magazines, who may also use 'morgue' when referring to collections of photos. – archivo

area make-up British term for *page layout*.

art Alternate term for *artwork*.

artboard Alternate term for *mechanical*. – boceto

art book Alternate term for *coffee table book*. – libro de arte

art director Person who plans and oversees the design and production of printed pieces.

An art director specifies and coordinates the work of photographers, graphic designers, printers, and others who contribute to the final product. Art directors are typically found in advertising and public relations agencies, large corporate marketing departments, and publishing companies. Sometimes they work with production managers; in other situations, one person does both jobs. – director de arte gráfico

art knife Knife with thin handle and sharp, pointed blade. Art knives are used to cut stencils, friskets, and elements for pasteup. Also called frisket knife, stencil knife, and by the brand name X-ACTO. – cuchilla para montaje

artotype Alternate term for *collotype*.

art paper British term for *gloss coated paper*.

artwork All original copy, including type, photos, and illustrations, intended for printing. Also called art. In Great Britain called repro. – arte final, boceto

ASA film speed See *film speed*.

ascender Part of lowercase letters, such as h and b, that rises above the x-height. Illustrated on page 259. – rasgo ascendente

ascending collate Alternate term for *forward collate*.

ASCII Acronym for *American Standard Code for Information Interchange*. Pronounced "ask-ey."

aspect ratio Ratio of width to height. A square has an aspect ratio of 1:1. The aspect ratio of a #10 envelope is 2.25:1; of any sheet in ISO paper sizes is 1:1.414; of a 35mm transparency is 3:2.

Aspect ratio is used to classify products such as mailing pieces, video screens, and bar codes. Mail not conforming to the aspect ratio for its class may require additional postage. An image not conforming to the aspect ratio of the medium used to display it may require cropping. A scanner may misread a bar code with the wrong aspect ratio. – índice de aspecto

ASPIC Abbreviation for authors symbolic prepress interfacing codes, commands developed by the British Printing Industries Federation to interface word processing files with typesetters.

assemble To bring together type, graphics, and other images in final form for reproduction. Assembly could take place at several points in the prepress process. – montar, arreglar
Image assembly brings together type and graphics on a computer screen. The computer may be part of a desktop publishing system or a computerized stripping system. Illustrated on page 75. – montar imagenes
Film assembly brings together pieces of film made by process cameras and scanners, thus is an alternate term for stripping. Illustrated on pages 64-65 – montar película

associate To overlay several webs coming off a web press prior to folding. Also called marry. – asociar

atlas Book of maps and other materials, such as tables and charts, dealing with demography, geography, and climate. – atlas

atlas paper Alternate term for *map paper.*

author 1) Person who writes materials such as books, articles, and manuals. 2) When used by a printer, can also be alternate term for 'customer.' For example, 'author alterations' can mean any changes made by the customer. – autor

author alteration Alternate term for *alteration.* Abbreviated AA. In Great Britain also called AC or Author Correction. – alteración del autor

autobiography Story of a life written by the person who lived it. Also called memoirs. – autobiografía

available light Photographic light from sources inherent to the scene, such as sunlight or normal room lighting, rather than from sources specifically for photography, such as electronic flash or spot lights. – iluminación disponible

AZERTY keyboard First six letters of keyboard layout standard on typewriters and computers in France.

B

backbone Alternate term for *spine*.

background Portion of a photograph or illustration behind or surrounding its main subject matter, as compared to foreground. Illustrated on page 233. – fondo

background tint Overall coverage of paper with a light colored ink or a screen tint. Also called base color.
  Printers use background tints to simulate colored paper. The blue of blue pages in telephone books comes from a tint printed on white paper, whereas the yellow of yellow pages is the color of the paper itself. – tinta de fondo

backing Creasing the back folds of gathered signatures to strengthen the binding and make the book easy to open.

backing paper 1) Strip of paper in a casebound book that reinforces the spine. Illustrated on page 23. 2) Alternate term for *release paper*.

backlight 1) Light falling onto a photographic subject from behind. Backlight shines into the camera and causes a rim of light along the edge of the subject. 2) Light in a process camera placed behind the copy. Used to burn out small imperfections so they will not appear on the film. – 1 & 2, luz de fondo

back lining Cloth added along the inside of the spine of a book to make the binding stronger. – gasa

back list List of books produced by a publisher more than a year ago but still available for purchase, as compared to front list. – lista de publicaciones viejas

back margin British term for *gutter*.

back matter Appendix, bibliography, glossary, and other elements of a book appearing after the main text. Also called end matter. – apéndice

back-of-the-book Pages in a publication that follow the main section. The back-of-the-book might contain classified ads in a magazine or sale items in a catalog. – anexo publicitario

back printing 1) Printing on the inner surface of a clear substrate, as compared to face printing the outside surface.

Back printing puts ink inside a bag or package, such as a bread bag, where it is less likely to scuff or get wet. It is also required when an image is viewed looking through the substrate, as with a decal.

2) Printing the second side of a sheet, often with generic information. Business forms are often back printed with terms and conditions of a contract.
– 1 & 2, impresión en el dorso

backslant Type slanted to the left, as compared to italic which is slanted to the right. – inclinación hacia atrás

backstep marks Alternate term for *collating marks.* – marcas guías

back up 1) To print on the second side of a sheet already printed on one side. 2) To adjust an image on one side of a sheet so that it aligns back-to-back with an image on the other side. For example, printers often make rules used with footers back up each other to prevent the rule on either side from showing through. – 1, imprimir en el reverso

backup copy Duplicate of an original made in case of loss or damage of the original. – copia de seguridad

bad break Incorrect or ungraceful hyphenation of a word or division of a sentence. For example, the hyphenation of 'typeset-ting' is grammatically correct, but could be considered a bad break. 'Type-setting' is more readable.
– separación incorrecta

baggy edge Wavy edge on a roll of paper caused by factors such as poor formation, too much tension along one side, or loose winding.
– orilla ondulada

balloon Circle enclosing copy in a cartoon. Also called bubble. – círculo

banding 1) Method of packaging using strips of rubber, fiberglass, paper, or steel to wrap individual bundles, or hold bundles or boxes tightly to a pallet. 2) Defect in halftone screens or screen tints output by laser printers or image-setters in which parallel breaks (stair steps) or streaks appear in the dot pattern. – 1, flejar, enfajillar; 2, rayas

bank British term for *onionskin.*

banker envelope Alternate term for *business envelope.* – sobre oficio

banknote paper Alternate term for *currency paper.* – papel cebolla

banner 1) Large headline, usually across the full width of a page. 2) Large sign printed on cloth or plastic and made to hang from strings or a pole. – 1, título; 2, bandera, pancarta

bar chart Chart using bars of varying heights or widths to express quantitative data. Illustrated on page 129. – gráfico de barras

bar code Pattern of vertical bars and spaces that encode information so that it is readable by scanning. For example, a bar code on a book indicates its ISBN and on a magazine its ISSN. See also *EMBARC, European Article Number (EAN), POSTNET, SPI,* and *Uniform*

Product Code (UPC).

There are many bar code formats, each having different requirements for aspect ratios, contrasts, and x dimensions. For example, in the US Postal Service bar code each digit is formed by combining two full bars with three half bars. – código de barras

bar code sorter Scanner that reads bar codes and sorts mail pieces according to the bar-coded data. – sorteadora de códigos de barras

baronial envelope Envelope shape used for invitations and greeting cards. Illustrated on page 209. – sobre baronial

barrel fold Alternate term for *letter fold.* – doblado continuo

baryta paper Alternate term for *repro paper.* The term comes from the chemical, barium sulfate, used in the coating to make the paper bright. – papel baritado

base art Copy pasted up on the mounting board of a mechanical, as compared to overlay art. Base art usually has the copy to be printed using black ink. Also called base mechanical. – boceto base

base color 1) Alternate term for *background tint.* 2) Color used as a starting point for creating another color. White ink is often used to provide a base color. – 2, color base

baseline Imaginary line, under a line of type, used to align characters. Illustrated on page 259.

Technically speaking, characters with square bottoms, such as 'w' and 'h', rest on the baseline, while characters with rounded bottoms, such as 'c' and 'o', fall slightly below the baseline. – línea base

base mechanical Alternate term for *base art.* – boceto base

basement Alternate term for *downstairs.* – sección inferior

base negative Negative made by photographing base art. Strippers assume that the base negative contains the most important copy with the images to which other copy should be registered. – negativo base

base side Side of paper that is not coated or of film that does not have emulsion. – lado base

base stock Underlying paper to which mills apply coatings to make coated paper. Also called body stock. In Great Britain called raw stock. – papel base

basic size The standard size of sheets of paper used to calculate basis weight in the US and Canada. Illustrated on page 115.

Each category of paper, such as bond and book, has a basic size. Basis weight is the weight, in pounds, of 500 sheets cut to the basic size.

Common basic sizes are:
- bond, writing, ledger
    17 x 22 inches (432 x 559 mm)
- text, offset, coated, bible
    25 x 38 inches (635 x 965 mm)
- cover
    20 x 26 inches (508 x 660 mm)
- newsprint
    24 x 26 inches (610 x 660 mm)

Basic size is used only to calculate basis weight. Paper is sold not only in the basic size, but in many other sizes as well. The basic size has no standard meaning other than its relationship to basis weight.
– tamaño básico

basis weight In the US and Canada, the weight, in pounds, of a ream (500 sheets) of paper cut to its basic size. Also called ream weight and substance weight (sub weight). In countries using ISO paper sizes, the weight, in grams, of one square meter of paper. Also called grammage and ream weight. Illustrated on page 115.

Labels on reams, cartons, and rolls of paper identify the basis weight of the paper they contain. In North America, they also typically identify the basic size used to calculate the basis weight. For example, the basic size of book paper is 25 x 38 inches, thus a 60-pound offset could be listed as 'BS 60 (25 x 38).'

When writing basis weight, the word 'pound' is abbreviated with the symbol '#.' Fifty-pound coated is written 50# coated. – peso base

bastard cut Any cut not at a 90° angle to one edge of the paper. – corte irregular

bastard progressives British term for *progressive proof.*

bastard size Any non-standard size of paper or type. – tamaño irregular

bastard title Alternate term for *half title.* – anteportada

baud Acronym for bits of audio data. Baud rate is the number of bits of information transmitted per second from one digital device to another, such as between modems. Common baud rates are 1200, 2400, and 9600. Sending at 1200 baud means sending approximately 120 characters per second. See also *data compression.* – baudio

bearer bars 1) Bars along the outside of bar codes that guide the scanner and reduce chances of error. 2) Ridges that parallel edges of a flexographic plate. Bearer bars make the impression pressure uniform across the plate, making ink density consistent. The bars print as solid lines along each edge of the substrate. – 1, barras guías; 2, bandas laterales de apoyo

bellows Collapsable section of a camera or enlarger that allows the lens to be moved in relationship to the film plane. – fuelle

belly band Sleeve that is narrower than the publication it protects, thus exposing both ends of the publication.

belt press Web press that uses rubber relief plates mounted on a flexible belt to produce tickets and mass market books. Because of the soft image carrier, the system can print quickly on rough paper. Also called by the brand name Cameron press. – prensa de correa

Benday 1) Obsolete generic name for screen tints or line patterns applied to a mechanical by ruboff techniques or pasting. The term originates with

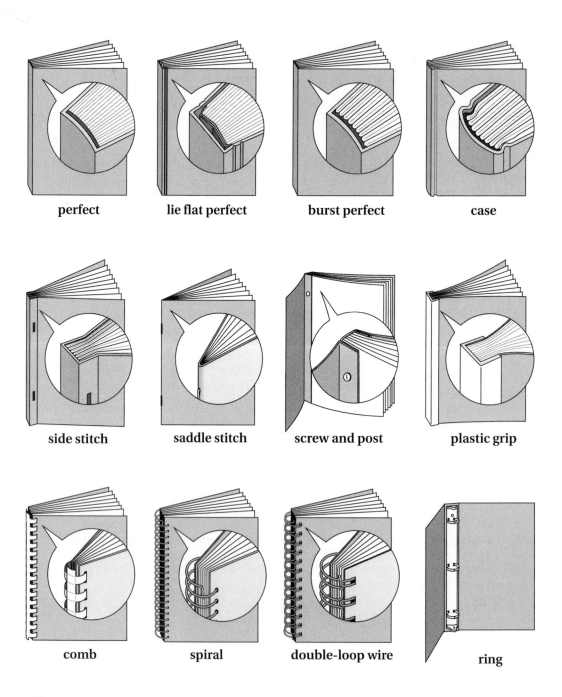

perfect   lie flat perfect   burst perfect   case

side stitch   saddle stitch   screw and post   plastic grip

comb   spiral   double-loop wire   ring

Benjamin Day, the inventor of an earlier process. 2) Alternate term for any screen tint or line pattern, regardless of how it is transferred to a printing plate.

beta test Test of computer software or other new product by a small group of users outside the organization that developed it. Beta testing occurs before releasing the product to the general public. – prueba beta

bevel Sloping surface on type or a die. Illustrated on page 247.– bisel

bible paper Very thin, opaque paper used for products such as bibles and dictionaries. Also called India paper. – papel biblia, papel india

bibliography 1) List of books and other printed sources consulted while doing research. 2) List of printed materials for reading or research about a specific topic. – bibliografía

bid Alternate term for *estimate* and *quotation.* – presupuesto

bill 1) Alternate term for *invoice.* 2) Alternate term for both *poster* and *flier.* – 1, factura; 2, cartel, circular

billboard Large, outdoor sign with advertising directed to motorists or spectators. – cartel publicitario

bill of lading List of goods included in a shipment. Also called manifest. – factura de envío

bind To fasten sheets or signatures and/or attach covers with glue, wire, thread, or other means. Binding creates the final product, such as a report, book, or magazine, and is one of the last steps in production. – encuadernar

binder 1) General term for a cover using devices such as rings, clamps, or screw posts to hold sheets. 2) Machine that binds. – 1, carpeta; 2, encuadernadora

binder's board Stiff, thick paper used to support the cover material of case bound books. Also called *case board.* – cartulina para encuadernación

bindery Place where printed products are collated, trimmed, folded, and/or bound. Because of their equipment and the production sequence of printing jobs, binderies may also die cut, emboss, foil stamp, and perform other finishing operations.

A bindery may be a department within a printing company or a separate business. – taller de encuadernación

bind-in card Card bound with glue or staples into a magazine, catalog, or book, as compared to blow-in card. – tarjeta encuadernada

binding edge Edge of a publication that is bound. Also called spine. On perfect bound books, often called grind edge.

When specifying the dimensions of a bound publication, it is common to state the binding edge second. For example, an 8½ x 11-inch book would be bound along its 11-inch side (in vertical format). A 6 x 9-inch, saddle-stitched catalog is stapled on the 9-inch side. – margen encuadernado

bind-in tabs Tabs on sheets of thick paper bound into books such as directories. Bind-in tabs are folded into the book during manufacture, then unfolded by the reader to reveal information on the tabs. – separadores encuadernados

binding lap Alternate term for *lap*. – orilla, labio

bind margin Margin between the bound edge and the live area. – margen de lomo

bingo card Alternate term for *reader service card*. – tarjeta de servicio

bit Contraction of binary digit, the smallest unit of information in a computer. – bit

bite 1) Referring to paper, alternate term for *tooth*. 2) Referring to sheetfed press, shortened form of gripper bite, meaning *gripper edge*.

bit map Computer image made up of dots (pixels). Each dot represents one bit. – transformación de bits

black-and-white photo Photograph made using film that reproduces images with varying shades of gray only, as compared to color photo. – fotografía en blanco y negro

black patch Alternate term for *window (3)*. – ventana

blackprint Alternate term for *blueline* and *photostat*.

black printer Flat, plate, or inking station that controls printing of black ink. In four-color process printing, also called key printer. Illustrated page 72. – plancha negra

blackstep marks Alternate term for *collating marks*. – marcas guías

black type Alternate term for *ultrabold type*. – letra ultranegra

blad Sample pages of a book bound as a booklet. Publishers distribute blads to explain and promote books. In Great Britain called taster. – folleto promocional

blade coating Method of coating paper that ensures a relatively thick covering and level surface, as compared to film coating. Also called knife coating.
   Gloss, dull, and matte papers are blade coated. Some are film coated first to yield even better ink holdout. – estucado de cuchilla

blank 1) Category of paperboard ranging in thickness from 15 to 48 points. Blanks may be C1S, C2S, or uncoated and are used for signs and posters. 2) Alternate term for *shell*. – 1, cartulina

blanket Rubber-coated pad, mounted on a cylinder of an offset press, that receives the inked image from the plate and transfers it to the surface to be printed. Illustrated on page 167. See also *offset printing*. – mantilla, caucho

blanket cylinder Cylinder that holds the blanket on an offset press. Illustrated on page 167. – cilindro de mantilla

blanket-to-blanket press One style of perfecting press. – prensa de caucho contra caucho

blast In gravure, to contact print a halftone with a bromide sheet.

Gravure prepress staff refer to blasting broms just as offset prepress staff refer to burning plates. – chorro

bleed 1) Printing that extends to the edge of a sheet or page after trimming. To ensure ink coverage to the bleed edge, printers need ⅛ inch (3 mm) of paper to trim away after printing. 2) Phenomenon of one ink color partially affecting another, such as red ink appearing slightly purple if printed over blue ink not yet dry. The wet blue ink bleeds through the red ink, causing the purple hue. 3) Alternate term for *feathering (1)*. 4) Alternate term for *lap register*. – 1, sangrado; 2, invasión del color

bleed through Alternate term for *strike through*. – invasión del color

blind British term for *blind emboss, blind deboss*.

blind deboss To deboss without added ink or foil on the image. In Great Britain called blind. – estampar bajo relieve sin tinta

blind emboss To emboss without added ink or foil on the image. In Great Britain called blind. – estampar en relieve sin tinta

blind folio Page number that is part of a sequence but that is not printed on the page as a numeral. Books that start printing page numbers on page 2 have page 1 as a blind folio. – folio sin tinta

blind image Image debossed, embossed, or stamped, but not printed with ink or foil. – imagen sin tinta

blinding Phenomenon of the image area on an offset plate refusing to accept ink because of wear, poor ink/water balance, or a defect in manufacturing. Blinding makes the printed image become pale as the run progresses. – cegado

blind stamp To stamp without adding ink or foil on the image. – estampar sin tinta

blister Small raised bubble in a coating. Blisters in paper coatings or film laminations may be caused by too much heat or moisture, or poor curing. Blisters in book covers or end sheets may happen when adhesives do not cover evenly or cure properly. – superficie quemada

blister card Package with products inside and a mounting card outside enclosed by a transparent plastic bubble. Also called bubble card and skin pack. In Great Britain called blister pack. – envoltura

blister pack 1) Packaging technique using sheets of plastic holding bubbles of air to wrap and cushion products. 2) British term for *blister card*. – 1, envoltura

block 1)Alternate term for *foil stamp*. 2) British term for *emboss*. – 1, estampar con láminas

block color Alternate term for *flat color*. – color plano

blocked up 1) Characteristic of areas in a halftone that lack detail because of underexposure or overdevelopment. 2) Characteristic of products that have experienced blocking. – 1, encerrado; 2, bloqueado

blocking Unwanted sticking together of printed sheets causing damage when the surfaces are separated. Blocking may happen when inks or coatings have not adequately dried before coming into contact with another surface. It can also happen when adhesives become moist or hot. – bloqueado

block out Alternate term for *opaque (2)*. – opacar

blockout pattern Pattern of small images printed on a check or business form to prevent writing from showing on that portion of the document. Illustrated on page 87. Also called safety pattern. – patrón de seguridad

block printing Alternate term for *letterpress printing*. – impresión tipográfica

blow-in card Loose card inserted into magazines by forced air, as compared to bind-in card. – tarjeta insertada por aire

blow up To enlarge an image either photographically by exposing it through a lens or digitally by using a computer. – ampliar

blue 1) Short for *blueline*. For example, a customer wanting to check bluelines might say, "Please send the blues to my office." 2) Commonly used, although imprecise, term for cyan.

blue book 1) Small, saddle-stitched notebook with a blue cover in which college students write answers to examination questions. 2) Generic term for any book that provides a list of people or services in a field. – 1, libreta azul; 2, directorio

blueline Prepress photographic proof made from stripped negatives where all colors show as blue images on white paper. Bluelines are used to check positions of images and pages and, in some situations, to evaluate color breaks.
   Because 'blueline' is a generic term for proofs made from a variety of materials that appear similar, it may also be called a blackprint, blue, blueprint, brownline, brownprint, diazo, dyeline, ozalid, position proof, silverprint, Dylux, or VanDyke. – prueba azul

blue pencil 1) Pencil that writes in the blue color that graphic arts film will not reproduce. Blue pencils and markers using non-reproducing blue ink are used for writing instructions on mechanicals. Also called non-repro pencil. 2) Traditional term for an editor's act of changing or deleting copy. – 1, lápiz azul; 2, correcciones del editor

blueprint 1) Diazo reproduction of a technical drawing used by architects and engineers. 2) Alternate term for *blueline*. – 1, cianotipo; 2, prueba azul

blur To reduce contrast on a photo in a computer file.

blurb 1) Brief quote taken from a review used to advertise a book. 2) Description of author or book printed on a book's cover. – 1, resumen en la solapa; 2, semblanza del autor

blush Gravure term for scum caused by a defective cylinder or doctor blade. – velo

BMC Abbreviation for *bulk mail center.*

board 1) Alternate term for *mechanical.* 2) British term for *board paper, mechanical.*

board paper General term for paper over 110# index, 80# cover, or 200 gsm. Commonly used for products such as file folders, displays, and post cards. Also called paperboard. – cartulina

body 1) Characteristic of ink referring to its viscosity. Press operators say that ink with good body flows evenly from the can and performs well on press, being neither too stiff nor too loose. 2) British term for *type size.* – 1, viscocidad

body copy 1) Copy set in text type, as compared to display type. Illustrated on page 164. 2) The bulk of a story or article, as compared to its headlines. In Great Britain called body text. – 1, tipo texto

body height Alternate term for *x height.* – altura x

body stock 1) Paper on which the text or main part of a publication is printed, as compared to cover stock. 2) Alternate term for *base stock.* – 1, papel texto

body type Alternate term for *text type.* – texto

boilerplate Paragraphs that are the same in every contract or policy manual and are simply inserted at the necessary points. Also called canned text. – párrafos comunes

bold type Type that appears darker than the text type of the same typeface. Illustrated on page 255. – negrillas

bond Certificate showing financial obligation of a government or organization. – bono

bond paper Category of paper commonly used for writing, printing, and photocopying. Also called business paper, communication paper, correspondence paper, and writing paper. Illustrated page 115.

Mills make bond in basis weights of 13, 16, 20, and 24 pound (48, 60, 75, and 90 gsm). Bond paper comes in a wide range of quality levels. Watermarked 100%, 50%, and 25% cotton bond is used for premium stationery, certificates, and legal documents. Premium #1 and #1 sulphite bond, made entirely from wood fiber, costs less, though it isn't as durable. Number 4 sulphite bond is used in photocopy machines, laser printers, and for everyday quick printing jobs.

Bond paper is not as opaque as offset paper and is designed to carry ink only on one side. It can be used for two-sided copies because it does not absorb toner as it would ink.

There are many bond papers made with special characteristics, such as dual-purpose bond, form bond, laser bond, and onionskin, defined elsewhere in this glossary.

The basic size for bond paper is 17 x 22 inches (432 x 559 mm). – papel bond

book 1) Set of printed sheets bound in any form of squared binding such as perfect, case, or comb. From a manufacturing standpoint, any product meeting this definition, whether a novel, directory, technical manual, or catalog, is a book. 2) Bound set of unprinted sheets or sheets with grids, such as a book for mounting photos or a book for keeping financial records. 3) Major section of a scholarly or literary work, such as a book of the Bible. 4) General term referring to any bound publication. For example, a magazine publisher might refer to the July issue as the 'July book.' 5) General term referring to a package of products held together in a convenient binding, such as a book of matches. 6) Script (libretto) of an opera or play. 7) Alternate term for *portfolio.* 8) (verb) In stripping, to assemble loose film into composite film. – 1-8, libro

bookbinder Bindery that specializes in binding books. May refer to any trade bindery. – encuadernador

book block Folded signatures gathered, sewn, and trimmed, but not yet covered. – encuadernación en rústica

book cloth Fabric used to cover the cases of casebound books.

Book cloth is available with several treatments that make it print and stamp well, and resist fading and mildew. Cloth impregnated with pyroxylin or acrylics is rated as A, B, or C, with C costing the most and having the highest thread count. Cloth filled with starch costs less than A cloth, thus could be considered commodity.

The term 'book cloth' includes thick paper and synthetic paper, sometimes known as nonwovens, made for case binding. Depending on their caliper, nonwovens cost less than woven cloth. – gasa

booklet Publication ranging from eight to 80 pages and typically bound using saddle stitching.

From a production standpoint, any product meeting this definition, whether a brochure, program, or directory, is a booklet. Technically speaking, saddled-stitched magazines and catalogs are booklets. Furthermore, there are no clear distinctions separating a thick pamphlet from a thin book. The definitions are imprecise. – folleto

booklet envelope Large envelope that opens on the long dimension and is designed to hold a booklet. Illustrated on page 209. – sobre para folleto

book paper Category of paper suitable for books, magazines, catalogs, advertising, and general printing needs. In Great Britain called cartridge.

Book paper is divided into uncoated paper (also called offset paper), coated paper (also called art paper, enamel paper, gloss paper, and slick paper), and text paper.

The basic size of book paper is 25 x 38 inches (635 x 965 mm). Because all categories of book paper use this basic size, their basis weights are comparable from one category to another. – papel libro

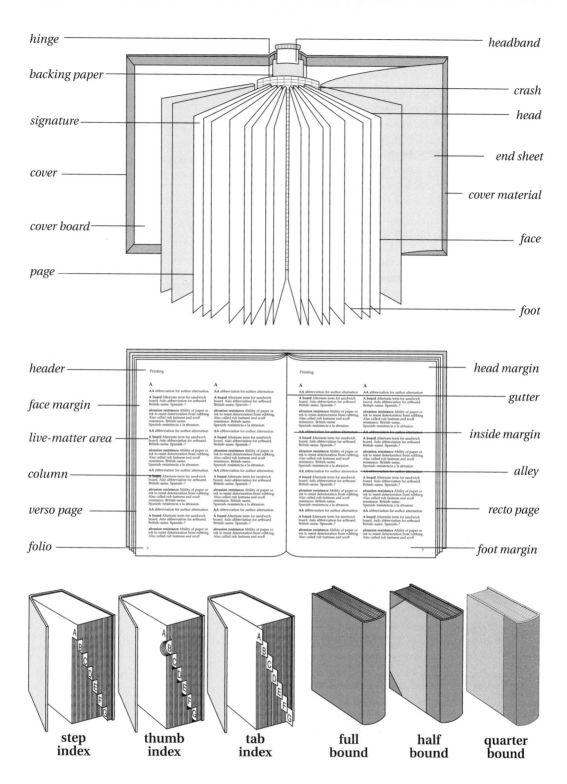

hinge

backing paper

signature

cover

cover board

page

headband

crash

head

end sheet

cover material

face

foot

header

face margin

live-matter area

column

verso page

folio

head margin

gutter

inside margin

alley

recto page

foot margin

step index

thumb index

tab index

full bound

half bound

quarter bound

book proof Folded and gathered signatures glued into cover and trimmed to simulate the final product. Book proofs, available before the book itself is out of bindery, show reviewers, salespeople, and others how the final product will appear. – prueba del libro

book rate Alternate term for *special fourth class rate.*

book size Term for letter size when applied to publications, not stationery. Book size includes 8½ x 11 inches (lettersize), and 8¼ x 10⅞ inches, a format suitable for many web presses and allowing for bleeds.

US Postal regulations classify book size as a flat for purposes of postal rates, as compared to postal rates for letters. – tamaño libro

book-weight type Medium weight type suitable for reading for long periods at a time. Illustrated on page 255.

booster 1) Lever that opens the rings of a ring binder. 2) Alternate term for *bump exposure.* – 1, palanca de apertura

border Decorative rule or design that frames type or graphics. – orilla, margen

bounceback Business reply card inserted into a publication or package. – tarjeta de suscripción

box 1) Rigid container made of chipboard, corrugated cardboard, or wood. Also called carton and case. 2) Area of a page framed by border lines. – 1, caja, cartón; 2, marco

B paper sizes One of five categories of *ISO paper sizes.*

Braille System of writing and printing using patterns of raised dots to create characters that blind people can 'read' by touch.

brass Alternate term for embossing or debossing die (although dies are made of many metals, such as aluminum, copper, and magnesium, as well as brass). – latón

BRC Alternate term for *business reply card.*

BRE Alternate term for *business reply envelope.*

break for color Alternate term for *color break.* – corte del color

breaking strength British term for *bursting strength.* – resistencia a la ruptura

break point Quantity level at which a unit price drops because of a change in equipment or process used, or because of the pricing structure of supplies, such as paper.

Some break points can save significant amounts of money. For example, the unit cost of a printing job might drop 8% if 23,000 copies are ordered instead of 20,000 copies because of the way paper is priced. Other break points are gradual and save relatively minor amounts of money. For example, an increase in quantity that merely adds a few minutes of press time would bring only a slight drop in unit price. – lugar del cambio

brick pack To alternate bundles on skids so they create a pattern like a brick wall. Brick packing helps distribute the load evenly and prevent units from shifting. Also called compensated stack. – apilar como ladrillos

bridge 1) Area of a gravure cylinder lying between its cells. 2) Alternate term for *crossover*. – 1, puente

bridging Alternate term for *fadeout*. – desvanecerse

brief cover Alternate term for *report cover*. – cubierta de informe

briefing book Collection of material given to an official, executive, or journalist to give the person background and insight about an issue or event. – informe

brightness Characteristic of paper or ink referring to how much light it reflects.

Mills express the brightness of papers as a numeral that corresponds to a percentage. Paper that reflects all the light falling on it would have a brightness rating of 100. Printing papers range in brightness from 60 to 95.

Brightness and whiteness are different features of paper. Brightness is a quantitative measure, whiteness a subjective judgment.

The brightness of a photograph or illustration refers to how much light it reflects or transmits. Many computer programs use the term 'brightness' when referring to adding or subtracting light from an image on the screen.

The brightness of ink, also called its reflectance, is affected by additives to the ink that make it glossy and by the surface of the paper on which it is printed. – brillantez, brillo

bristol paper General term referring to paper 6 points or thicker with basis weight between 90# and 200# (200-500 gsm). Used for products such as index cards, file folders, and displays. – papel bristol

British Standards Institute Organization in Great Britain that sets standards for many procedures and products. Abbreviated BSI.

broadsheet Sheet of a newspaper open to the full size of two pages.

broadside 1) Alternate term for *flier,* especially when referring to a large flier that is folded for mailing but unfolded for reading. Fliers and broadsides have two pages, each one side of the full sheet. 2) British term for *parent sheet.* – 1, apaisado

broadside format Alternate term for *horizontal format.* – formato apaisado

brochure Printed piece promoting a product, service, or idea. Brochures are distinguished from other printed products by purpose rather than specifications. From a production standpoint, a small brochure may be a flier or pamphlet and a large brochure may be a booklet. – folleto

broke Trimmings, defective sheets, and other waste paper collected at the mill.

broken carton Carton of paper from which some of the sheets have been sold. 'Broken carton' is a selling unit referring to any amount of paper less than one full carton. Paper merchants charge higher prices for paper from broken cartons because of the extra handling required. Also called less carton. – caja incompleta

broker Agent who sells printing from many printers or paper from many sources, as compared to a sales representative working for just one company. Also called jobber. In Great Britain called print farmer. – intermediario

brom Abbreviation for *bromide*.

bromide Photographic print that is scanned in the HelioKlischographic process of making cylinders for gravure printing. Abbreviated brom.
Bromides are halftone positives that resemble Velox prints, but are sturdier and more glossy than Veloxes. They are made by contact printing separation negatives and negatives of type that has been halftoned. Broms are mounted on a drum and scanned using machines similar to drum scanners used to make color separations. – bromuro

brownline Alternate term for *blueline*.

brownprint Alternate term for *blueline*.

BSI Abbreviation for *British Standards Institute*.

bubble card Alternate term for *blister card*. – tarjeta de burbuja

buckram 1) Coarse cloth used to cover binder's boards on case bound books. 2) Embossed finish on paper that simulates the look and feel of buckram cloth.

buffer Computer memory designed to hold information while waiting to process it. A common example of a buffer is in the printer, used to hold data waiting to be printed so the memory of the computer itself is free for other tasks. – buffer

bug 1) Error in a computer program that prevents it from working properly. 2) Alternate term for *union bug*. – 1, error

build a color To overlap two or more screen tints to create a new color. Such an overlap is called a build, color build, stacked screen build, or tint build. Illustrated on page 79.
Color builds are often used in four-color process printing jobs when screen tints of two or more process colors are overlapped to simulate additional colors, such as spot colors. Some speakers refer to building colors only when speaking of using combinations of process colors. Others use the term referring to combinations of screen tints of any colors. – construcción del color

buildups Alternate term for *working film*. – película de trabajo

bulk 1) Thickness of paper relative to its basis weight. An uncalendered sheet is relatively bulky compared to a calendered sheet of the same basis weight. Gloss coated paper has little bulk; uncoated paper has moderate bulk; reply card paper has high bulk. Bulk is expressed as a bulking number or pages per inch (ppi). See also *caliper*. 2) Thickness of a book without its cover. In Great

Britain called bulk between boards.
– 1, gruesor; 2, libro en rústica

bulking book paper Paper made to have high bulk, resulting in a thick book relative to the number of pages. Also called novel paper.
– papel grueso

bulking dummy Dummy assembled from the actual paper specified for a printing job.

A bulking dummy shows how thick the product will be when printed and bound. Bulking dummies are used to determine the correct size for type on the spine of a book. Binders use them as guides when setting up bindery equipment. Customers use them to help plan packaging and mailing.
– muestra del gruesor

bulking number Number of sheets of paper in a one-inch stack. Because one sheet has two pages, multiplying the bulking number by two yields pages per inch (ppi). – número de gruesor

bulk mail General term for presorted mail handled in bundles, sacks, or pallets, as compared to mail handled as individual pieces. To qualify items as bulk mail, the sender needs a permit from the post office and must presort the mail according to postal regulations. – correo en bulto

bulk mail center US Postal Service facility designed to handle bulk mail. Abbreviated BMC.

bulk pack To pack printed pieces in boxes without first strapping

or wrapping the pieces in bundles.
– empacar flojo

bulky mechanical British term for *high bulk paper*.

bullet Bold dot used for typographic emphasis or to identify elements in a list. Illustrated on page 163.
– punto señalizador

bulletin Special announcement of timely information printed in a periodical or as a flier or small poster. – boletín

bull's eye 1) Alternate term *hickey*. 2) Alternate term for *register mark*.

bump Alternate term for *hit*.

bump exposure Short exposure given a halftone without using a screen to increase highlight detail and soften harsh whites. Also called booster, bump, and no-screen bump. – exposición suplementaria

bumper bars Alternate term for *bearer bars (2)*.

bumper sticker Label designed to attach to the bumper of an automobile. Bumper stickers promote a product, service, or idea, or make a statement that some may find clever or offensive. – calcomanía

bundle 1) Printed pieces tied with string, strapped with a band of rubber, paper, or metal, or shrink wrapped. Bundles may contain any convenient handful or armload or may contain uniform quantities as specified by the customer. 2) Batch of signatures faced with wooden boards and strapped for secure shipment to bindery. 3) US Post

Office designation for two or more packages secured together as one unit for bulk mailing. See also *package (3)*. – 1 - 3, bulto

burn 1) In lithography, to make a proof or plate by contact exposing it with film. 2) In photography, to give extra exposure to a specific area of a print in order to darken that area, as compared to dodge. Burning is usually done to increase details in highlights. Illustrated on page 232. Also called print in. – 1, exposición de la plancha

burned out Characteristic of film, paper, or plates exposed to light for so long or at such intensity that details do not appear. Also refers to an image printed by burned out film or plate. – velado

burnish 1) To smooth and seal into place by rubbing elements stuck to a mechanical. 2) To smooth rough edges on a die. – 1 & 2, bruñir

burst Design or die cut looking like an exploding star. – estrella

burst bind Alternate term for *burst perfect bind*.

bursting strength Ability of paper to resist rupture. Measured using a Mullen tester. Also called pop strength. In Great Britain called breaking strength. – resistencia a la ruptura

burst perfect bind To bind by forcing glue into notches along the spines of gathered signatures before affixing a paper cover. Burst perfect binding is stronger than perfect binding because the backs of signatures are not ground off. Also called burst bind, notch bind, and slotted bind. Illustrated on page 16. – encuadernación a la americana ranurada

business cabinet Alternate term for *stationery*. – papelería

business card Small card giving business information such as name, title, address, phone and fax number. In the US and Canada, the common size is 2 x 3½ inches (51 x 90 mm). Countries using ISO paper sizes have no standard size, although 55 x 90 mm is common. Also called calling card and visiting card. – tarjeta de presentación

business envelope Envelope with opening and flap along the long edge, such as the #10 in the North American sizes and the DL in ISO sizes. Also called banker envelope, commercial envelope, and official envelope. Illustrated on page 209. – sobre oficio

business form General term referring to any printed document with spaces or lines used to record information, such as purchase orders, invoices, manifests, checks, and personnel records. – forma comercial

business graphics Alternate term for *infographics*. – gráficas financieras

business paper Alternate term for *bond paper*. – *papel bond*

business reply card Pre-addressed card meeting postal regulations for size, caliper, bar coding, and prepayment. Also called BRC and reply card.

Business reply cards in card decks or publications, or included with packaging, make it easy to request information, register serial numbers, and supply other data. – tarjeta de servicio del lector

business reply envelope Pre-addressed envelope meeting postal regulations for bar coding and pre-payment. Also called BRE and return envelope.

Business reply envelopes bound into catalogs or included with invoices make it easy for customers to order products or send payments. Although business reply envelopes are commonly #6 envelopes in North America and C7/6 in ISO sizes, they may be any size or format that meets postal regulations. Illustrated on page 209. – sobre de servicio del lector

butt fit Alternate term for *butt register.* – registro de contacto

butt line Line at which inks or substrates meet precisely, as compared to lap line. – borde de corte

butt register Register where ink colors meet precisely without over-lapping or allowing space between, as compared to lap register. Also called butt fit and kiss register. – registro de contacto

butt roll Roll of paper with some of the paper already used. If it contains enough paper, a printer may return a butt roll to inventory to use later on another job. Also called stub roll. – colilla del rollo

buy out To subcontract for a service that is closely related to the business of the organization. Also called farm out. Work that is bought out or farmed out is sometimes called outwork or referred to as being out of house.

A printer might buy out separations or case binding. Accounting or food services, however, would not be considered buyouts when purchased by a printer. – subcontratar

byline Printed line, in a newspaper or magazine article, showing author's name. Illustrated on page 160. – línea del nombre

byte Group of eight bits representing one letter, numeral, or other character in computer memory. – byte, octeto

C

C Roman numeral for one hundred (100). For example, CWT stands for hundredweight, which is commonly used to express quantities of paper.

CA Abbreviation for customer alteration which is an alternate term for *alteration.*

cab Abbreviation for *cabriolet.*

cabinet Collection of paper swatchbooks and unprinted samples from many mills. Cabinets are assembled by a paper merchant and supplied to printers, agencies, and other major customers. – vitrina

cabriolet Masking material once used to make flats for gravure printing, thus gravure term for *flat.*

calendar Printed product showing months and days of the year. Also alternate term for both *schedule* and *agenda.* – calendario

calender To make the surface of paper smooth by pressing it between steel rollers during manufacture. Calendering affects paper in a variety of ways because it compresses fibers as it smooths the surface. Illustrated on page 31.

The correct spelling is calender (a verb meaning to roll out), not calendar (a noun referring to a graphic representation of time). – calandrar

calf paper Paper colored and embossed to resemble the leather that is occasionally used in book binding. – papel cuero

California job case Alternate term for *case (1).* – caja California

caliper 1) Thickness of paper or other substrate expressed in thousandths of an inch (mils or points), pages per inch (ppi), thousandths of a millimeter (microns), or pages per centimeter (ppc). 2) Device on a sheetfed press that detects double sheets or on a binding machine that detects missing signatures or inserts. – 1 & 2, calibre

calligraphy Ornamental or highly decorative handwriting. – caligrafía

calling card Alternate term for *business card.* – tarjeta de visita

callout 1) Word that identifies part of an illustration. 2) Reference within

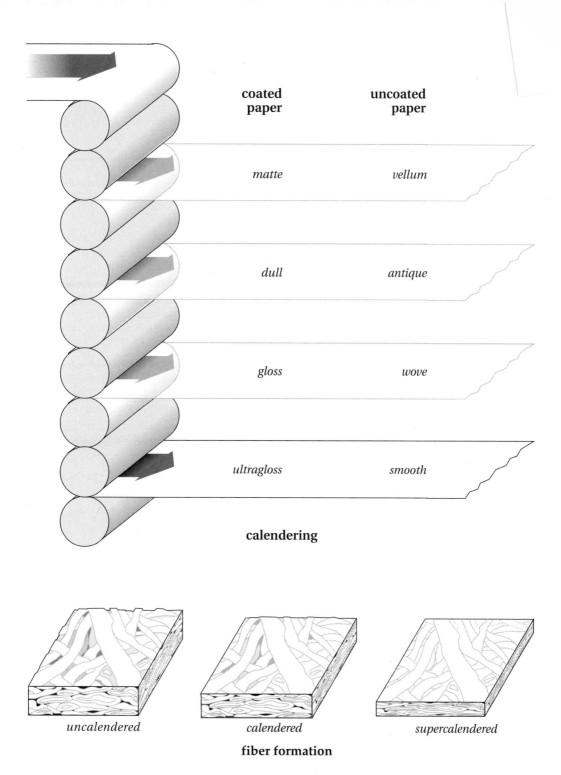

coated paper	uncoated paper
matte	*vellum*
dull	*antique*
gloss	*wove*
ultragloss	*smooth*

calendering

uncalendered   *calendered*   *supercalendered*

fiber formation

text to another part of a publication, such as 'See Appendix A.' **3)** Screen density required when making a color build. For example, the cyan callout might be 30%. **4)** Alternate term for *pull quote.* – 1 & 2, referencia; 4, cita

cameo Alternate term for *emboss.*
– estampar en relieve

cameo type Alternate term for *reverse type.* – tipo invertido

camera, graphic arts Alternate term for *process camera.*

camera lucida Device used by illustrators to enlarge or reduce images so they can be copied by hand to the desired size. A camera lucida is a simple device that works on the same principles as an overhead projector. Also called lucy.
– ampliadora

camera-ready copy Mechanicals, photographs, and art fully prepared for reproduction according to the technical requirements of the printing process being used. Also called finished art and reproduction copy. In Great Britain called line mechanical.
  Copy that is truly camera ready has corrections pasted in position on the mechanical; technically correct overlays; photos shown by keylines, position stats, or windows; register and trim marks; and clear, complete instructions. Photos should be keyed to mechanicals and have cropmarks and other instructions clearly indicated.
– copia lista para cámara

camera separation Separation made using a process camera, as compared to a scanner separation. Separations to reproduce paintings or other originals that do not wrap conveniently around the drum of a scanner are sometimes made using a process camera. – separación por cámara

camera service Business using a process camera to make photostats, halftones, plates, and other elements for printing. Also called prep service and trade camera service.
– negocio de reprografía

Cameron press Brand name for *belt press.*

cancellation proof Final press sheet of a limited or fine-art print run certifying that plates have been destroyed by showing scratches in the image. – prueba de cancelación

canned text Alternate term for *boilerplate.* – párrafos comunes

cap height Height of capital letters in one type size of a font. Illustrated on page 259. – altura de mayúscula

capital letters Letters used to begin sentences and proper nouns. Also called majuscules and uppercase letters. See also *small caps.* – letras mayúsculas

caption Identifying or descriptive text accompanying a photograph, illustration, map, chart, or other visual element. Illustrated on pages 160 and 162. Also called cutline, legend, and underline. – subtítulo, leyenda

captive printer 1) Alternate term for *in-plant printer.* 2) Printing company doing a major portion of its business with only one customer. – 1 & 2, imprenta exclusiva

carbonless paper Paper coated with chemicals that enable transfer of images from one sheet to another with pressure from writing or typing. Also called action paper, impact paper, NCR paper, and self-copy paper.

Carbonless paper may be CB (coated back), CF (coated front), or CFB (coated front and back) and comes in both parent sheets and cut sizes. – papel autocopiante

carbon paper Paper coated with black wax that transfers to another sheet with pressure from writing or typing. Carbon paper may be semi-coated (coated one side) or full coated (coated both sides). – papel carbón

carbro British term for *continuous tone copy.*

cardboard General term for stiff, bulky paper such as blanks, index, tag, or bristol. – cartulina

card deck Collection of business reply cards sent as a package to a direct mail market. Each card in the deck describes a different product and is returned to a different advertiser. – conjunto de tarjetas

carding Alternate term for *feathering (2).* – espaciado entre líneas

card stock Paper used to make products such as postcards and index cards. – cartulina

carload Selling unit of paper. Abbreviated CL.

A carload may weigh anywhere from 20,000 to 100,000 pounds (9,090 to 45,454 kilos), depending on which mill or merchant uses the term. The 20,000 pound figure represents a fully-loaded trailer truck; the 100,000 pound figure a fully-loaded rail car. The mill or merchant using the term may, however, have in mind some amount in between these figures, such as 40,000 pounds (18,180 kilos). – carga total de un furgón

carousel carrier Screen printing machine with arms each holding a screen for a single color, rotating around an axis, and positioning the screens over the item to be printed. A carousel carrier keeps the substrate in a fixed position while printing.

carrier sheet 1) Sheet with indicia and address label inserted into a polybag along with a publication to be mailed. 2) Alternate term for release paper.

car sign Advertising poster mounted at standing eye level inside buses and trains. Car signs are commonly 11 x 28 or 11 x 42 inches. – cartel para autobuses

car sign board Board paper for car signs. It is approximately .02 inch thick and coated on one side. – cartulina ahulada

cartography Art and science of making maps. – cartografía

carton 1) Shipping and selling unit of paper weighing approximately

150 pounds (60 kilos). A carton can contain anywhere from 500 to 5,000 sheets, depending on the size of the sheets and their basis weight.
2) Alternate term for *box (1)*.
– 1 & 2, caja

cartoon Humorous drawing in a newspaper or magazine. – caricatura

cartouche 1) Highly decorated area on a map used to enclose its name and often its legend. 2) Any ornate border made to look historic or antique. – recuadro tipo antiguo

cartridge paper Uncoated paper from 70# book through 65# cover (100 gsm to 200 gsm). – papel guarro

case 1) Shallow tray with compartments to store individual pieces of metal type for letterpress printing. Also called California job case.
2) Covers and spine that, as a unit, enclose the pages of a casebound book. 3) Rarely used shipping unit of paper containing four cartons, approximately 600 pounds.
4) Alternate term for *box (1)*.
– 1, caja tipográfica; 2, tapa; 3 & 4, caja

case bind To bind using glue to hold signatures to a case made of binder board covered with fabric, plastic, or leather. Illustrated on page 16. Also called cloth bind, edition bind, hard bind, and hard cover.
– encuadernación con tapas rígidas

case board Alternate term for *binder's board*. – cartulina para encuadernación

cassette Small box used to protect and carry products such as audio tape, video tape, and film. – cassette

cassette cover Alternate term for *J card*. – tarjeta del cassette

cast-coated paper High gloss, coated paper. Mills achieve the gloss by pressing the paper against a hot, polished, metal drum while the coating is still wet. – papel estucado de lujo

cast off Alternate term for *copyfit*. – calibración del texto

catalog Publication advertising a variety of goods or services offered for sale by one organization.
Catalogs are distinguished from other printed products by purpose rather than specifications. From a production standpoint, a small catalog may be a pamphlet and a large catalog may be a book. Most catalogs are thick booklets similar to magazines. – catálogo

catalog envelope Large envelope that opens on the short dimension and is designed to hold a catalog or magazine. Illustrated on page 209. – sobre para catálogo

Cataloging in Publication Procedure used by the US Library of Congress to assign catalog numbers and information to books before publication. Publishers print the identifying information on the verso of title pages. Cataloging in Publication data help librarians classify new books quickly and accurately. Abbreviated CIP.

catalog paper Coated paper rated #4 or #5 with basis weight from 35# to 50# (50 to 75 gsm) commonly used for catalogs and magazines. – papel para catálogos

catalog sheet Single sheet that advertises goods or services and tells how to order them. – hoja de catálogo

catchlight Alternate term for *specular highlight.* – zona clara especular

catch line Temporary title of a manuscript used prior to publication. – título provisional

catch up Alternate term for *scum (1).*

cathode ray tube Tube where flat end forms the screen for computers and television sets. Also called CRT.

CB Abbreviation referring to carbonless paper coated on its back side only.

CCD Abbreviation for *charge coupled device.*

CCP Abbreviation for *computer controlled press.*

CD-I Abbreviation for compact disc interactive, an optical disc that plays visual information (type, graphics, photos) and auditory information (words, sounds, and music). A CD-I plays through the screen and speaker of either a computer or a television set and may be accessed like a computer memory.

CD-ROM Abbreviation for compact disc, read only memory, an optical disk that plays both visual and auditory information but, unlike a CD-I, may not be randomly accessed.

cell 1) Alternate term for *well.* 2) Location of a single unit of information, such as one box in the matrix of a spread sheet or type table. – 2, celda

cellophane Thin, transparent paper used for packaging and windows in envelopes. – celofán

celluloid proof Alternate term for *overlay proof.* – prueba de celuloide

centered type Type with the middle of each line aligned with the middle of the column. Illustrated on page 270. In Great Britain called quad or range centre. – texto centrado

centerline Imaginary vertical line through the middle of a page or layout. The centerline is used to align type and visual elements on the layout. – línea central

center marks Lines on a mechanical, film, printing plate, or press sheet indicating the center of a page or press sheet. – marcas del centro

center spread Spread located in the middle of a signature. Also called center truck and natural spread. – centrado

center truck Newspaper term for center spread.

central processing unit Part of a computer that calculates data and executes instructions. Central processing unit sizes, expressed in bits, tell how much data they can process at one time. Abbreviated CPU. – unidad central de proceso

CEPS Abbreviation for *color electronic prepress system.*

certificate Document that confirms status, ownership, or performance. – certificado

CF Abbreviation referring to carbonless paper coated on its front side only. – tratado por el frente

CFB Abbreviation referring to carbonless paper coated on its front and back sides. – tratado por ambos lados

CGA Abbreviation for *color graphics adapter.*

chain dot 1) Alternate term for *elliptical dot,* so called because midtone dots touch at two points and look like links in a chain. 2) Generic term for any midtone dots whose corners touch. – 1 & 2, punto en cadena

chain lines 1) Widely-spaced lines in laid paper. Chain lines run vertically and with the grain. 2) Blemishes on printed images, caused by tracking. – 1, líneas de cadena; 2, manchas de cadena

chalking Deterioration of a printed image caused by ink that either absorbs into paper too fast or has long exposure to sun and wind. Chalking makes printed images look dusty as ink pigments separate from the solvent. Chalked ink can be rubbed off the sheet as a powder. Also called crocking.

change order Written instructions about changes to a job already in progress. – cambio de orden

chapbook Small, inexpensive book of poems, short stories, or essays that is perfect bound or saddle stitched. Derived from 18th Century English 'cheapbook.' – libro de bolsillo

chapter Major division of a book. – capítulo

chapter drop White space between the name of a chapter and its first line of text. – espacio de capítulo

chapter head Title and/or numeral at the beginning of a chapter. – título de capítulo

character Any letter, numeral, punctuation mark, or other alphanumeric symbol. – carácter

character alignment Vertical placement of characters so they rest uniformly on a baseline. – alineación de caracteres

character compensation Alternate term for *tracking.*

character count Number of characters in a specific unit of text such as a line or page. For purposes of copyfitting, character count includes spaces as well as characters. – recuento de caracteres

character fit British term for *letter spacing.*

character set Complete collection of characters available in one font. – juego de caracteres

character spacing Alternate term for *letter spacing.* – espacio entre caracteres

characters per inch/pica Average number of characters of a specific typeface and size that fit into one horizontal inch or pica of type.

Number of characters per inch or pica changes in response to changing typeface and type size and using techniques such as extending and condensing. – caracteres por pulgada/pica

characters per second Number of characters of text type that a printer or imagesetter can produce in one second. Characters per second is one method of expressing output speed. Abbreviated CPS. – caracteres por segundo

character user interface Instructions given to a computer by entering letters or numerals, as compared to graphic user interface. – interface a base de caracteres

charge coupled device Silicon chip containing photoreceptors that digitize light by converting it into magnetic impulses. Abbreviated CCD. Scanners, electronic cameras, and other photographic devices use CCDs.

chart paper Alternate term for *map paper.* – papel de marca mayor

chase 1) Metal frame holding type assembled for letterpress printing. 2) Stencil and screen ready for screen printing. – 1, bastidor de cierre; 2, esténcil

check copy 1) Production copy of a publication verified as printed, finished, and bound correctly. Both the printer and the customer keep check copies as a record of how all other copies should look. 2) One set of gathered signatures approved by

the customer as ready for binding. – 1, prueba definitiva; 2, juego de signaturas

checker Alternate term for *galley proof.* – prueba de galera

check paper Alternate term for *safety paper.* – papel para cheques

chemical pulp Pulp for paper made by using chemicals to remove lignin and separate chips into fibers, as compared to mechanical pulp. – pulpa química

Cheshire labels Names, titles, and addresses printed on wide computer paper in a format that can be cut into labels and affixed by machines developed by the Cheshire Company. Also called four-up labels.

Cheshire labels are printed in a format known as four up east/west: there are four columns of labels. The ZIP code sequence runs across rows, then down to the next row, identical to reading a western language. – etiquetas Cheshire

chilled type Type with blurred edges or that is smudged.

China clay Alternate term for *clay.*

chipboard Inexpensive, single-ply board usually brown or gray. Also called cardboard and fiberboard. Chipboard is commonly used as the backing for note pads and point-of-purchase displays. – cartoncillo

choke Technique of slightly reducing the size of an image. Also called shrink and skinny. Illustrated on page 60.

Printers use a choke to create a hairline trap or to outline an image by revealing paper or another ink color behind it. A choke can be created photographically using a contact frame or digitally using image assembly software. – contraer

choke roll Roller, on a flexographic press, that floods the substrate with a background color.

chroma Strength of a color as compared to how close it seems to neutral gray. An ink containing lots of pigment yields a vivid color having strong chroma. Illustrated on page 79. Also called depth, intensity, purity, saturation, and strength. – intensidad

chrome Alternate term for *transparency (1)*. – cromo

chrome plating Thin layer of chromium applied to an etched gravure cylinder to make it last longer on press. – cromado

chrome stripping To remove the chromium from a gravure cylinder. Also called dechrome and strip. – remover el cromo

chromo paper Thick paper especially suited to color printing because of its thick coating. – papel cromo

cicero Typographic unit in the Didot system that expresses a linear measure equal to 4.55 mm (.1776 inches). Each cicero contains 12 Didot points. Illustrated on page 259. Also called Didot pica. – cícero

CIE Abbreviation for *Commission Internationale de l'Eclairage.*

CIE LAB System of describing colors according to the three character-istics of hue, lightness, and saturation. 'Hue' refers to the color itself, 'lightness' to its relative lightness or darkness, and 'satur-ation' to its density. See also *color, language of.*

The CIE system was developed to organize colors into logical relationships. Its concepts and language are widely used in the graphic arts by companies that make software, computer printers, press controls, and instruments such as spectrophotometers.

CIP Abbreviation for *Cataloging in Publication.*

circle chart Alternate term for *pie chart.* – gráfica circular

circles of confusion Circles of light that a lens forms in front of and behind its point of precise focus. The circles become larger as their distances from the point of focus increases. As the circles grow, that dimension of the subject matter becomes more out of focus. Illustrated on page 229.

circular Alternate term for *flier.*

CL Abbreviation for *carload.*

clasp envelope Envelope with a flexible metal clasp that helps hold the flap shut and allows for reuse. Illustrated on page 209. – sobre con broche

classified advertising Advertising consisting mostly of words, not art, and placed into categories with

other ads for similar products or services, as compared to display advertising. Classified ads are usually set in agate type.
– anuncio clasificado

clay Fine-grained natural material, usually aluminum silicate, used to make coating for coated paper. Paper mills use clay as a coating for paper to enhance its smoothness, opacity, and ink holdout. Also called China clay. – porcelana

clean copy Manuscript copy with few errors or flaws, as compared to dirty copy. Also called fair copy.
– copia limpia

clean up To remove errors, such as typos, from a manuscript, or defects, such as spots, from film.
– corregir

clearance merchant Alternate term for *job lot merchant.*

cleat sew To bind by sewing separate sheets, as compared to sewing signatures. – costura de estremo

cleat stitch Alternate term for *side stitch.* – costura de estremo

clip art Copyright-free drawings available for purchase for unlimited reproduction. Clip art illustrations are printed on glossy paper or stored on computer disks. They are ready to place on mechanicals or pages designed using a computer. Illustrated on page 165. Also called standard artwork.
– dibujos recortados

clogging Phenomenon of ink drying in holes of a screen stencil, thus blocking ink from the substrate and causing poor printing. Also called drying in. – atascarse

cloning Computerized technique of duplicating portions of an image, then using the duplicate to replace unwanted portions of the image.
– copiar

closed gate fold Alternate term for *double gate fold.* – doblado de puerta doble

closed heads Signature with folds at tops of the pages.

close formation Relatively uniform distribution of fibers in paper.
– formación compacta

close out Paper merchant term for sale on papers needing to be cleared from inventory. – barata

close register Alternate term for *tight register.* – registro exacto

close up To make a layout seem more unified by removing white space. – acercar comiento

close-up lens Alternate term for *macro lens.* – lente macro

closing date Last date on which a periodical says it will accept articles or advertisements for a specific issue. Also called copy date.
– fecha de cierre

cloth bind Alternate term for *case bind.* – encuadernación en tela

club run Press sheet containing products for several customers, such as labels of different shapes and sizes.

CMYK Abbreviation for cyan, magenta, yellow, and key (black), the four process colors. Illustrated on page 78.

coarse mesh Screen printing fabrics with relatively few threads and apertures per inch or centimeter. – trama ancha

coarse papers Papers made for linings, wrappings, and other industrial uses, as compared to fine papers for writing and printing or sanitary papers such as napkins and tissues. Also called industrial papers. – papeles burdos

coarse screen Halftone screen with ruling of 65, 85, or 100 lines per inch (26, 34, or 40 lines per centimeter). Coarse screens are used when printing on highly absorbant papers, such as newsprint, and with quick printing. – trama ancha

coated cartridge British term for *book paper, coated paper.*

coated paper Paper with a coating of clay and other substances that improves reflectivity and ink holdout. In Great Britain called coated cartridge.

Mills produce coated paper in four major categories of surface shine:

Cast coated is smoothest and most expensive. Only a few mills make cast coated. In Great Britain called machine glazed.

Gloss coated is shiny and comes in a range of levels from premium to #5. Gloss-coated paper is also called art paper, chromo paper, enamel paper, and slick paper.

Dull coated is slightly less shiny than gloss and comes in two levels, premium and #1.

Matte coated is slightly less shiny than dull and comes in three levels, #1, #2, and #3.

Coated paper comes in a wide range of basis weights, from 30# (44 gsm) for catalogs and magazines to 110# (165 gsm) for annual reports and posters. Many commercial printers use #2 gloss in 70# (100 gsm) as a house sheet for products such as brochures and booklets.

Because coated paper is usually printed using four-color process inks, it is available mostly in white and off-white hues such as cream and ivory. Higher grade paper has better ink holdout and more brightness than lower grade stock. – papel tratado, papel estucado

coating Layer of clay and other substances applied to base stock to create the surface of coated paper. – estucado, tratado

cocked-up initial British term for *raised cap.*

cockle finish Slightly puckered surface on bond paper. Mills create a cockle finish by passing the paper through an air dryer during manufacture. – acabado martelé

cockling Unwanted wavy edges on paper caused by absorption of moisture. – ondulado

coffee table book Large book with lavish illustrations or photos for viewing as a work of art as well as for reading. Also called art book. – libro grande ilustrado

coil bind Alternate term for *spiral bind.* – encuadernación con espiral

coin envelope Small envelope with flap on the short dimension used to hold money. – sobre coin

cold colors Blues, greens, and some grays. Also called cool colors because they suggest cool places or scenes. – colores fríos

cold-set ink Alternate term for *non-heat-set ink.* – tinta de secado en frío

cold-set web Alternate term for *non-heat-set web.* – prensa de bobina sin horno

cold type Type from typewriters, dry transfer materials, laser printers and photo type machines, as compared to hot type. – composición en frío

collage Image created by assembling different kinds of elements, such as photos, illustrations, and maps, into one visual whole. Illustrated on page 156. – collage

collate To assemble sheets of paper into proper sequence. – intercalar

collateral Printed pieces, such as newsletters and brochures, that support or supplement display or broadcast advertising. – colateral

collating marks Short lines printed on the spines of signatures showing the sequence in which they should be gathered. Also called backstep marks, blackstep marks, and spine marks. – marcas guías

collotype Method of printing using a plate coated with gelatin that hardens when exposed to light. Also called albertype, artotype, helio-type, and hydrotype.

How hard the gelatin becomes depends upon how much light falls on it. During printing, the gelatin absorbs ink in proportion to the hardness of the image. Ink is transferred to the paper in varying amounts, allowing collotype to reproduce almost continuous tones.

Collotype is suited to very short runs of very high quality printing jobs. Because it does not rely on halftone dots, the technique is also used to make translites.
– fotogelatinografía, albertipia

colophon 1) Production notes, such as information about typeface and paper, printed near the end of a book. 2) Logo that identifies a printer or publisher. – 1 & 2, colofón

color, language of No topic in the graphic arts has less precise language than color. Experts use different terms to describe identical features. Terms flow informally through the industry and find their way into books, software manuals, classes, seminars, and other media.

Consider, for example, the term 'chroma.' The terms 'depth,' 'intensity,' 'purity,' and 'saturation' all mean the same as 'chroma.' You can hear and read them all used as often as 'chroma,' and sometimes interchangeably for each other. The same confusion exists for the term 'value' and its alternates 'tone,' 'shade,' and 'brightness.' To confuse matters further, 'lightness' is used as an alternate term for both 'value' and 'chroma.'

See also *CIE LAB, HVS* and *Munsell Color System.*

color, typographic General darkness or lightness giving visual impact to a page of type. Typeface, leading, and alignment affect typographic color. Light type set with lots of leading has a relatively light color. Bold type set with little leading has a relatively dark color.

color balance 1) Regarding proofs or printed products, refers to amounts of cyan, magenta, yellow, and black that simulate the colors of the original scene or photograph. The process colors are in balance if the customer, the printer, and others involved in the job feel satisfied. They are out of balance if images have an unwanted color cast or hues that don't look correct.
2) Regarding photographic film, refers to emulsion and chemistry that matches film to light sources such as daylight, studio flash, and tungsten lights. Balanced film reproduces images free from color casts when exposed using the light for which it is balanced. Illustrated on page 82. – 1 & 2, balance del color

color bar Alternate term for *color control bar.* – barra de colores

color blanks Press sheets printed with photos or illustrations, but without type. Also called shells. Publishers use color blanks if they plan editions in various languages. They may save blanks for later printing when there will be changes in text copy. – hojas ilustradas sin texto

color booth Alternate term for *viewing booth.* – cabina de inspección

color break In multicolor printing, the point, line, or space at which one ink color stops and another begins. Also called break for color. In Great Britain called colour split. – corte del color

color build See *build a color.*

color cast Unwanted color affecting an entire image or portion of an image. Illustrated on page 82.
Color casts can appear in photographs or reproductions. They can also contaminate a solid color. For example, a color photo might have a blue cast. A gray intended to appear neutral might have a magenta or yellow cast.
On photos, casts originate with incorrect filters, improper lighting conditions, or poor development of film or prints. On proofs, they originate with uncorrected separations or incorrect screen tints. On press sheets, casts can originate with dot gain or out of balance process inks. – contaminación de color

color compensating filters Filters that correct color cast or balance. – filtros correctores de color

color comprehensive Alternate term for *comprehensive dummy.*

color control bar Strip of small blocks of color on a proof or press sheet to help evaluate features such as density, dot gain, and gray balance. Illustrated on page 62. Also called color bar, color guide, and standard offset color bar.

Color control bars have screen rulings appropriate to the paper and press used for the job, such as 150 lpi for sheetfed commercial printing on coated paper, 133 lpi for web on publication-grade coated paper, 120 lpi for sheetfed on uncoated, 100 lpi for web on uncoated, and 85 lpi for newsprint. Typically they contain 25%, 50%, and 75% screen tints of each process color in addition to solids, gray balance targets, and overprints to test wet trapping.

Many organizations produce color control bars, including GATF, GCA, FIPP, FOGRA, 3M, and System Brunner. Printers and separators use the one that best suits their process needs. – barra de colores

color correct To adjust the relationship among the process colors to achieve desirable colors. Color correcting is done by dot etching, masking, re-scanning, or other techniques that are part of making separations. – corrección del color

color curves Instructions in design and page assembly software that allow users to change or correct colors. The curves are look-up tables with options that can be applied to each primary color, either additive or subtractive. Also called HLS and HVS tables. – gráficas de los colores

color electronic prepress system Computer, scanner, printer, and other hardware and software designed for image assembly, color correction, retouching, and output onto proofing materials, film, or printing plates. Abbreviated CEPS.

CEPS installations vary greatly in speed, capabilities, and cost, ranging from desktop systems to high-end color separation systems. Many interface with personal computers. Most can retain images as files on magnetic tape, diskettes, or optical disks for later use.

colorfast Ability of an ink color to retain its original density and resist fading as the product is used or stored. – color fijo

color fringe Printing defect resulting when builds or trapped solids are printed slightly out of register, or when a choke or spread is incorrect. The fringe appears along the edge of an image, showing as one color where a blend should appear. – franja del color

color gamut The entire range of hues possible to reproduce using a specific device, such as a computer screen, or system, such as four-color process. Illustrated on page 78. – gama de colores

color graphics adapter Circuit board, for IBM computers and clones, that supports a color monitor at 640 x 200 resolution, as compared to higher resolution EGAs and VGAs. Abbreviated CGA. – adaptador gráfico a color

color guide 1) Alternate term for *color control bar*. 2) Alternate term for *OK sheet*. 3) Sheet showing colors commonly used by a publication. A color guide reveals how colors look when created by specific techniques or software and printed by specific presses on production paper. 4) British term for *color break*. – 3, guía de los colores

Color Key Brand name for an overlay color proof. Sometimes used as a generic term for any overlay color proof.

color matching system System of numbered ink swatches that facilitates communication about color. See also *Colorcurve, Focaltone, Pantone Matching System,* and *Trumatch*. – sistema de igualación de colores

color model Way of categorizing and describing the infinite array of colors found in nature. Two color models relevant to the graphic arts are *CIE LAB* and *Munsell Color System*. – modelo de colores

color photo Photograph made using film that reproduces images in color, as compared to black and white photo. See also *C print* and *R print*. – fotografía de color

color process printing Alternate term for *four-color process printing*. – cabina de inspección

color reversion Alternate term for *yellowing*. – amarillento

color scanner Electronic device that separates a continuous-tone color image into cyan, magenta, yellow, and black so that the image can be output as four film halftones, one for each of the four process colors. – scanner de colores

color separation 1) Technique of using a camera, scanner, or computer to divide continuous-tone color images into four film halftones ready for stripping, proofing, and platemaking for four-color process printing. Illustrated on page 72.
2) The product resulting from color separating and subsequent four-color process printing.
3) Technique of preparing film or plates for a job requiring two or more colors. In this sense, color separating could take place in computer output, pasteup, or stripping. Color separating for letterpress is done by making separate forms for each color. Also called separation. – 1 - 3, separación de colores

color separation service Business making color separations for four-color process printing. Also called engraver, prep service, separator, and service bureau. – servicio de separación de colores

color sequence Order in which inks are printed. With process colors, the sheetfed sequence is often black first, then magenta, cyan, and yellow last. The web sequence is often cyan, magenta, yellow, with black either first or last. Also called laydown sequence and rotation. In Great Britain called printing sequence. – secuencia de colores

color shift Change in image color resulting from changes in register, ink densities, or dot gain during printing. – cambio de color

color station Alternate term for *printing unit*. – mecanismo impresor

color swatch Small sample of paper or printed ink. – muestra de color

color temperature System of expressing the color of light. Equal amounts of red, green, and blue light produce a color temperature of 5000 degrees Kelvin, the standard light for evaluating color for the graphic arts industy in the US and Canada. – temperatura del color

color transparency Alternate term for *transparency (1)*.

color wheel Circular chart showing colors of the visible spectrum. Illustrated on page 78. – muestrario circular de colores

colour comp print British term for *R print*.

colour etch British term for *dot etch*.

colour overleaf proofs British term for *overlay proof*.

colour split British term for *color break*.

column 1) Vertical arrangement of type on a page or in a table, as compared to a row. Illustrated on pages 23 and 164. 2) Article, in a periodical, that appears regularly and is written by the same author or about the same topic. – 1, columna; 2, artículo

column inch One inch measured vertically up or down a column. Column inches are used most often to measure space for display advertising. – pulgada de columna

column rule Thin vertical line that separates columns. – línea de columna

co mail To join two or more publications to reduce postage costs. Co mailing could take place by collating or fastening pieces in the bindery or by inserting pieces into one envelope, bundle, sack, or pallet. All pieces must be mailed within the same class of mail.

comb bind To bind by inserting the teeth of a flexible plastic comb through holes punched along the edge of a stack of paper. Also called plastic bind and GBC bind (a brand name). Illustrated on page 16.
    Plastic combs are available in many sizes and colors and may be screen printed so information appears on the spine of the publication. – encuadernación con peine

combination board Board paper usually consisting of three plies (layers). – cartulina de combinación

combination line and tone British term for *composite film, composite art*.

combination plate Printing plate including both line art and halftones. – plancha mixta

combination run Alternate term for *gang (2)*. – tiraje de combinación

comet Defect in gravure printing caused when a tiny piece of dirt gets stuck under the doctor blade, causing ink to streak. Looks like the tail of a comet.

comic book Book or booklet using cartoons to tell a story. – historieta, cuento

comic strip Sequence of cartoons telling a story. – tira cómica

coming and going British term for *work and turn.*

commercial envelope Alternate term for *business envelope.* – sobre oficio

commercial film Film used to make continuous-tone photographs, as compared to graphic arts film. – película comercial

commercial match Acceptable difference between the color on a sample of ink or paper, or the color on a proof, and the color achieved on press. Printing jobs produced according to commercial match have goals that do not require extensive effort to reproduce colors precisely and budgets that do not allow for it. – igualación aproximada

commercial printer Printer that produces a wide range of products such as announcements, brochures, posters, booklets, stationery, business forms, books, and magazines. Commercial printers typically use metal plates made from negatives, as compared to quick printers using paper or plastic plates made directly from mechanicals. Also called job printer. – imprenta comercial

commercial register Informal trade recognition that acceptable quality allows slight variation of register during the press run. – registro satisfactorio

commercial signs Typographic symbols such as © (copyright), $ (US dollars) £ (pounds sterling),

and % (percentage). – signos comerciales

Commission Internationale de l'Eclairage International Commission on Light. Abbreviated CIE.

commodity Refers to paper or printing produced quickly and in high volumes, thus relatively inexpensive. – común

communication paper Alternate term for *bond paper.* – papel bond

comp 1) Abbreviation for *comprehensive dummy.* 2) Abbreviation for *complementary copy.*

comparable stock Alternate term for *equivalent paper.*

compendium Synopsis or summary of a book or other relatively long publication. – compendio

compensated stack Alternate term for *brick pack.*

complementary colors Colors directly opposite each other on the color wheel. – colores complementarios

complimentary colour removal British term for *grey component replacement.*

complementary flat(s) The second or additional flat(s) used when making composite film or for two or more burns on one printing plate. See also *double burn.* – montajes complementarios

complimentary copy Free copy of a book or other publication. – ejemplar gratuito

compose 1) To set type. 2) To make (strip) composite film from pieces of working film. – 1, componer; 2, ensamblar

Composer Brand name for strike-on typesetting machine no longer made.

composite art Mechanical on which copy for reproduction in all colors appears on only one surface, not separated onto overlays. Composite art has a tissue overlay with instructions that indicate color breaks. In Great Britain called combination line and tone. – arte compuesto

composite film Film made by combining images from two or more pieces of working film onto one film for making one plate. In Great Britain called combination line and tone. – película compuesta

composite photo Photo made by combining two or more images. – fotografía compuesta

composite proof Proof of color separations in position with graphics and type. Also called final proof, imposition proof, and stripping proof. In Great Britain called imposed colour proof. – prueba compuesta

composition 1) In photography, the manner in which an image is arranged and framed to give an overall effect. 2) In typography, the assembly of typographic elements, such as paragraphs, into pages ready for printing. 3) In graphic design, the arrangement of type, graphics, and other elements on the page. – 1, marcado; 2 & 3, composición

composition proof Alternate term for *integral color proof.* – prueba compuesta

composition type Alternate term for *text type.* – tipo de texto

compositor Alternate term for *typesetter (2),* especially with reference to hot type.

comprehensive dummy Simulation of a printed piece complete with type, graphics, and colors. A comprehensive dummy is the closest possible representation of the final printed product until it is represented by color proofs. Also called color comprehensive and comp. In Great Britain called comprehensive layout. – croquis, muestra definitiva

comprehensive layout British term for *comprehensive dummy.*

computer-controlled press Press with many features operated by using a computer. Abbreviated CCP.
Typical features controlled by computers on a press include ink and water flow, register, and paper feed. – prensa computarizada

computer graphics Charts, maps, illustrations, and other images created using a computer. – gráficos de computador

computer memory Ability of a computer to retain information.
Some memory, such as RAM, exists only when the machine is turned on. Other memory, such as

that on disks and tapes, is storage that exists regardless of whether the machine is on or off.

Memory is expressed as number of bytes. Kilobytes, megabytes, and gigabytes are the most common categories.

Many computer applications in the graphic arts need relatively large amounts of memory, especially when handling operations involving halftone dots. Memory required for halftones depends on many factors, including number of pixels per dot, screen ruling, screen angle, dot shape, and size of the image.
– memoria de computador

computer program Alternate term for *software.*

concentric circle screen One of many special effect screens.– trama de círculos concéntricos

concertina fold Alternate term for *accordion fold.* – doblado tipo acordeón

concordance Alphabetical index of words or phrases and their contexts as found in a specific publication, such as a religious text. – concordancia

condensed type Characters relatively narrow in proportion to their height, thus seeming tall and tightly-spaced. Illustrated on page 255.
– letras condensadas

condition To keep paper in the pressroom for a few hours or days before printing so that its moisture level and temperature equal that in the pressroom. Improperly conditioned paper may curl, go out of register, or develop other problems on press. Also called cure, mature, and season. – curar

C1S Abbreviation for *coated one side.* In Great Britain called one-sided art paper.

confirming proof Any proof considered final and provided as evidence that a job was done correctly. – prueba final

console British term for *terminal.*

consolidate Alternate term for *amalgamate.* – consolidar

consumer magazine Magazine published for the general public, as compared to a trade journal.
– revista para consumidores

contact platemaker Alternate term for *vacuum frame.* – pasador de planchas de contacto

contact print 1) Photographic print made by exposure of film in contact with paper, as compared to enlargement. 2) Screen print made with a stencil in contact with the substrate.
– 1 & 2, copia por contacto

contact screen Alternate term for the screen used to make screen tints or halftones. – pantalla de contacto

contact sheet Alternate term for *proof sheet.* – hoja de contacto

container Large metal box used to enclose goods for shipment via rail car or ship.

Containers come in two standard sizes. A small container holds 24 pallets with standard European dimensions and loads, a large container holds 48 pallets. Many pallets, however, do not carry standard loads, so the capacity of a container varies. – contenedor

container printing Screen printing of objects, such as bottles, that are not flat. Also called geometric printing.

continuous paper Paper for business forms or general computer printing with each sheet attached to other sheets as part of an accordion-folded supply. Continuous paper has sprocket holes along two sides and perforations that divide the sheets. Also called fan fold paper and reel paper. – papel continuo

continuous-tone copy All photographs and those illustrations with a range of shades not made up of dots, as compared to line copy or halftones. Abbreviated contone. In Great Britain called carbro.

Continuous-tone copy must be converted to halftones for faithful reproduction using a printing press. The conversion process may be done either photographically, or using a computer or a scanner. These methods use screens, called either line-conversion screens or halftone screens, to make halftones or color separations. – copia de tonos continuos

contone Abbreviation for *continuous-tone copy.*

contouring Alternate term for *tone breaks.* 'Contouring' is often used to refer to tone breaks in output from non-impact printers.

contract artist Alternate term for *freelancer.*

contrast Difference between the lightest and darkest portions of an image. Illustrated on page 226.

Continuous-tone copy and halftone copy, such as photographs, may be relatively high or low in contrast, depending on the original scene, techniques of exposure, developing, and printing, and the paper used.

Line copy, such as type, is by definition high contrast. To be legible, dark images should stand out from light backgrounds. Printing plates and graphic arts film and paper are made to reproduce only high-contrast images—line art and halftone dots. – contraste

contrast grade Rating of photographic paper that helps match it to the negative to achieve desired effects in the final print. The most common contrast grades are 1 soft, 2 medium, 3 hard, 4 extra hard, and 5 ultra hard. Litho paper for reproducing line copy has a contrast grade of 6 or more.

Contrast grades are not standardized. Results on one brand rated #3 may be different from results on another brand with the same rating. – grado de contraste

contrast ratio 1) Measure of opacity of paper expressed as a percentage of light it reflects when backed by a black surface as compared to light reflected when backed by a white surface. 2) Alternate term for *density range.* – 1 & 2, proporción de contraste

control ball Alternate term for *track ball.* – bola de control

control character Alternate term for *delimiter*. – carácter de control

conversion service Business that specializes in data conversion. – servicio de conversión

convertable press Press that can be changed from perfecting to printing one side only. – prensa convertible

converter Business that makes products such as bags, envelopes, and displays. A converter uses unprinted paper as raw material, as when making envelopes, or printed sheets, as when making boxes from chipboard laminated to paper. – convertidor

cool colors Blues, greens, and other colors that suggest cool places or scenes, as compared to warm colors. Cool colors have lower color temperatures than warm colors. – colores fríos

co palletize To place on one pallet a variety of items, such as different catalogs or magazines, addressed to the same destination, to reduce costs and speed delivery.

copier Alternate term for *photocopy machine*. – copiadora

copier paper Smooth, white paper made for everyday use in photocopy machines and laser printers. Also called xerocopy paper. – papel para copiadora

copy 1) For an editor or typesetter, all written material. 2) For a graphic designer or printer, everything to be printed: art, photographs, and graphics as well as words. 3) Dup-

licate made using a photocopy machine. 4) Any duplicate of an original. – 1 & 2, original; 3, copiar; 4, copia

copy area Alternate term for *image area*. – área de la copia

copyboard Surface or frame on a process camera that holds copy in position to be photographed. – portaoriginales

copy camera 1) Alternate term for *process camera*. 2) Camera with a macro or process lens. Used to make photographic reproductions of documents. – cámara de foto-reproducción

copy date Alternate term for *closing date*. – fecha de cierre

copy editor Person who checks and corrects a manuscript for spelling, grammar, punctuation, inconsistencies, inaccuracies, and conformity to style requirements, as compared to a visual editor. Also called line editor. – corrector del texto

copyfit 1) To calculate the space that text requires in a specific typeface and point size. 2) To edit writing and adjust typography for the purpose of making text fit a layout. Also called cast off. In Great Britain called white out. – calcular

copy preparation 1) In typesetting, marking up a manuscript and specifying type. 2) In paste up and printing, making mechanicals and writing instructions that ensure proper placement, printing, and finishing of each component of the mechanical. – preparación del original

copy range Alternate term for *density range.* – rango de densidad

copyright Ownership of creative work by the writer, photographer, artist, or programmer who made it, or, if work for hire, the organization that paid for it. – derechos de autor

copyright notice Statement of copyright ownership that has three elements: the word 'copyright' or symbol ©; the year of publication; and, the name of the copyright owner. For example, 'Copyright 1992 Mark Beach.' – aviso del copyright

copyright page Page of a book showing copyright information and Cataloging in Publication. Usually verso of the title page. Also called biblio page.

copy shop Print shop that uses photocopy machines, not offset presses, to reproduce originals. – servicio de fotocopias

copywriter Person who writes advertising copy. – publicista

core curl Alternate term for *roll set.* – abarquillamiento del núcleo

core waste Paper near the center of a roll that is unusable because of roll set or splicing techniques, as compared to strip waste. – desperdicio del centro del rollo

corner marks Lines on a mechanical, negative, plate, or press sheet showing locations of the corners of a page or finished piece.
   Corner marks appear outside the image area or trim size so they do not show on the finished piece. Strippers and printers use them as register guidelines; bindery staff use them as guidelines for folding and trimming. – marcas de esquina

corner stitch To bind with one staple through a corner, usually the upper left. – engrapado en esquina

corporate identity Personality or image of an organization as conveyed by features such as logo, colors, graphic design, and style of writing. – identidad corporativa

correction marks Alternate term for *proofreader marks.*

correspondence paper Alternate term for *bond paper.* – papel bond

corrugated board Board made by sandwiching fluted kraft paper between sheets of paper or cardboard. Used for making boxes.
   Single-wall boards have one sheet glued to one side of the corrugation; double-wall boards have one sheet glued to each side; triple-wall boards have two corrugated layers and three sheets, one in the middle and one on each side. – cartón

cotton content paper Paper made from cotton or linen fibers instead of, or in addition to, tree fibers. Mills use percentages to express the amount of cotton fibers used, with 25% cotton and 100% cotton being most common. Also called rag paper. – papel con algodón

count Number of pieces printed, bound, delivered, or charged for. Also called final count and finished count. – cuenta

counter 1) Gauge on a press or bindery machine that records the number of pieces that have passed through the machine. 2) Alternate term for *female die* in foil stamping and embossing. – 1, contador; 2, matriz

counter card Small display made to stand on a counter or table. Illustrated page 87. – tarjeta de mostrador

counter display Alternate term for *point of purchase display*. – cartel de mostrador

counter stack To assemble catalogs or magazines in spine-to-front groups to achieve a level pile. For mailing purposes, counter stacking must meet postal regulations about number of turns and orientation of addresses. – flejar, amarrar

coupon Small certificate that entitles the owner to a payment, discount, or privilege. – cupón

coupon book Book of coupons that are perforated for easy removal. – libro de cupones

coupon page Sheet of coupons inserted into newspapers and other publications. – página de cupones

courtesy line Alternate term for *credit line.*

courtesy reply envelope Pre-addressed envelope for which the sender pays postage, commonly a #6 business envelope in North America and a C7/6 in ISO sizes. – sobre para servicio del lector

cover Thick paper that protects a publication and advertises its title. Illustrated on pages 23 and 53.

Parts of covers are often described as follows: Cover 1 = outside front; Cover 2 = inside front; Cover 3 = inside back; Cover 4 = outside back. – cubierta

coverage Extent to which ink covers the surface of a substrate. Ink coverage is usually expressed as light, medium, or heavy. – capacidad de cubrir

cover board Board paper used to make cases for casebound books. Illustrated on page 23. – cartulina para cubiertas

cover date Date of issue printed on the cover or front page of a periodical. – fecha de edición

covering power British term for *opacity (2).*

cover paper 1) Category of thick paper used for products such as posters, menus, folders, and covers of paperback books. Illustrated on page 115.

Many brands of cover paper are made to coordinate with corresponding brands of bond, book, or text paper to give products a unified design. Compatible stocks have identical colors and surfaces, differing only in basis weight and thickness. Bond paper for letterhead can match cover paper for business cards; text paper for a brochure can match cover paper for a presentation folder.

Mills make cover paper in two common weights, 65# (175 gsm) and 80# (215 gsm). Cover papers are also commonly specified by caliper instead of basis weight, with 8

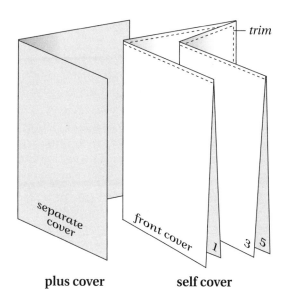

plus cover **self cover**

trim

separate cover

front cover 1 3 5

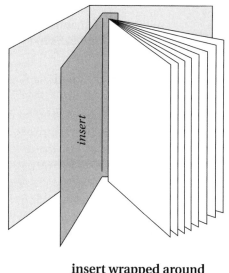

insert

**insert wrapped around
16-page signature**

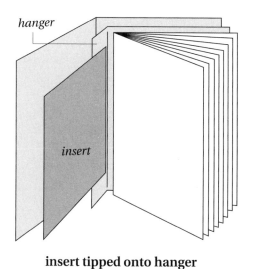

hanger

insert

insert tipped onto hanger

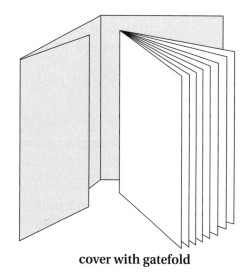

cover with gatefold

point, 10 point, and 12 point being the most common calipers.

2) Paper used for the cover of a publication or catalog, as compared to its text paper. – 1 & 2, papel para cubiertas

cover price Retail price of a publication. – precio de portada

cover stock Paper used to make the cover of a publication. – papel para cubiertas

cover wrap Four-page wrap over the actual cover of a magazine or catalog that protects it in the mail. Also called outsert and wraparound. – envoltura de cubierta

C paper sizes One of five categories of ISO paper sizes.

CPI Abbreviation for *characters per inch.*

CPP Abbreviation for *characters per pica.*

C print Color photographic print made from a negative using Kodak C Print paper and processing. Often used generically to refer to any color print made from a negative. In Great Britain called C type or negative-positive print. – impresión C

CPS Abbreviation for *characters per second.*

CPU Abbreviation for *central processing unit.*

crash 1) Coarse cloth embedded in the glue along the spine of a book to increase strength of binding. Illustrated on page 23. Also called gauze , mull, and scrim. **2)** Sudden

failure of a machine, such as a computer, or sequence of activities, such as a program or schedule. – 1, gaza; 2, avería

crash finish Finish on text paper similar to crash cloth used to bind books. Also called homespun finish.

crash numbering Letterpress printing on multipart forms so that numeral printed on the top sheet simultaneously transfers to all other sheets in each set.

crash printing Letterpress printing on multipart forms so that the image printed on the top sheet simultaneously transfers to all other sheets in each set.

crease Alternate term for *score.* – rayar

credit line Line of relatively small type next to a photo or illustration giving its source and/or the name of the photographer or artist. May include copyright notice. Illustrated on pages 160 and 162. Also called courtesy line. – línea de reconocimiento

creep 1) Phenomenon of middle pages of a folded signature extending slightly beyond outside pages. Illustrated on page 223. Also called feathering, outpush, push out, and thrust. See also *shingling.*

2) In screen printing, the phenomenon of ink or varnish spreading into non-image areas due to poor drying.

3) In flexography, phenomenon of sagging or changing shape of rubber plate which has been improperly mounted or stored.

4) Also in flexography, the tendency of images to print out of register near the end of the plate. – 1 - 4, deslizarse

crocking Alternate term for *chalking.*

Cromalin Brand name for integral proof. Often used generically to refer to any integral proof.

crop To eliminate portions of an image so the remainder is more useful, pleasing, or able to fit the layout. Illustrated on page 233. – recortar

crop marks Lines near the edges of an image indicating portions to be reproduced. Illustrated on page 233. Also called cut marks and tic marks. In Great Britain called dimension marks. – marcas de corte

cropping angles Alternate term for *cropping Ls.* – recortes de cartón en "L"

cropping Ls Pieces of paper cut into L shapes which, when overlapped, can be adjusted to frame a photograph. Cropping Ls are used to view possible ways of cropping an image. Also called cropping angles. – recortes de cartón en "L"

cross direction British term for *against the grain.*

cross fold British term for *against the grain.* – contra la fibra

cross grain Alternate term for *against the grain.* – contra la fibra

crosshatching Shading created by closely-spaced sets of lines. – rayado cruzado

crossline screen Halftone screen scribed into glass. Also called Levy screen. – trama de líneas cruzadas

cross marks Alternate term for *register marks.* – cruz de registro

crossover Type or art that continues from one page across the gutter to the opposite page. Also called bridge, gutter bleed, and gutter jump. – cruzado

CRT Abbreviation for cathode ray tube, the computer screen.

CSR Abbreviation for customer service representative.

C2S Abbreviation for *coated two sides.*

C type British term for *C print.*

CUI Abbreviation for *character user interface.*

cultural papers Alternate term for *fine papers.* – papeles culturales

cup Alternate term for *well.*

cure **1)** To dry inks, varnishes, or other coatings after printing to ensure good adhesion and prevent setoff. Curing is usually done under heat or special light in a curing oven in line with the press. The term may, however, refer simply to allowing sufficient time to pass before beginning the next step in manufacturing. **2)** Alternate term for *condition.* – 1 & 2, curar

curl Tendency of paper to bend parallel to its grain direction due to uneven moisture content. – abarquillamiento

currency paper Premium 100% rag content paper made to be strong and durable for products such as money and bonds. Typically sub 24 (90 gsm). Also called banknote paper. – papel moneda

cursive Alternate term for *script (1)*.

cursor Marker displayed on a computer screen designating which character or location will be affected by the next action. Also called insertion point. – cursor

cursor arrows Alternate term for *arrow keys*. – flechas del cursor

customer alteration Alternate term for *alteration*. – alteración del cliente

customer service representative Employee of a printer, service bureau, separator, or other business, who coordinates projects and keeps customers informed. Abbreviated CSR.

A CSR works inside an organization as the person everyone depends on for quick answers and smooth flow of work. Often a CSR works with the customers of one or two specific sales representatives. – representante para servicio de los clientes

customs, printing trade See *trade customs*.

cut 1) (verb) To remove copy from a manuscript, mechanical, or computer file. 2) (noun) An illustration or halftone ready for letterpress printing. Because letterpress images are engraved, they are all known as 'cuts.' The small type that identifies and

explains them is a cutline. – 1, reducir; 2, clisé

cut ahead To trim paper without regard for where the watermark appears on the sheet.

cutaway illustration Illustration drawn to reveal the inside of an object. Illustrated on page 195.

cut-back bind Alternate term for *perfect bind*. – encuadernación perfecta

cut-back film Film that has been extensively etched to compensate for relatively large dot gain, as with offset on newsprint or flexography on kraft paper.

cut-back proof Proof made from cut-back film.

cut flush Alternate term for *flush cover*. – cortado al ras

cut-in headline Headline that is embedded in a paragraph so that text runs around it at the top, right, and bottom. – título marginal intercalado

cut-in index Alternate term for *thumb index*. – índice recortado

cutline 1) Alternate term for *caption*. 2) Defect sometimes appearing on a printed product when one piece of film is patched into another or when an element is pasted onto a mechanical. – 1, leyenda; 2, sombra del corte

cut marks Alternate term for *crop marks*. – marcas de corte

cutoff Circumference of impression cylinder of a web press, therefore also the length of the printed sheet that the press cuts from the roll of paper.

The cutoff of a press usually results in a sheet of paper with the same dimensions as a common sheet size. For example, a 22-inch press with a 17-inch cutoff yields sheets that are 17 x 22 inches. Knowing the size and cutoff of a web press allows designing for efficient use of paper.

When a web press runs without cutting sheets at the delivery end, such as when printing labels that will rewind onto a roll, the circumference of the impression cylinder is called the repeat length.
– límite de cada impresión

cutoff rule Horizontal floating rule between classified ads that separates one ad from the next.

cut sizes Paper sizes used with office machines and small presses. North American cut sizes are 8½ x 11 inches (letter size), 8½ x 14 inches (legal size), and 11 x 17 inches (tabloid size). ISO cut sizes are A4 (210 x 297 mm) and A3 (297 x 420 mm). – pliegos cortados

cutting tolerances Allowable variations in dimensions resulting from trimming or die cutting. Common cutting tolerance for trimming is $\frac{1}{32}$ inch (.8 mm), for die cutting $\frac{1}{64}$ inch (.4 mm).
– tolerancias de cortes

cut to register To trim paper so the watermark appears at close to the same location on every sheet.

CWT Abbreviation for *hundred-weight* using the Roman numeral C for 100.

cyan One of the four process colors. Illustrated on pages 72 and 78. – cian

cyan printer Film, plate, or ink station that controls the printing of cyan ink. Illustrated on page 72.
– plancha cian

cylinder 1) Large roller on a printing press. Offset presses have plate cylinders, blanket cylinders, and impression cylinders. 2) The plate in gravure printing. Illustrated on page 117. – 1 & 2, cilindro

cylinder gap Open space along the width of a press cylinder that houses clamps and grippers.
– ranura del cilindro

D

daisy wheel Circular print element used on some typewriters and computer printers. Called a daisy wheel because the keys spread from the center like petals on a daisy flower. Also called print wheel. – margarita

dampener fountain Alternate term for *water fountain*. – mecanismo mojador

dampener solution Alternate term for *fountain solution*. – solución mojador

dampening rolls Alternate term for *water rolls*. – rodillos mojadores

damper British term for *water fountain*.

dandy roll Wire-mesh drum on a papermaking machine. The dandy roll presses watermarks and surface patterns into paper while it is still 90% water. – rodillo escurridor

darken Technique of using a computer to increase highlight detail in an image appearing on a screen, as compared to lighten.

When photographic techniques are used in a darkroom to increase highlight detail, it's called burning. – oscurecer

dark printer Negative or plate that carries lower midtones and shadows for a duotone. – plancha oscura

darkroom Room sealed from outside light and equipped for film development and photographic printing while illuminated by safe light. – cuarto oscuro

dash Typographic mark indicating a break between thoughts. An em dash (—) is longer than an en dash (–) and much longer than a hyphen (-). – guión

database Collection of information categorized according to fields and records and organized for efficient access by a computer.

A database could contain anywhere from hundreds to millions of records; each record could contain anywhere from a few fields to several dozen. A computer can access the information quickly and randomly to search or analyze a database. – base de datos

database publishing Publishing products, such as directories, encyclopedias, price lists, and technical documentation, using information kept in a database. – base de datos para publicar

data card Sheet or card that gives rental costs and reports demographics of a mailing list. In Great Britain called media data form. – tarjeta de datos

data compression Technique of reducing the amount of storage required to hold a digital file. For example, a 35mm transparency requires approximately 18 megabytes of memory to store at photographic resolution. Using data compression, the same image requires approximately 4 megabites to store on a photo compact disk.

Data compression reduces the disk space the file requires and allows it to be processed or transmitted more quickly. Compression works most efficiently with text files and with files containing images having relatively little detail, such as screen tints. – compresión de datos

data conversion Technique of changing digital information from its original code so that it can be recorded by an electronic device using a different code.

Data conversion is often required when copy has been created using one kind of computer or software and will be prepared for printing using another kind. Data must also be converted for various output devices, such as when RGB colors are converted to CMY colors. – conversión de datos

data manual Book giving technical information and illustrations about computers and other complex machines. – manual de datos

dated material Documents, such as price lists and schedules, containing information accurate or useful only until a certain date. – material fechado

dateline 1) Line of type giving the date of publication. Illustrated on page 162. 2) Line of type at the beginning of a news article giving the location from which it was written. – línea de fecha

DDCP Abbreviation for *direct digital color proof.*

DDES Abbreviation for *digital data exchange standard.*

deadline Final day or hour by which a project must be complete or delivered. Also called due date. – fecha límite

dead matter Images in forms or on plates that have been printed and are no longer needed, as compared to live matter. – composición no útil

deboss To press an image into paper so it lies below the surface. Also called tool. Illustrated on page 247. In Great Britain called platesunk. – estampar bajo relieve

debug To remove flaws from a computer program or any process requiring a precise sequence of actions. – remover errores

decal Short for decalcomania, designs or logos printed on film or paper to allow easy transfer of the design to glass, cloth, or other

posterization

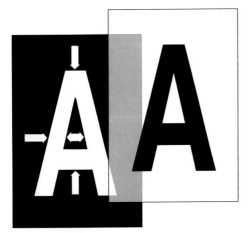

choke

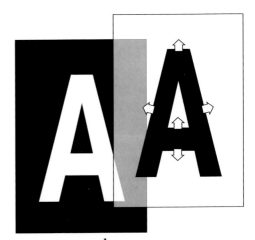

spread

untrapped ink colors

trapped ink color

surface. Decals may release under heat and pressure, when soaked in water, or may transfer after peeling off a backing material. – calcomanía

decal paper Smooth, flexible paper used as backing for decals. – papel para calcamonias

dechrome Alternate term for *chrome stripping.*

deck 1) Alternate term for *printing unit.* 2) Alternate term for *subhead.* – 1, unidad impresora; 2, subtítulo

deckle edge Edge of paper left ragged as it comes from the papermaking machine instead of being cleanly cut. Also called feather edge. – barba del papel

dedicated Equipment assigned to one task that it performs especially well. For example, a web press with a custom cutoff to produce only four-color rack brochures would be a dedicated press. – dedicado

dedication Inscription on a manuscript or near the front of a book that honors a family member or friend. – dedicatoria

deep-etch halftone British term for *dropout halftone.*

default Action that computer program automatically performs unless instructed otherwise by operator. For example, word processing software defaults to ragged right unless instructed to justify. – default

definition Alternate term for *focus.* A photo with good definition is in focus. – definición

dégradé Alternate term for *graduated screen tint* and *vignette.*

delimiter Symbol that identifies the beginning or end of a character string, separating instructions to a computer from data to be processed. In the preparation of electronic manuscripts, the most common delimiters are '<' and '>'. Also called control character and precedence code. – delimitador

delivery date Date on which goods arrived or legal possession changed hands. Some printers consider delivery date when finished products leave the bindery, not when they arrive at the customer's place of business. In the case of paper, delivery date may be when the ship arrives at the loading dock of the mill or merchant, not at the site of the printer. – fecha de entrega

delivery memo Document signed by customer to verify receipt of goods and agreement to contract terms. – memorándum de entrega

demographic edition Edition of a publication using selective binding, ink jet printing, and other techniques to tailor the publication to a specific audience as defined by factors such as income, age, location, and/or buying habits. – edición demográfica

densitometer Instrument used to calculate density.
Printers use densitometers to ensure proper exposure and processing for film and appropriate ink coverage on press. Reflection densitometers measure light

Graphic Arts Technical Foundation, 1992

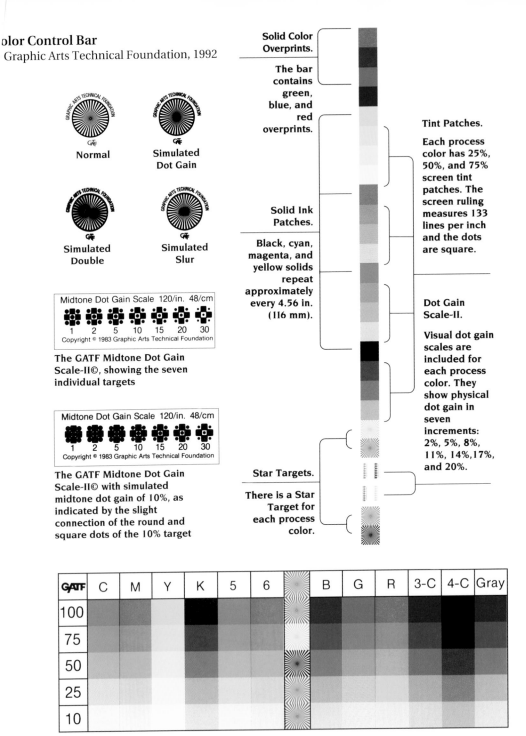

Normal

Simulated Dot Gain

Simulated Double

Simulated Slur

Midtone Dot Gain Scale 120/in. 48/cm

1 2 5 10 15 20 30

Copyright © 1983 Graphic Arts Technical Foundation

The GATF Midtone Dot Gain Scale-II©, showing the seven individual targets

Midtone Dot Gain Scale 120/in. 48/cm

1 2 5 10 15 20 30

Copyright © 1983 Graphic Arts Technical Foundation

The GATF Midtone Dot Gain Scale-II© with simulated midtone dot gain of 10%, as indicated by the slight connection of the round and square dots of the 10% target

Solid Color Overprints.

The bar contains green, blue, and red overprints.

Solid Ink Patches.

Black, cyan, magenta, and yellow solids repeat approximately every 4.56 in. (116 mm).

Star Targets.

There is a Star Target for each process color.

Tint Patches.

Each process color has 25%, 50%, and 75% screen tint patches. The screen ruling measures 133 lines per inch and the dots are square.

Dot Gain Scale-II.

Visual dot gain scales are included for each process color. They show physical dot gain in seven increments: 2%, 5%, 8%, 11%, 14%, 17%, and 20%.

Color Reproduction Guide II

reflected from paper and other surfaces; transmission densitometers measure light transmitted through film and other materials. – densitómetro

density 1) Regarding ink, a way of expressing the approximate thickness of a layer of printed ink. See also *densitometer* and *target ink densities.*

2) Regarding color, the relative ability of a color to absorb light reflected from it or block light passing through it. Dark colors are more dense than light colors. High-percentage screen tints are more dense than low-percentage tints.

3) Regarding paper, the relative tightness or looseness of fibers. The density of paper affects its bulk, finish, and ink holdout.

4) Regarding floppy disks and other electronic media, the relative amount of data that fits into a given medium. For example, double-density disks hold twice as much data as single-density disks.

5) Regarding type, the degree of blackness. Type that is too dense or not dense enough doesn't read well when printed. – 1 - 5, densidad

density, of bar code Number of characters per inch in a bar code.

density of tone Alternate term for *total area coverage.* – área total cubierta

density range Difference between the darkest and lightest areas of copy. Also called contrast ratio, copy range, and tonal range.

The density range of an image determines its contrast. A photo having relatively dark highlights or relatively light shadows has a small density range, thus low contrast.

Density range is measured using a densitometer. For example, a bright highlight on coated paper might have a density of .10 and a dark shadow a density of 1.90. The density range of the image is 1.80 (1.90 minus .10).

The density range achievable by photographic paper and film is far greater than that achievable by printing inks. See also *tone compression.* – rango de densidad

depth Alternate term for *chroma.* – profundidad

depth of field 1) Distance in front of a camera within which its lens can render acceptably sharp focus of a subject. Illustrated on page 228.
2) Difference between closest and farthest distances at which a scanner can read information, such as a bar code. – profundidad de campo

descender Portion of a lower case letter falling below its baseline. Illustrated on page 259. – rasgo descendente

descending collate Alternate term for *reverse collate.*

design brief Written description of how a printed piece is intended to look and the requirements for reproducing it. A design brief is a narrative description, not a list of technical specifications. – descripción resumen

mechanical to printed piece

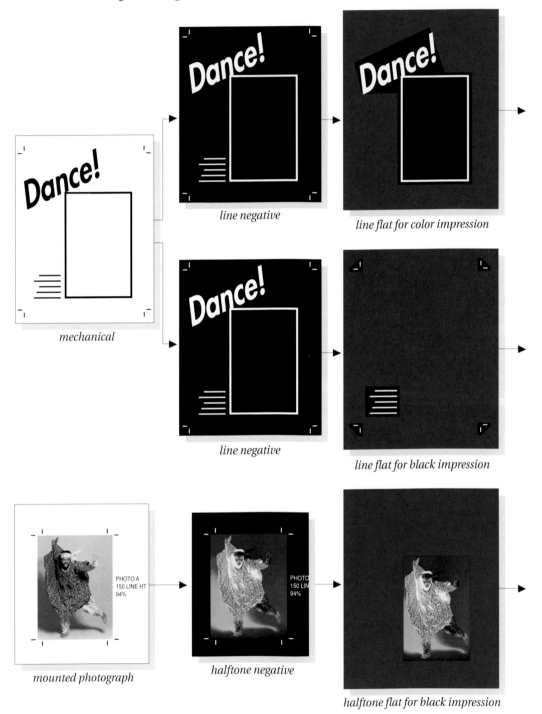

line negative

line flat for color impression

mechanical

line negative

line flat for black impression

mounted photograph

halftone negative

halftone flat for black impression

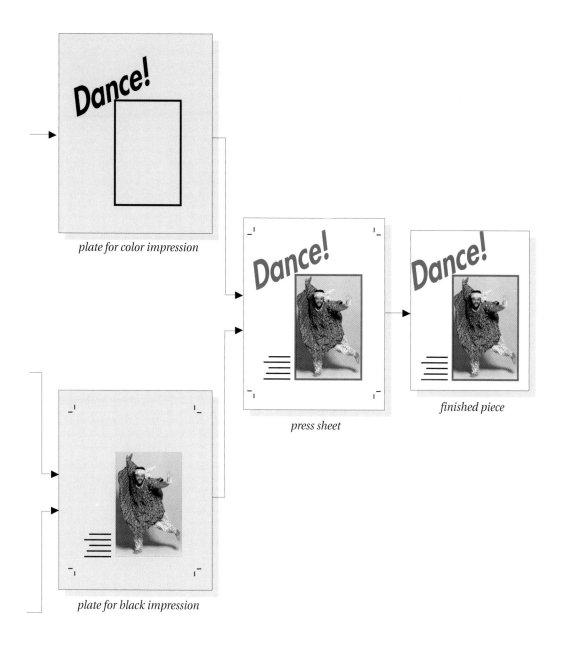

plate for color impression

press sheet

finished piece

plate for black impression

desk copy Free copy of a book given by the publisher to a teacher whose students will all use copies of the book as a classroom text. – ejemplar de cortesía

desktop publishing Technique of using a personal computer to design images and pages, and assemble type and graphics, then using a laser printer or imagesetter to output the assembled pages onto paper, film, or printing plate. Used to design products ranging from small display ads to entire books. Abbreviated dtp.

develop To bring out the latent image on an exposed film, paper, printing plate, or stencil by treating the emulsion with water or special chemicals. – revelar

device independent colors Hues identified by wavelength or by their place in sytems such as CIE LAB. 'Device independent' means a color can be described and specified without regard to whether it is reproduced using ink, projected light, photographic chemistry, or any other method. – colores independientes de aparatos

diacritic Accent mark, such as the acute accent (´) and tilde (~), showing how to pronounce a word. – signo diacrítico

diagnostic program Program that finds flaws in computer hardware or software and may identify potential solutions. – programa de diagnóstico

diagram Illustration that represents a process or shows how parts fit together. Illustrated on page 129 and 195. – diagrama

dialog box Window appearing on a computer screen giving the user a choice of commands. – ventana de diálogo

diazo Chemical, sensitive to ultra-violet light, used to coat paper or film for making prints. – diazo

dictionary Alphabetical list of words in a book or computer file giving complete definitions and guide to pronunciations. Also called lexicon. – diccionario

Didot type system System for expressing type size used in most of Europe and in other countries that do not use the Anglo American type system. – sistema Didot

die Device for cutting, scoring, stamping, embossing, and debossing. Illustrated on page 247.

Most dies are metal and have two parts: the male die provides the shape, the female die provides either resistance to or reinforcement of the shape. A cutting or stamping die works when pressed against paper backed by hard rubber. Embossing and debossing dies mold paper between their halves.

A laser beam used for die cutting works in conjunction with a computerized pattern, which may be thought of as the die giving shape to the cut. – troquel

die cut To cut irregular shapes in paper or paperboard using a die.

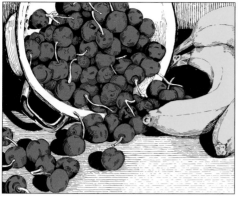

multicolor printing

4-color process printing

multicolor enlarged to 600%

4-color process enlarged to 600%

4-color process out of register

4-color process in register

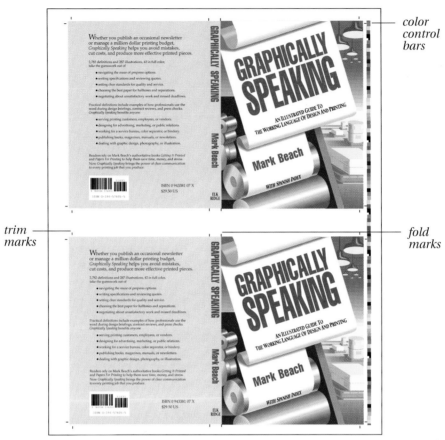

color control bars

trim marks

fold marks

press sheet 2-up

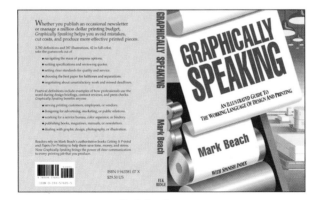

finished cover

blueline

loose proof

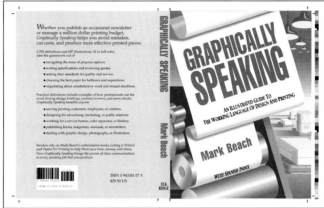

composite proof, integral

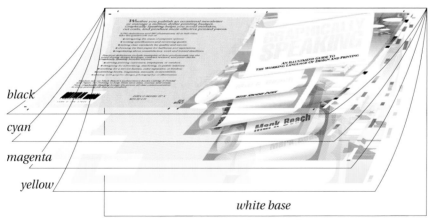

black

cyan

magenta

yellow

white base

overlay proof

Die cutting is done using a letterpress and produces products such as door hangers, presentation folders, and table tents. Intricate patterns can be die cut using lasers. Illustrated on page 247. – troquelar

die score To score paper using a die. – rayar con troquel

die stamp To stamp images using a die. – estampar con troquel

diffuse highlight Lightest highlight still showing detail, as compared to a dropout or specular highlight. A white flower might create a diffuse highlight in a photo. Illustrated on page 226. – clara por difusión

diffusion transfer Process of reproducing line copy and making halftone positives ready for pasteup. After original art is exposed to photosensitive paper, a print is made by pressing the exposed sheet against a receiving sheet. Chemicals bathing the two sheets release the image so it transfers without needing a negative. – transferencia por difusión

digest Shortened version of an article or book. Also called abridgement. – resumen

digest size Trim size approximately half of letter size. Three popular digest sizes are 5 x 7 inches as used by *The Reader's Digest*, 5½ x 8½ inches (exactly half of letter size), and 5⅜ x 8⅜ inches, which suits many web presses and allows for bleeds.

US Postal Service regulations classify digest size as a letter for purposes of postal rates, as compared to postal rates for flats. – tamaño resumen

digit Any Arabic numeral 0, 1, 2, 3, 4, 5, 6, 7, 8, or 9. – dígito

digital camera Camera that uses a charge coupling device to display images on a computer screen, manipulate their shadows, midtones, and/or highlights, then record them as electronic files. – cámara digital

digital data exchange standard Standard for formatting computer files that include graphics, such as photographs, and assembled pages so that files produced using one brand of machine or software can be read or output using another brand. Typically found only in color electronic prepress systems. Abbreviated DDES.

digital dot Dot created by a computer and printed out by a laser printer or imagesetter. Digital dots are uniform in size, as compared to halftone dots whichvary in size. – punto digital

digital photography Photography using a camera that records the scene as pixels, not as a continuous-tone image. – fotografía digital

digital proof Alternate term for *direct digital color proof*. – prueba digital

digital type Characters made of dots. Imagesetters and most modern typesetters produce digital type. – tipo digital

digitize To convert information, such as type or photographs, to digital form. – digitalizar

dimensional stability Ability of paper or film to retain its exact size despite the influence of temperature, moisture, or stretching. – estabilidad dimensional

dimension drawing Cross-section drawing used in technical manuals, as compared to exploded drawing. Also called inspection drawing. – dibujo con medidas

dimension marks British term for *crop marks.*

dimple Small depression in a glass or plastic bottle. Used as a guide to register printing. – hoyuelo

DIN Abbreviation for Deutsches Institut für Normung, the German standards organization similar to ANSI and BSI.
  The International Organization for Standardization (ISO) adopted the DIN system of paper sizes. Many printers and merchants, however, continue to say 'DIN sizes' as an alternate term for 'ISO sizes.' DIN standards for classifying light sensitivity of photographic films were also adopted by ISO and are used internationally.

dingbat Typographic symbol, such as a bullet (•), used for emphasis or decoration. See also *pi character.* – punto señalizador

diploma Certificate confirming graduation from a school, college, or educational program. – diploma

diploma paper Alternate term for *parchment paper.* – papel pergamino

DIP switch Abbreviation for *dual in-line package switch.* Pronounced "dip switch."

direct digital color proof Color proof made on paper or other substrate without needing to make separation films first. The proof is made by a laser, ink jet printer, or other computer output device. Abbreviated DDCP. Also called digital proof. – prueba directa de color digital

direct impression British term for *strike-on type.*

direct mail Mail created to motivate readers to respond with a purchase, donation, or other action called for by the advertising. – correo directo

direct order Order for paper filled from inventory at a mill rather than at a paper merchant. – orden directa

directory 1) Publication giving names, addresses, and phone numbers. 2) List of files in electronic storage on a computer. – 1 & 2, directorio

directory paper Very thin groundwood used for products such as directories and almanacs. – papel para directorios

direct positive copy Copy reproduced without needing intermediate negatives. Xerography, photomechanical transfer, and photostat are direct positive processes. – copia directa positiva

direct process duplicate Alternate term for *spirit duplicate.*

dirty copy Copy unsuitable for reproduction, as compared to clean copy. Copy may be dirty because

color separation

original transparency

yellow printing negative

magenta printing negative

cyan printing negative

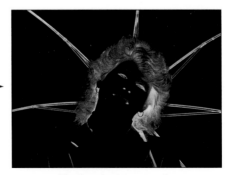

black printing negative

impression from yellow plate

yellow impression

impression from magenta plate

yellow & magenta impression

impression from cyan plate

yellow, magenta & cyan impression

impression from black plate

yellow, magenta, cyan & black impression

it has dust or scratches, or because it has mistakes, typographic errors, or type that is badly set. – copia sucia

dirty paper Paper that causes picking or other press problems related to unwanted particles contaminating the inking system. – papel sucio

diskette Alternate term for *floppy disk*. – disquete

disk operating system Computer program with instructions for how the computer should read or write disks used with that computer.
– programa de operación del disco

display Exhibit of products or materials. – pantalla

display advertising Advertising in publications, such as newspapers and magazines, combining display type with photos or illustrations, as compared to classified advertising.
– anuncio publicitario con gráfico

display board Plastic, wood, or thick paper used to make a display. In Great Britain called panel.

display type Type used for headlines, advertising, and signs. Also called headline type.
Most authorities say that display type is any type larger than 14 points, but disagree about whether 14-point type is display or text size. In practice, it depends on context.
– tipo para títulos

distortion factor Slight amount by which images on a flexographic plate must be changed to compensate for the thickness and stretch of the plate. – factor de distorción

distributing rollers British term for *ink rollers.*

distributor Business that buys goods from manufacturers and sells them to retailers. Paper distributors buy from mills and sell to printers. Also called jobber, merchant, and wholesaler. – distribuidor

dither Computer technique of creating or re-arranging pixels to retouch an image or correct its colors.
– interpolación

Ditto Brand name for *spirit duplicating.*

divider Tabbed sheet of heavy paper, such as index, used to separate sections of a book or binder. – divisor

docket Alternate term for *job ticket.*
– orden de trabajo

doctor blade Flexible metal strip that controls thickness of a substance such as ink. Illustrated on page 117.
In gravure printing, a doctor blade spreads ink evenly and cleans excess ink from a cylinder prior to each impression. A doctor blade may also be used to remove excess ink in screen printing or to remove excess coating when making coated papers. Also called flood bar in screen printing. Some pasteup waxers use a doctor blade to ensure a uniform wax layer. – cuchilla tangente

document Any written or printed product. – documento

documentation 1) Books, drawings, and other printed materials that

35mm transparencies ↓ *scanned into digital memory* ↓

electronic image assembly

original

electronic retouching of one original image

accompany a machine or program to tell how to use or repair it. 2) Any written or printed materials that explain or verify information, such as for court cases or writing history. – 1 & 2, instructivo

dodge To block light from selected areas while making a photographic print, as compared to burn. Dodging is usually done to increase details in shadows. Illustrated on page 232. – desvanecer

door hanger Printed product that is die cut to hang over a door knob, such as the 'Do not disturb' notice in a hotel room. – anuncio para puerta

DOS Acronym for *disk operating system*. Pronounced "doss."

dot area Alternate term for *dot percent*. – área de puntos

dot etch Method of color correcting separation negatives or positives. Also called etch. In Great Britain called colour etch.

Dot etching is done using chemicals on film (wet etch), photographic contacting techniques on film (dry etch), or computer programs on digital images. All reduce the size of dots. Dot etching may be done to compensate for dot gain or to make color corrections. – grabado de puntos

dot gain Phenomenon of halftone dots printing larger on paper than they are on films or plates, reducing detail and lowering contrast. Illustrated on pages 62 and 202. Also called dot growth, dot spread, and press gain.

Dot gain is expressed as a percent. For example, a 50% screen tint that measures 70% on the press sheet has a 20% dot gain.

Dot gain is most noticeable in midtones and shadows, where dots are largest, and least noticable in highlights, where dots are smallest.

Every printing job involves some dot gain. With offset printing, gain can range from 5% for sheetfed printing on premium coated paper to 40% for web printing on newsprint. With flexography, gain can range from 25% to 40%, depending on the substrate, kind of plate, and specific press.

Because dot gain is a predictable phenomenon, not a flaw, a prepress service can estimate how much gain to expect with a given paper and style of press. Camera and scanner operators can control halftones and separations to compensate for some dot gain.

See also *mechanical dot gain* and *optical dot gain*. – ganancia de puntos

dot gain scale Test pattern, printed on a press sheet, that reveals the amount of dot gain. Illustrated on page 62. – escala de ganancia de puntos

dot growth Alternate term for *dot gain*. – ganancia de puntos

dot loss Phenomenon of halftone dots printing smaller on paper than they are on film or plates, making images less dense and colors seem weak. Also called sharpening.

Dot loss is most noticeable in highlights, where dots are smallest, and least noticeable in midtones and shadows, where dots are largest. – pérdida de punto

dot matrix printer Computer printer using patterns of dots to form characters and other images. This term is usually limited to pin printers. – impresora de matrix de puntos

dot percent Percent of paper that dots cover when using a specific screen. A screen with a dot percent of 20 is a 20% screen. Also called dot area. See also *screen density*. – porcentaje de puntos

dot pitch Alternate term for *dots-per-inch*.

dot size Relative size of halftone dots as compared to dots of the screen ruling being used.

There is no unit of measurement to express dot size. 'Large dots' could indicate too much dot gain or be evidence of dense shadows; 'small dots' could mean the bump exposure was too long or be evidence of vivid highlights. Dots are too large, too small, or correct only in comparison to what the viewer finds attractive.

When describing or discussing dots, they are referred to by the percentage of paper that they cover. For example, a printer who says "The 25% dots seem too big" means that the dots that should cover 25% in fact cover more. – tamaño de puntos

dots-per-inch Measure of resolution of input devices such as scanners, display devices such as monitors, and output devices such as laser printers, imagesetters, and monitors. Abbreviated dpi. Also called dot pitch.

Expressions of dots-per-inch state the horizontal measurement first, the vertical measurement second. For example, an EGA monitor with a resolution of 640 x 350 displays 640 pixels per inch horizontally and 350 pixels per inch vertically.

Dots per inch is different from screen ruling. Dpi expresses the frequency of digital dots, which are all the same size. Screen ruling expresses the frequency of halftone dots, which are all the same size on a screen tint and have different sizes on a halftone. – puntos por pulgada

dot spread Alternate term for *dot gain*. – ganancia de puntos

double black duotone Duotone printed from two halftones, one shot for highlights and the other shot for midtones and shadows. Both halftones are printed using black ink to increase the tonal range of the reproduction. A double black duotone needs two plates, as compared to a double dot halftone which needs only one plate. – bitono de dos negros

double black printing Using two ink stations to print black.

Double black printing might be done to print a double black duotone. It might also be done by heavily inking the plate carrying type to yield dense type and lightly inking the plate carrying halftones to avoid plugging up their shadows. – impresión con dos negros

double bump To print a single image twice so it has two layers of ink. A double bump might be necessary to

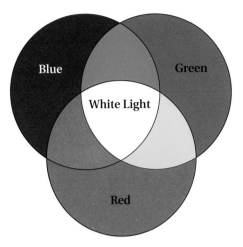

additive primary colors
red, green, blue
RGB

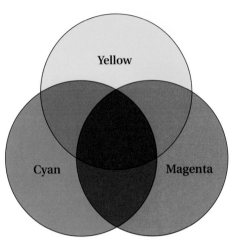

subtractive primary colors
cyan, magenta, yellow
CMYK: cyan, magenta, yellow + black
are the process colors

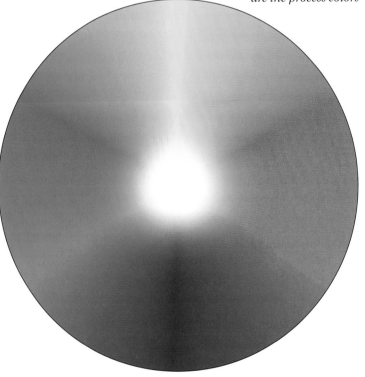

color wheel

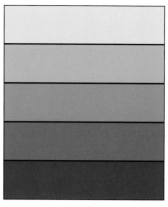

hue	chroma	value
color	saturation, depth, intensity, purity, value	tone, lightness, brightness, shade

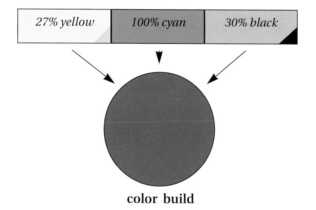

27% yellow	100% cyan	30% black

color build

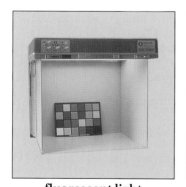
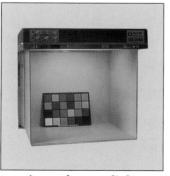
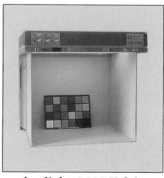

fluorescent light   **incandescent light**   **day light, 5000 Kelvin**

The Judge color matching booth courtesy of Macbeth ®

produce a strong image using light ink on dark paper or when printing a large, dark solid. – impresión doble

double burn   To expose film or a plate twice to different negatives and thus create a composite image.

Double burns are typically done to expose line copy with one burn and halftone copy with the second burn. They may also be used to add corrected copy to a plate. For example, a headline containing a typo could be masked on one flat and a correct headline double burned from a second flat (often called a complementary flat).

Theoretically, there is no limit to the number of burns possible onto one plate. Triple burns are common, but more than four burns are rare. If a plate requires images from a large number of negatives, use of composite film ensures better fit than multiple burns and reduces the chances of dirt contaminating the image. – exposición doble

double dot halftone   Halftone that is double burned onto a plate from two halftones, one shot for shadows, the second shot for midtones and highlights. A double dot halftone is printed using only one plate, as compared to a double black duotone needing two plates. – mediotono de doble punto

double etch   To expose a gravure cylinder to two carbon prints or two film positives and thus create a composite image. Double etches are typically done to expose line copy with the first etch and halftone copy with the second etch. – grabado doble

double exposure   Two images exposed onto one frame of film, thus appearing as one composite image. – doble exposición

double faced   Sign or display printed on both sides. – doble cara

double-faced board   Alternate term for *double-walled board*. – cartón con dos caras planas

double-faced paper   Alternate term for *duplex paper*. – papel duplex

double gate fold   Alternate term for *closed gate fold*. – doblado de puerta doble

double page spread   Layout of two facing pages as a single unit. Called double truck in newspapers. – página doble

double post card   Two postcards, one of which is a BRC, attached by a perforated score so they are easy to tear apart. The two are mailed as one unit so the recipient can remove the BRC and mail it back to the sender. – tarjeta postal doble

double truck   Newspaper term for *double page spread*.

double-walled board   Corrugated board with sheets glued to both sides of the corrugation. Also called double-faced board. – cartón con dos caras planas

double wire bind   Form of mechanical binding using parallel strands of wire. Illustrated on page 16. Also called by the brand name *Wire-O*. – encuadernación de doble argolla

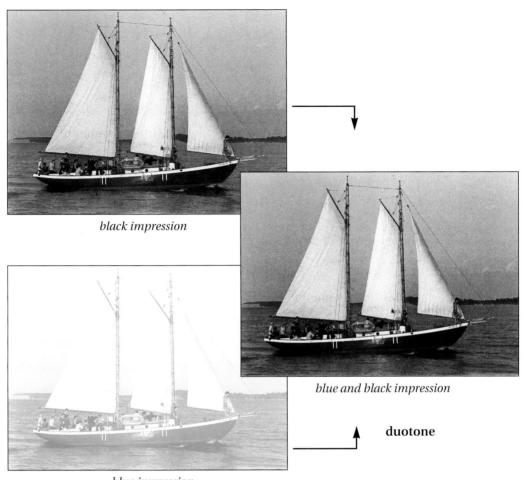

black impression

blue and black impression

duotone

blue impression

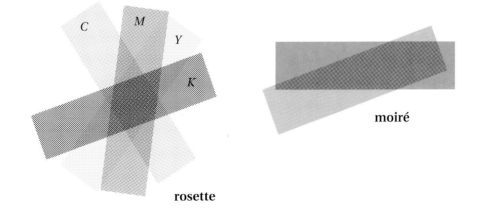

rosette

moiré

balanced exposure

blue color cast

underexposure

overexposure

doubling Printing defect appearing as blurring or shadowing of the image. Doubling may be caused by problems with paper, cylinder alignment, blanket pressures, or dirty cylinders. In Great Britain called prekissing. – doblado de imagen

doughnut 1) In lithography, a form of hickey that has a spot of ink surrounded by a small circle without ink. 2) In gravure, defect of printing the circumference of a cell without printing its interior.
– 1 & 2, mota

down 1) Not functioning, as compared to up. A broken press is down; a press working properly is up. 2) Referring to color sequence. For example, a printer might say "Black is the first color down."
– 1, fuera de funcionamiento

downlink To bring information from a satellite down to an earth station, as compared to uplink.

download To receive information at one computer from another, as compared to upload. – descargar

downstairs 1) Lower half of a newspaper page, as compared to upstairs. Also called basement. 2) Alternate term for horizontal format.
– 1, mitad inferior; 2, formato horizontal

down style Typographic format for headlines using the same rules of grammar and capitalization that apply to sentences, as compared to up style. – estilo de minúsculas

down time Time that a machine or system is not working properly, as compared to up time. – período de paro

DP bond paper Abbreviation for *dual purpose bond paper.*

dpi Abbreviation for *dots per inch.*

draft Preliminary version of a manuscript or drawing. A final product might go through many drafts, such as rough draft, second draft, and final draft. – borrador

draft mode Computer printing using a printer adjusted for relatively few dots per inch, thereby printing quickly but at low resolution.
– modo para borrador

drawdown 1) Sample of the inks specified for a job applied to the substrate specified for the job. Drawdowns are made using an ink knife and are used to evaluate color and opacity. Also called pulldown. 2) Process of forcing two materials, such as film and plate, into tight contact with each other by squeezing them together in a vacuum frame.

drawn-on cover British term for *perfect bind.*

drill To bore holes in paper. – perforar

drop folio Page numeral appearing at the foot of a page. – folio al pie

drop out Halftone dots or fine lines eliminated from highlights by overexposure during camera work. The lost copy is said to have dropped out. Drop outs may be done on purpose or accidentally, thus may be enhancements or defects.
– perder

dropout blue Alternate term for *non-reproducing blue.* – azul no reproducible

dropout halftone Halftone in which contrast has been increased by eliminating dots from highlights. Illustrated on page 219. In Great Britain called deep-etch halftone. – medios tonos perdidos

dropout highlight Alternate term for *specular highlight.* – zonas claras perdidas

dropout type Alternate term for *reverse type.* – tipo invertido

drop shadow Screen tint or rule touching an illustration, box, or type to give a three-dimensional shadow effect. Illustrated on page 162. Also called flat shadow. – sombra bajada

dropped cap Large capital letter that extends down into the first two or more lines, as compared to raised cap. Used as a design element. Illustrated on pages 160 and 263. – mayúscula bajada

DRUPA Acronym for Druck und Papier, an international exhibition of printing equipment and supplies held in Dusseldorf, Germany. DRUPA is scheduled for 1995, 2000, and every five years thereafter.

dryback Phenomenon of printed ink colors becoming less dense as the ink dries. Wet ink looks darker (more dense) than dry ink because it reflects more light. For purposes of measurement, ink is considered wet the instant it's printed and dry 24 hours later. – densidad al secar

dry down Alternate term *dry back.*

dryer Alternate term for *drying oven.*

dry gum paper Label paper with glue that can be activated by water. – papel con goma seca

drying in Alternate term for *clogging.*

drying oven Heated tunnel on some web presses that dries ink as paper passes through the tunnel. Web presses with drying ovens are called heatset webs. Some presses for screen printing also have drying ovens. Also called dryer. – horno secador

drying time Time required for ink or varnish to dry sufficiently so that it will not smear or set off during another pass through the press or in bindery operations. Drying time could range from an hour to several days, depending on ink coverage, paper surface and moisture, and pressroom climate. – tiempo de secado

dry offset printing Alternate term for *letterset printing.* – impressión offset seco

dry proof Alternate term for *prepress proof.* – prueba de pre-impresión

dry transfer lettering Type that can be rubbed off its backing sheet onto another surface. Also called alphabet sheet, instant lettering, press-on type, rub-on lettering, transfer lettering, and transfer type. In Great Britain called rub-down lettering. – letras transferibles

dry trap To print over dry ink, as compared to wet trap. Dry trapping requires drying, then another pass through a press, but ensures better adhesion for the second color or varnish. – atrapar con tinta seca

DTP Abbreviation for *desktop publishing*.

dual in-line package switch Switch that selects compatible settings on computer printers and other electronic devices. Commonly called "dip switch." – interruptor interior

dual-purpose bond paper Bond paper suitable for printing by either lithography (offset) or xerography (photocopy). Abbreviated DP bond paper. – papel de doble uso

duct Alternate term for *fountain* on an offset press. – tintero

due date Alternate term for *deadline*. – fecha límite

dull Characteristic of paper, ink, or varnish that reflects relatively little light. – mate

dull finish Flat (not glossy) finish on coated paper; slightly smoother than matte. Also called suede finish, velour finish, and velvet finish. Illustrated on page 31. – acabado mate

dull ink Ink that dries to a flat finish, as compared to gloss ink. Also called matte ink. – tinta mate

dull varnish Varnish that dries to a finish that reflects diffuse light, as compared to gloss varnish. Also called matte varnish. – barniz mate

dummy 1) Mockup simulating the final product. Dummies range from very simple, showing only size or rough layout, to very complicated, showing position and color of type and art. Various forms of dummies include paper dummy, thumbnail sketch, rough layout (rough), and comprehensive (comp). Also called mockup. 2) Empty box or package used only for display. – 1 & 2, muestra

dummy duotone Alternate term for *fake duotone*. – bitono falso

dump Free-standing rack or bin designed to display products from a specific company.

duograph Alternate term for *fake duotone*. – bitono falso

duotone Black and white photograph reproduced using two halftone negatives, each shot to emphasize different tonal values in the original. Illustrated on page 81. In Great Britain called double printing.
   Duotones are usually printed using black ink and one other ink color. They can also be printed using two black plates (see *double black duotone*) or combinations of any two ink colors. – bitono

dupe Abbreviation for a duplicate, such as a dupe transparency, film, or print. – duplicado

duplex halftone Sometimes used as alternate term for both *fake duotone* and *duotone*.

duplex paper Thick paper made by pasting together two thinner sheets, usually of different colors. Also called double-faced paper and two-tone paper.

Duplex paper is usually made by combining two sheets of 80# text and calling the result 88# cover.
– papel duplex

duplex press Alternate term for *perfecting press.* – prensa de retiración

duplicate Identical copy of an original, such as duplicate film used to strip for 2-up printing. – duplicado

duplicator 1) Offset press made for quick printing. Duplicators use paper 12 x 18 inches (A3) or smaller and have only one or two inking units. Typically they lack grippers, multiple roller stacks, anti-offset sprayers, and other devices required to print close register, heavy ink coverage, and coated paper.
2) Any office machine that prints using mimeograph, photocopy, lithography, or spirit duplicating.
– 1 & 2, multicopista

dust Alternate term for *anti-offset powder.* – polvo

dust cover Printed cover wrapped loosely around casebound books. Also called jacket. – sobrecubierta

dusting Technique of making printed images look metallic. Dusting requires printing an image with size, varnish, or some other sticky fluid, then allowing powdered metal to stick to the image.
– espolvoreado

Dvorak keyboard Arrangement of keys claimed to be more rational and to allow faster, more accurate typing than standard keyboard arrays. – teclado Dvorak

dwell time Time that a section of a moving web spends within the drying oven.

dyeline Alternate term for *blueline.*

Dylux Brand name for photographic paper used to make blueline proofs. Often used as an alternate term for blueline.

dynamic link Automatic connection between two computer programs. For example, if copy is written in word processing and designed using typesetting software, a dynamic link means that revising the copy in word processing will automatically revise it in type-setting. – enlace dinámico

dynamic range Extent to which a scanner can capture the complete tonal range of an original. – rango dinámico

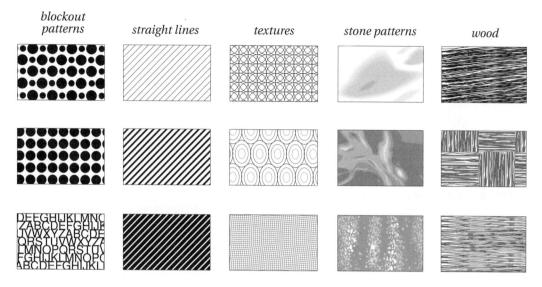

| *blockout patterns* | *straight lines* | *textures* | *stone patterns* | *wood* |

Special effect screens

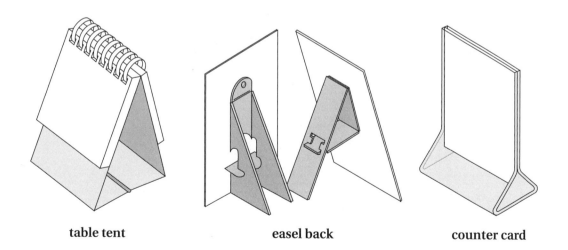

table tent　　　　**easel back**　　　　**counter card**

E

earth colors Tones of green, brown, and other colors common in nature. – colores de la tierra

easel back Device on the back of a display or binder allowing it to stand upright without additional support. Illustrated on page 87.
Easel backs are laminated to printed products, not printed themselves. They have single or double wings. – soporte dorsal

ED Abbreviation for *emulsion down.*

EU Abbreviation for *emulsion up.*

edge coloring Using dyes or metallic inks to color the trimmed edges of books. – coloración del borde

edge enhancement Alternate term for *unsharp masking.*

edition One version of a publication, such as the first edition of a book or the regional edition of a magazine. – edición

edition bind Alternate term for *case bind.* – edición encuadernada

editor 1) Person who selects words and visual elements, such as photographs, to accomplish communication goals.
2) Executive in a publishing company responsible for a specific management function, such as the acquisitions editor who seeks new books or the city editor who controls the city edition of a newspaper.
3) Writer or reporter responsible for a topic in a publication, such as thesports editor. – 1 - 3, editor

editorial matter All copy, other than advertising, in a magazine or newspaper. Editorial matter includes photos as well as text. For example, a publisher might say, "We have 40% advertising and 60% editorial." – texto del editorial

EF Abbreviation for *English finish* on paper.

EGA Abbreviation for *enhanced graphics adapter.*

eggshell antique British term for *eggshell finish.*

eggshell finish Paper simulating the surface and color of an egg. Eggshell finish is smoother than wove, rougher than smooth. In Great

Britain called eggshell antique. – acabado cáscara de huevo

eight-page press Alternate term for half-web press. See *web press.*

Ektachrome Brand name for *transparency film* processed in E6 chemistry.

electronic camera Camera that uses a charge coupling device to record a still image on a disk. – cámara electrónica

electronic engraving Engraving done with a stylus guided by a scanner reading the image to be engraved. Electronic engraving of gravure cylinders is called by the trade name HelioKlishography. – grabado electrónico

electronic front end General term referring to a prepress system based on computers. In addition to a central processing unit, the system would include a laser printer, imagesetter, or other output device. It might also include a scanner, modem, and other peripherals such as magnetic tape drives.

There is a wide range of power and sophistication of both hardware and software for electronic front end systems, ranging from simple desktop publishing setups to complex systems for scanning, manipulating, and making proofs of full-color images. – sistema electrónico de entrada

electronic image assembly Assembly of a composite image from portions of other images using a computer. Illustrated on page 75. – composición electrónica de imagen

electronic mechanical Mechanical existing exclusively in electronic files. – boceto final electrónico

electronic page assembly Assembly and manipulation, using a computer, of page elements such as type and graphics. – composición electrónica de página

electronic publishing 1) Publishing by printing with a device, such as a photocopy machine or ink jet printer, driven by a computer that can change the image instantly from one copy to the next. 2) Publishing via output on fax or other electronic medium. – 1 & 2, publicación electrónica

electronic retouching Using a computer to enhance or correct a photo or illustration that has been scanned and digitized. Illustrated on page 75. – retocado electrónico

electrostatic printing Alternate term for *photocopy.* – impresión electrostática

element One part of an image, page, or publication. Elements of an image may include subject, background, and foreground. Elements of a page may include headlines, body copy, and halftones. Elements of a publication may include title page, logo, and index. – elemento

elite type Smaller of the two standard typewriter type sizes, usually 10 point and 12 pitch. – tipo elite

ellipsis Three dots (...) indicating that a few words, or even a few sentences, have been omitted from a quoted passage. An ellipsis is a typographic character, not merely three periods. – puntos suspensivos

elliptical dot   One of several shapes of dots available for halftone screens. Some printers believe that elliptical dots produce more dense shadows and smoother midtone gradations than round or square dots. Illustrated on page 218. Also called chain dot. – punto elíptico

em   Space the width of an imaginary square whose sides equal the height of the type in use. In most type-faces, this width is the same as the letter 'M.' Dashes and paragraph indents are often expressed in em spaces. Illustrated on page 259. Also called mutt. – eme

emblem   Alternate term for *logo*.

emboss   To press an image into paper so it lies above the surface. Illustrated on page 247. Also called cameo and tool. In Great Britain called block.
Embossing uses a letterpresss to squeeze paper between two dies, leaving a sculpted, raised image. – estampar en relieve

embossed finish   Surface pattern pressed into dry text paper and having a name such as linen, pebble, or canvas. Mills emboss paper after it's off the papermaking machine, as compared to machine finishes. – acabado estampado

em dash/space   Dash/space one em long. – guión/espacio de eme

emulsification   Problem during printing when fountain solution on a plate pollutes the ink, causing washed out colors and/or mottling. – emulsificación

emulsion   Coating of light-sensitive chemicals on papers, films, printing plates, and stencils. – emulsión

emulsion down/emulsion up   Film whose emulsion side faces down (away from the viewer) or up (toward the viewer) when ready to make a plate or stencil. Abbreviated ED/EU. Also called E down/E up and face down/face up.
Complete specifications for plate-ready film make clear whether the emulsion side should be down or up. See also *RRED* and *RREU*. – emulsión abajo/emulsión arriba

emulsion side   Side of film or paper coated with emulsion. In cameras, the emulsion side faces the lens. In contact printing photos or printing plates, the emulsion side is usually in contact with the emulsion of the receiving surface. – lado de emulsión

en   Half an em. Also called nutt. – ene

enamel paper   Alternate term for *gloss coated paper*. – papel cromo

encapsulated PostScript file   Computer file containing both images and PostScript commands. Abbreviated EPS file.
Images in EPS files can be manipulated on screen for design purposes without changing the contents of the file. Furthermore, EPS files can be transferred from one machine to another. For example, they can be printed out for proofing at 300 dpi on a laser printer, then printed out as camera-ready copy at 2,400 dpi on an imagesetter. – archivo PostScript encapsulado

encyclopedia Book or set of books with articles about many branches of knowledge or relating detailed knowledge about a specific field. – enciclopedia

en dash/space Dash/space one en long. – guión/espacio de ene

end book price The lowest price for paper shown in a price book, so called because it is often found listed at the ends of columns of numerals. The end book price is low because it applies to high-volume purchases.

end matter Alternate term for *back matter*. – apéndices

endorsement 1) Recommendation by a qualified or famous person or organization. Also called testimonial. 2) Instructions about delivery or handling printed on the outside of a mailing piece. – 1, endoso; 2, instrucciónes

end product Printed piece in its final form. – producto final

end sheet Sheet that attaches the inside pages of a case bound book to its cover. Illustrated on page 23. Also called pastedown. – hoja final

end user Person or organization for whom a product is intended. – usuario final

English finish Smooth finish on uncoated book paper; smoother than eggshell, rougher than smooth. – acabado inglés

engrave To cut an image into the surface of metal. Engraving can be done by hand, machines, chemicals, or lasers. – grabar

engraver 1) Person or business who prints by engraving. 2) Out-of-date term for person or business that makes halftones, color separations, printing plates, or dies. Alternate terms such as color separator and service bureau are more common. – 1& 2, grabador

engraving 1) Printing method using a plate, also called a die, with an image engraved into it. Engraving is considered a prestigious method of printing and is imitated by thermography. US currency is printed in part using engraving. Illustrated on page 246.
2) Illustration made using an engraved plate. Also called cut. – 1& 2, grabar

engrossing Formal calligraphy used on certificates.

enhanced graphics adapter Computer board supporting a color monitor that displays 16 colors at 640 x 350 resolution, as compared to lower resolution CGA and higher resolution VGA. Abbreviated EGA. – adaptador para gráficos aumentados

enlargement Image printed larger than the original from which it was made. – ampliación

enlarger Device that projects an image from photographic film onto paper that will be developed to become the print. – ampliadora

en space Space one en wide.

envelope Paper enclosure used for mailing. Abbreviated ep. – sobre

ep Abbreviation for envelope. Commonly made plural. For example, the phrase 'color eps' in a price book refers to envelopes made of colored paper.

epilogue Last section of a book or article. Intended to bring the reader up to date or let the author make a few final comments. – epílogo

EPS file Abbreviation for *encapsulated PostScript file.*

equal spacing Typographic system of allocating the same amount of space to each character regardless of its width, as compared to proportional spacing. In equal spacing, 'i' gets the same space as 'p' or 'w' or a punctuation mark. Typewriters use equal spacing. Also called monospacing and unit spacing. – espaciado equitativo

equivalent paper Paper that is not the brand specified, but looks, prints, and may cost the same. Also called comparable stock. – papel equivalente

equivalent weights Differing basis weights that, although they describe different papers, are in fact identical because they are computed using different basic sizes. For example, 24# bond is equivalent to 70# book, meaning that a ream of 11 x 17-inch 24# bond weighs the same as a ream of 11 x 17-inch 70# book. – pesos equivalentes

erasable bond Bond paper with surface treated for easy erasure. – papel bond borrable

erratum Piece of paper, inserted into a book, pointing out errors and making corrections after the book has been printed. – lista de erratas

E scale Sheet of clear plastic with capital Es printed on it in various type sizes. Used to measure type size. – escala de caracteres E

esparto Coarse grass whose fibers yield strong, economical paper. Also called Spanish grass. – esparto

esquisse Alternate term for *rough layout.* – bosquejo

essay Written analysis of a literary, political, or social topic. – ensayo

estimate Price that states what a job will probably cost. Also called bid and tender.

Graphic arts professionals use the terms 'estimate' and 'quotation' interchangeably, recognizing that no one can precisely forecast the final price of most jobs. Some professionals use 'estimate' as an informal guess and 'quotation' as a formal offer.

Estimates are based on specifications provided by customers and are prepared by an employee called an estimator. Estimators compile data about the costs of paper and supplies, prepress and press time, and dozens of other factors to predict the cost of a printing job and determine what to charge the customer. Color separators, binderies, and other graphic arts businesses also have estimators who perform functions similar to those at printers. – presupuesto

etch 1) To use chemicals to carve an image into metal, glass, or film. Dies for engraving and embossing are etched, as are some cylinders for gravure printing. Printed electronic circuits are etched after screen printing is used to print a resist. 2) Alternate term for *dot etching*. – 1& 2, grabar

E up/ E down Alternate term for *emulsion up/ emulsion down.*

European Article Number Twelve-digit bar code used on retail products in Europe to enable scanners to read prices and keep inventory records. Abbreviated EAN. The format and use of EANs is similar to that of Uniform Product Codes in North America.

exact rerun Reprint of a publication that requires no changes. – retiraje exacto

examination copy Free book given for marketing purposes by the publisher to a teacher to evaluate for use as a classroom text. Also called inspection copy. – ejemplar de cortesía

excerpt Portion of text from a long publication that is reproduced in a magazine, newspaper, or anthology. – extracto

expanded type Characters wide in proportion to their height, thus seeming fat. Illustrated on page 255. Also called extended type. – letras anchas

expansion envelope Envelope with gussets so it can expand to hold many documents. Also called accordian envelope and portfolio. – sobre expandible

exploded view Technical illustration showing parts drawn related to each other but not connected. Exploded views make clear how parts fit together. Illustrated on page 195. – sección amplificada

expose To allow light to strike photosensitive emulsion.
    Exposure time and intensity of light affect proper exposure. Intensity of light is determined by strength of the light source, its proximity to the emulsion, and the size of the aperture. – exponer

exposure meter Alternate term for *light meter.* – fotómetro

exposure time Time allowed for one exposure. – tiempo de exposición

extended type Alternate term for *expanded type.* – letras ancha

extent Alternate term for *page count.* – número de páginas

eyelet Metal or plastic reinforcement for holes in a banner, folder, or tag. A large eyelet may also be called a grommet. – ojete

eye markers In flexography, color control images consisting of small squares of process color printed outside of image areas.
    Eye markers are used for automatic control of density and register and to guide slitting and trimming machines. They may be seen on inside flaps of packages containing consumer goods, such as food or cosmetics. – marcas de ojos

F

face 1) Edge of a bound publication opposite the spine. Illustrated on page 23. Also called foredge.
2) Alternate term for *typeface*.
– 1, canto; 2, ojo de tipo

face cut Alternate term for *kiss die cut*. – corte de canto

face down Alternate term for *emulsion down*. – emulsión abajo

face margin Margin between the face trim and the start of printing. Illustrated on page 23. – margen del canto

face material Substrate that forms the top layer of a self-adhesive label. – material del canto

face printing Printing on the outer surface of a roll of plastic or other substrate, as compared to back printing. – impresión del anverso

face trim Trim along the face of a publication, as compared to a head, foot, or spine trim. – recorte del canto

face up Alternate term for *emulsion up*. – emulción arriba

Facing Identification Marks Pattern of nine vertical bars near the top of business reply mail that identifies the category of mail to automatic sorting machines. Abbreviated FIM. The US Postal Service provides camera-ready FIMs. – marcas de identificación

facsimile Approximation of an original, as compared to a duplicate. – facsímil

factor number Average width of characters in various typefaces and sizes. Factor numbers are used to help copyfit type.

fadeback Alternate term for *ghosting (2)*. – fantasma

fadeout Printing defect occurring when graduated dots end abruptly instead of blending into the background. Fadeout is especially likely to occur with flexography and gravure which have difficulty reproducing less than 5% dots. Also called bridging. – desvanecerse

fade-out blue Alternate term for *non-reproducing blue*.

fade-resistant inks Inks made to withstand the bleaching effects of wind and sun, so are useful for products such as bumper stickers and window displays. In Great Britain called permanent inks. – tintas indecoloras

fair copy Alternate term for *clean copy.* – copia limpia

fair dealing Alternate term for *fair use.*

fair use Concept in copyright law allowing, without permission from copyright holder, short quotations from a copyrighted product for purposes of reviewing or teaching. Also called fair dealing.

fake color printing Printing one ink over another, either screen tints or solids, with the intent of creating a third color different from either of the first two. – impresión de colores falsos

fake duotone Halftone in one ink color printed over screen tint of a second ink color. Also called dummy duotone, duograph, duplex halftone, false duotone, flat tint halftone, and halftone with screen. – bitono falso

false duotone Alternate term for *fake duotone.* – bitono falso

family of type Alternate term for *type family.* – familia de tipos

f & gs Abbreviation for folded and gathered sets of unbound book signatures sent to reviewers and often stored by the printer pending request from the publisher to bind them into finished books.

fan fold Alternate term for *accordion fold.* – doblado tipo acordeón

fan fold paper Alternate term for *continuous paper.* – papel en zig-zag

fanzine Short for fan magazine, a small and usually inexpensive magazine for special interests and audiences. – revista para aficionados

farm out Alternate term for *buy out.*

fast color inks Inks with colors that retain their density and resist fading as the product is used and washed. Fast inks are appropriate for clothing and products, such as flags, exposed to water and strong light. In Great Britain called lightfast ink. – tintas indecoloras y lavables

fast film Film that requires relatively little light (short exposure or small aperture opening) to record an image, as compared to slow film. Film rated ISO 400 or over is considered fast. – película rápida

fast lens Lens capable of being opened to a large aperture, such as f/1.9, thus allowing photography in low light conditions, at short shutter speeds, and/or using slow films, as compared to a slow lens. – lente rápido

fatty 1) Alternate term for *spread (3).* 2) Excess ink deposit that enlarges an image. 3) Photographic negative that is underexposed or under-developed.

feather edge Alternate term for *deckle edge.* – borde adelgazado

feathering 1) Effect of ink spreading as it sinks into paper, thus making the image lose sharpness. Also called bleeding. 2) Increasing leading to lengthen a column

of type. Also called carding.
3) Alternate term for *creep (1)*.
– 1, expansión de la tinta; 3, deslizarse

feature Article, in a periodical, that provides general knowledge, entertainment, or background on the news. Feature articles are usually longer than news articles. – crónica

feeder British term for *feeding unit.*

feeding edge Alternate term for *gripper edge.* – orilla alimentadora

feeding unit Component of a printing press that moves paper into the register unit. In Great Britain called feeder. – alimentador de hojas

feed lap Alternate term for *lap.*

feet per minute Measurement of the rate at which paper passes through a web press or at which a Fourdrinier machine makes paper. Abbreviated fpm. – pies por minuto

felt Continuous cloth belt on a papermaking machine. The felt picks up paper from the Fourdrinier wire and carries it into the dryers. – fieltro

felt finish Soft woven pattern in text paper. A true felt finish is applied while the paper is still 90% water. Felt finishes can also be embossed, but their patterns are not as deep as those made on the Fourdrinier wire. – acabado de fieltro

felt side Side of the paper that was not in contact with the Fourdrinier wire during manufacture as compared to wire side. – lado de fieltro

female die Die that receives pressure during embossing or debossing. Illustrated on page 247. Also called counter. – matriz

fiberboard Alternate term for *chipboard* and *cardboard.*

fiber puff Phenomenon of paper fibers popping up when subjected to the heat of a drying oven. Fibers in groundwood papers are more likely to puff than those in free sheets. The defect is most noticeable in areas of heavy ink coverage. Also called heat-set roughening. – levantamiento de la fibra

fidelity Extent to which color in a printed piece matches color in the original scene, product, or art. – fidelidad

field One line of information, such as a name or postal code, that is part of a record in a database. – campo

field of view 1) Amount of scene as seen through the lens or viewfinder of a camera. Illustrated on page 229. 2) Width of an image, such as a bar code, that a scanner can read in one pass. – 1 & 2, campo visual

fifth color Ink color used in addition to the four needed by four-color process.
    A fifth color is often used to print a logo or to enhance a critical hue. Fifth colors are also used to print background colors that would be difficult to simulate or keep in balance using four-color process printing. – quinto color

figure General term for any illustration, graph, table, map, photo, or other visual element in a technical publication. – figura

file Collection of data treated by a user or computer as one unit. – archivo

file server Computer with large memory dedicated to central storage for a local area network. – servidor de archivos

filled in Alternate term for *plugged up*. – tapado

fillers 1) Short items, such as proverbs or announcements, kept on hand to fill small blank spaces in a layout. 2) Clay and other materials added to paper to increase opacity or brightness. – 1, textos de relleno; 2, arcillas

fill-in flash Photographic flash used to supplement or enhance available light. Increases light, and therefore detail, in shadows.

fill pattern Alternate term for *screen tint* and other patterns produced using software for graphics, desktop publishing, and presentations.

film assembly Alternate term for *strip (1)*. – montaje de películas

film coated paper British term for *lick-coated paper, size coated paper*.

film coating Method of coating paper that leaves a relatively thin covering and rough surface, as compared to blade coating. Film-coated papers are often sold as uncoated or offset sheets and don't have designations such as gloss and matte. Illustrated on page 202. – tratamiento del papel

film gauge Thickness of film. The most common gauge for graphic arts film is 0.004 inch (0.1 mm), the gauge recommended in SWOP standards. – espesor de película

film laminate Thin sheet of plastic bonded to a printed product, such as a book cover or record jacket, for protection or increased gloss. – película plástica en envolturas

film mechanical Alternate term for *flat (1)*. – montaje

film speed Measure of light sensitivity of photographic film. Fast film is highly sensitive, slow film less sensitive.

The system of rating film speeds doubles or halves the amount of light required for a proper exposure. Film with a speed of 100 requires twice as much light as film rated 200 and four times as much light as film rated 400. – velocidad de película

filter Colored glass or gelatin that reduces or eliminates specific colors from white light before it strikes a photosensitive emulsion.

Photographers often use filters to enhance images. They may be used with both black and white or color photography to accent or reduce certain colors. When making halftones, operators use filtering to improve flesh tones, eliminate color casts, and compensate for the selective way that film records certain colors.

Filters are required when making color separations using a process camera. They are built into the optical systems of scanners. – filtro

FIM Abbreviation for *facing identification marks.*

final count Alternate term for *count.*

final film Film with all corrections made and approved, thus ready for platemaking. – película final

final proof Alternate term for *composite proof.* – prueba definitiva

fine mesh Relatively large numbers of threads and apertures per inch or centimeter in screens for screen printing. Screens over 300 meshes per inch (120 per centimeter) are considered fine mesh screens. – retícula fina

fine papers Papers made specifically for writing or commercial printing, as compared to coarse papers and industrial papers. Also called cultural papers and graphic papers. – papeles finos

fine screen Screen with ruling of 150 lines per inch (80 lines per centimeter) or more. – trama fina

finish 1) Surface characteristics of paper, such as laid or linen finish.
2) General term for trimming, folding, binding, and all other post press operations. Sometimes additional printing by methods such as die cutting and foil stamping are also considered finishing.
3) In gravure printing, inclusive term for color correcting and all other steps needed between engraving a cylinder and having it ready to print. – 1, acabado del papel; 2, operaciones finales

finished art Alternate term for *camera-ready copy.* – arte listo para cámara

finished count Alternate term for *count.* – recuento

finished size Size of product after production is complete, as compared to flat size. Also called *trim size.* – tamaño final

FIPP Abbreviation for Federation International of the Periodical Press, an organization that develops printing guidelines similar to SWOP guidelines. FIPP guidelines for offset printing have been adopted by national organizations of printers in 15 European countries.

first class mail US Postal Service classification for letters, post cards, invitations, and other personal messages. – correo de primera clase

first color down The first color printed. In four-color process printing, some printers use black as the first color down. Others prefer cyan. Some prefer yellow. – primer color de impresión

first proof Alternate term for *loose proof.* – primera prueba

first run 1) Printing the first side of the sheet. 2) The first time that a publication is printed. For example, a publisher might say, "Our first run was 5,000 copies." – 1, primera impresión; 2, primer tiraje

fish eye 1) Alternate term for *hickey.* 2) Defect in screen printing caused by slight bubbling of ink. **3**) Very wide angle lens, such as an 18mm lens in 35mm format. – 1 - 3, ojo de pescado

fit **1**) Refers to ability of film to be registered during stripping and assembly. Film that doesn't fit well may have images that can be stripped in register near one or two edges, but not near other edges. Good fit means that all images register to other film for the same job.

Fit is determined primarily by the accuracy of the output device, but can also be affected by the stability of the film base and atmospheric conditions during storage and stripping. **2**)British term for *register*. – 1, acomodar

fixative Clear, protective spray applied to a mechanical to seal elements in place and protect them from dirt and moisture. – fijador

fixed costs Costs that remain the same regardless of how many pieces are printed, as compared to variable costs. The costs of copywriting, photography, and design are examples of fixed costs. – costos fijos

fixer Chemical that neutralizes developing chemicals used with film or paper, thus preventing overdevelopment of the image. Also called hypo. – fijador

flag **1**) Banner with political logo. **2**) Slip of paper inserted between printed sheets of paper in a pile to mark the stop or start of a count or to show location of a flaw. **3**) Title and logo of a newspaper appearing at the top of page one. Illustrated on page 160. – 1, bandera; 2, tira divisora; 3, cabecera

flap **1**) Portion of a book's cover or dust jacket that lies folded inside the cover. **2**) Alternate term for *hanger*. – 1 & 2, solapa

flare Unwanted photographic effect caused by stray light falling on film.

flash Short burst of light used to illuminate a scene for photography.

flash exposure Short exposure, through a halftone screen, given a halftone to extend its density range, thus increase its shadow detail. A flash exposure makes shadow dots larger, darkening the deepest areas of shadows. – exposición auxiliar

flat **1**) Printer's assembly of film taped to a carrier sheet ready for platemaking. Also called film mechanical, Goldenrod and, in gravure printing, cabriolet. In Great Britain called photomechanical.

2) US Postal Service term for a piece of mail with length from 6 to 15 inches and height from 6 to 12 inches, as compared to letter mail which has smaller dimensions. Flats include large envelopes and publications such as most magazines, catalogs, and newsletters.

3) Characteristic of a photo or other image that seems lifeless, usually because it lacks contrast. Illustrated on page 226. – 1, montaje; 2, plano; 3, opaco

flat artwork British term for *reflective copy*.

flat-back bind To case bind leaving the spine flat before insertion into the case, as compared to round-back bind. Also called square-back bind. – encuadernación de lomo plano

flatbed press Press that holds the plate on a flat surface while printing. Illustrated on page 246.
– prensa plana

flatbed scanner Scanner that holds original art on a flat surface while scanning. – scanner plano

flat color 1) Any color created by printing only one ink, as compared to a color created by printing four-color process. Also called block color and spot color. 2) Color that seems weak or lifeless. – 1, color plano; 2, color opaco

flat contrast Characteristic of an image that lacks contrast.
– contraste mate

flat finish Alternate term for *low finish.* – acabado mate

flat plan Diagram of the flats for a publication showing imposition and indicating colors. – esquema de montaje

flat shadow Alternate term for *drop shadow.* – sombra bajada

flat size Size of product after printing and trimming, but before folding, as compared to finished size.
Flat and finished sizes may be identical, as when 8½ x 11 sheets are printed for letterhead. If, however, those sheets are folded in half for the final product, then the flat size is 8½ x 11 and the finished size is 5½ x 8½. – tamaño de hoja

flat view Illustration showing its subject straight from the front, with no perspective. Illustrated on page 195.

flat tint halftone Alternate term for *fake duotone.* – bitono falso

flexo Abbreviation for *flexography.*

flexography Method of printing on a web press using rubber or soft plastic plates with raised images. Also called aniline printing because flexographic inks originally used aniline dyes. Illustrated on page 101. Abbreviated flexo.
Flexography is a relatively simple and inexpensive printing process and requires little makeready time or waste. Using ink that dries instantly, it's suited to high speed and high volume printing on a variety of substrates, including newsprint, foil, cardboard, plastic film, and waxed paper. It is popular for printing paper bags and cups, food packaging, boxes, labels, and similar products. Most bread bags, comic books, and Sunday newspaper comics are printed using flexography. The process requires light pressure, so works well for very lightweight papers in products such as directories.
Flexo inks are water based, not oil based like most litho inks, so are easy to recycle and require no solvent for washup. – flexografía

flier Small poster or advertising handout. Also called bill, broadside, circular, handbill, insert, leaflet, and slick. Also spelled flyer. – circular

float 1) To place an element on a separate overlay or piece of film

flexography

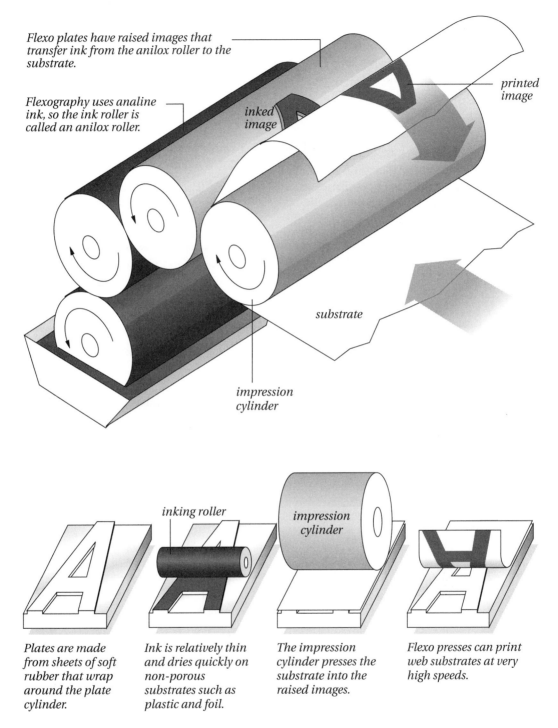

Flexo plates have raised images that transfer ink from the anilox roller to the substrate.

Flexography uses analine ink, so the ink roller is called an anilox roller.

inked image

printed image

substrate

impression cylinder

inking roller

impression cylinder

Plates are made from sheets of soft rubber that wrap around the plate cylinder.

Ink is relatively thin and dries quickly on non-porous substrates such as plastic and foil.

The impression cylinder presses the substrate into the raised images.

Flexo presses can print web substrates at very high speeds.

even though it is to be printed in the same ink as other elements. For example, prices in a catalog might float, allowing them to be coveniently changed for another printing without changing the film holding product descriptions and illustrations.

2) Refers to a design element, such as an illustration or block of type, that does not appear visually linked to other elements. Elements that seem loose in the layout are said to float. – 1 & 2, flotar

floating rule Rule, usually between columns, whose ends do not touch other rules. Illustrated on page 165. – línea flotante

floating type Type kept separate from other images printed in black. A negative with floating type might carry copy to be double burned with graphics instead of being composed into one piece of film. The fact that the type floats means it can be easily changed for reruns or editions in different languages. – tipo flotante

flood To print a sheet completely with an ink or varnish. Flooding with ink is also called painting the sheet. – inundar

flood bar Screen printing term for *doctor blade.*

floor sheet Alternate term for *house sheet.* – hoja de la casa

flop To change the orientation of an image so it is the mirror image of its orginal. Illustrated on page 219. In Great Britain called lateral reverse. – inversión lateral

floppy disk Portable computer storage device 5¼ inches or 3½ inches in diameter and holding anywhere from 360,000 to 2.5 million bytes of data. Also called disk and diskette. – disco flexible

flow chart Chart showing a process or sequence of events. Illustrated on page 129. – diagrama de flujo

flowout Ability of screen printed ink to spread slightly, covering areas not receiving ink because of threads in the screen. Too little flowout leaves a mesh of fine lines in the image; too much flowout causes the image to lose sharpness.

fluid duplicate Alternate term for *spirit duplicate.*

fluorescent 1) Ability to emit light when struck by ultraviolet radiation. Fluorescent papers and inks are treated with chemicals that make them seem to have internal light sources. 2) Light emitted by fluorescent tubes, as comapred to incandescent light. Fluorescent light is considered cool and may produce a green color cast on color photos. Illustrated on page 79. – 1 & 2, fluorescente

flush cover Cover trimmed to the same size as inside pages, as compared to overhang cover. Perfect bound books have flush covers. Also called cut flush. – cubierta exacta

flush left Type aligning vertically along the left side of the column. Illustrated on page 270. Also called left justified. In Great Britain called quad left or ranged left. – alineado a la izquierda

flush right Type aligning vertically along the right side of the column. Illustrated on page 270. Also called right justified. In Great Britain called quad right or ranged right. – alineado a la derecha

flute Paper pleat between walls in corrugated cardboard. Also called liner.

Flutes are in categories according to height and number per inch as follows: A flute is $^3/_{16}$ inch high, 35 flutes per inch; B flute is $^3/_{32}$ inch high, 50 flutes per inch, C flute is $^5/_{32}$ inch high, 40 flutes per inch, E flute is $^1/_{16}$ inch high, 90 per inch. – estría

flyer Alternate spelling for *flier*.

fly fold Sheet folded once horizontally. Also called four-panel fold.

flying ink Alternate term for *misting*.

flyleaf Leaf at the front and back of a casebound book that is the one side of the end paper not glued to the case. – guarda

foam board Light sheet of plastic foam or corrugated plastic laminated with smooth surfaces. Used for products such as lawn signs and store displays.

FOB Abbreviation for *free on board*.

focal length Distance from the optical center of a lens to the film surface when the lens is focused at infinity. Focal length is commonly expressed in millimeters.

A normal focal length is equal to the diagonal of the film being used. On a 35mm camera, a 50mm lens is considered normal. Lenses on a 35mm camera with focal lengths shorter than 50mm, such as 28mm and 35mm, are wide angle lenses. Lenses with focal lengths longer than 50mm, such as 105mm and 200mm, are telephoto lenses. – distancia focal

focal plane The plane on which a lens forms an image that is in focus. In a camera, the side of the film that faces the lens is at the focal plane. – plano focal

Focoltone Colour System System of specifying color based entirely on four-color process. Printers can reproduce any of the 763 hues using either four-color process or spot color mixed from process inks.

focus To adjust the lens of a camera so that an image appears clearly. Such an image is said to be in focus, be sharp, or have good definition. Illustrated on page 229. – enfocar

fog Defect looking like haze appearing on photographic film or paper after developing. Fog occurs because of light leaks in the camera or darkroom or because of wrong developing chemicals. – velo

foil 1) Extremely thin sheet of metal used for foil stamping. 2) Sheet of plastic that simulates metal foil. – 1, lámina; 2, hojuela

foil emboss To foil stamp and emboss an image. Also called heat stamp. – estampar con láminas

foil papers Papers with surfaces that seem metallic. – papeles metalizados

foil stamp Method of printing using a letterpress and dies. Images created by foil stamping use foil that releases from its backing when stamped with the heated die. Also called block print, hot foil stamp, and stamp. Illustrated on page 247.

Foil stamping allows printing with colors and effects that inks cannot achieve, especially because foil is opaque and ink is not. For example, light foil on dark paper yields a clean image, whereas light ink on dark paper may almost disappear. – estampar con láminas

folder 1) Product made of stiff paper and designed to store letters and documents. 2) Machine for folding paper. – 1, carpeta; 2, plegadora, dobladora

folding dummy Dummy made of paper specified for the job. A folding dummy shows imposition and how thick the product will be and reveals potential problems with grain direction, cracking, and binding. – muestra de plegado

fold marks Lines on a mechanical, film, printing plate, or press sheet indicating where to fold the final product. – líneas de doblado

foldout Gatefold sheet bound into a publication, often used for a map or chart. Also called gatefold and pullout. In Great Britain called throwout. – hoja plegada encuadernada

folio 1) Page number. 2) Sheet of paper folded once, yielding four pages. 3) Alternate term for *presentation folder.* – 1 - 3, folio

folio lap Alternate term for *lap.*

folio size 1) Alternate term for *parent size.* 2) Alternate term for *oversize.* – tamaño folio;

font Complete assortment of upper and lower case characters, numerals, punctuation, and other symbols of one typeface. Illustrated on page 255. In Great Britain called fount.

A font is a concept, not a physical object. Fonts can be held in the storage or memory of a computer, on sheets of transfer lettering, on film, or in cases holding metal type. – fuente

foot Bottom of sheet or page. Illustrated on page 23. – pie

footband Small strip of decorative cloth at the bottom of the spine of a casebound book. Also called tailband. – banda de pie

footer Information, such as a chapter title, that appears at the bottom of every page of a publication. Also called running foot. – línea de pie

foot margin Margin at bottom of sheet or page. Illustrated on page 23. – margen inferior

footnote Comment, explanation, or citation that explains text. Footnotes may appear at the bottom (foot) of the page, at the end of a chapter, or as an appendix to the document as a whole. – nota al pie

foot of page Bottom of the page. In Great Britain called tails.

common folds

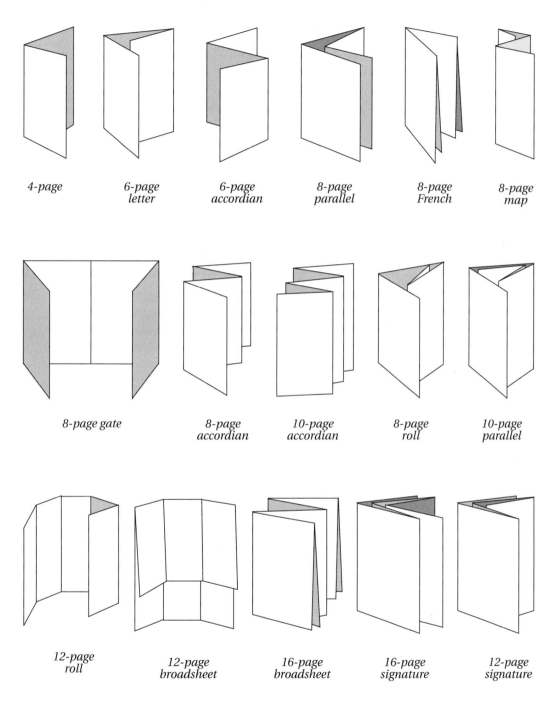

4-page

6-page
letter

6-page
accordian

8-page
parallel

8-page
French

8-page
map

8-page gate

8-page
accordian

10-page
accordian

8-page
roll

10-page
parallel

12-page
roll

12-page
broadsheet

16-page
broadsheet

16-page
signature

12-page
signature

force card Alternate term for *male die*. – contramatrix acuñadora

foredge Alternate term for *face (1)*.

foreground Portion of a photo or illustration in front of its center of attention, as compared to background. Illustrated on page 233. – primer plano

foreword Short introduction to a book. Written by a famous or authoritative person other than the author. – prólogo

form Each side of a signature. Also spelled forme.

Precisely speaking, the term 'form' refers to an array of images, not to a physical object. Saying "Let's print the second form" means "Let's print the images that go on the second side of the sheet." For that reason, 'form' can refer to type ready for printing, a flat, a plate, or one side of a press sheet. – forma

format Size, style, shape, layout, organization, or typography. Format is a general term whose meaning depends on context. All the following examples are correct.

size "The format of that book is 8½ x 11 inches." "She photographs using 35 mm format."

style "We plan a coffee-table format." "Their catalog is digest format."

shape "The annual report has an album format." "I need a computer screen in portrait format."

layout "Our catalog has a newspaper format." "Simple newsletters use a one-column format."

organization "We transmit data using the serial format." "The INIT command formats disks for a specific computer."

typography "Use a one-eme indent format on all paragraphs." "The book has three formats for subtitles and captions." – formato

formation Characteristic of paper referring to the distribution of fibers as perceived when the sheet is lighted from behind. Good formation means fibers appear uniform; poor formation means they appear in clumps. In Great Britain called look through. – formación

forme British spelling of *form*.

form bond Lightweight bond, easy to perforate, made for business forms. Also called register bond. – papel bond para formas

former fold First fold given paper coming off a web press, often before the paper is cut into sheets. The former fold is in the direction of the web, thus parallel to the grain.

form roller(s) Roller(s) that come in contact with the printing plate, bringing it ink or water. – rodillos de planchas

formula pricing Printing prices based on standard papers, formats, ink colors, and quantities. – precios base

form web press See *web press*.

for position only Refers to inexpensive copies of photos or art used on mechanicals to indicate placement and scaling, but not intended for reproduction. Abbreviated FPO.

The abbreviation FPO is often boldly written on the image to ensure that nobody mistakes it for the correct original art. – para posición solamente

forward collate To collate from first page to last, as compared to reverse collate. Also called ascending collate.

foundry type Individual pieces of hot type made for repeated use, as compared to lines of type cast for just one job. Foundry type is made of much harder metals than line casting type. – tipo por fundición

fount British term for *font.*

fountain Trough or container, on a printing press, that holds fluids such as ink, varnish, or water. Also called duct. – tintero

fountain roller Roller that revolves in contact with an ink or water fountain. Fountain rollers pick up ink or water to start its movement through the printing unit toward the paper. Illustrated on page 167. – rodillo del tintero

fountain solution Mixture of water and chemicals that dampens a printing plate to prevent ink from adhering to the non-image area. Also called dampener solution. – solución mojadora

four-color process printing Technique of printing that uses process colors—black, magenta, cyan, and yellow—to simulate full-color images. Illustrated on pags 67

and 72. Also called color process printing, full color printing, and process printing. See also *process colors.* – impresión cuatricolor

Fourdrinier machine Machine used to make paper by catching furnish on a wire called a Fourdrinier wire. – máquina Fourdrinier

Fourdrinier wire Screen on a paper-making machine that catches furnish and carries it while it begins to form into paper. – alambre Fourdrinier

four-panel fold Alternate term for *fly fold.* – doblado de cuatro paneles

four-stop photography Technique of measured photography to yield photos with four-f/stop tonal ranges that reproduce faithfully using four-color process printing on gloss coated paper.

fourth class mail US Postal Service classification for books, records, and other relatively heavy parcels that may travel slowly and at low cost. – correo de cuarta clase

four-up labels Alternate term for *Cheshire labels.*

foxing Yellow or brown spots on old paper. Foxing is caused by chemical impurities and poor storage conditions. – manchas de moho

fpm Abbreviation for *feet per minute.*

FPO Abbreviation for *for position only.*

frame 1) One unit in a series of photos, such as one image on a contact sheet or one transparency on a light table. 2) Alternate term

for *stretch frame.* 3) Lines to enclose type or graphics on a page.
– 1, marco; 3, caja

frame grabber Computer utility that freezes one image from a video signal and inserts into a page layout.

freelancer Professional, such as writer or photographer, who is self-employed, thus free to accept work from many clients. Also called contract artist. – independiente

free on board Refers to the location from which shipping charges are calculated. Abbreviated FOB.

FOB printer's location means the printer loads the job onto a truck and the customer pays for shipping to the final destination.

free sheet Paper made from cooked wood fibers mixed with chemicals and washed free of impurities, as compared to groundwood paper. Also called woodfree paper.

Because free sheet contains little lignin and other substances found in groundwood, it resists yellowing with age. Bond, text, offset, and most cover and coated papers for commercial printing are free sheets.
– hoja libre

free-standing insert Insert that is loose between pages or sections of a publication, such as a newspaper, as compared to a bound insert. Abbreviated FSI. – inserción suelta

French fold Two folds at right angles to each other. Illustrated on page 105. Also called right angle fold.
– doblado frances

fringe Alternate term for *halo effect.*

frisket Mask used to prevent ink from reaching non-image areas. Friskets are used in airbrushing and in letterpress and screen printing.
– frasqueta

frisket knife Alternate term for *art knife.* – cuchilla para frasqueta

frontispiece Photograph or illustration facing the title page of a book or chapter. – portada

front list List of books recently produced by a publisher, usually within the last year, as compared to back list. – lista de publicaciones receintes

front matter Foreword, acknowledgments, and other elements of a book appearing before the start of the main text. Also called preliminaries.

Front matter traditionally is numbered using lowercase Roman numerals. Pages appear in the following sequence: half title, title, copyright (on verso of title page), dedication, preface, foreword, acknowledgments, table of contents, list of illustrations, and introduction. Each section starts on a right hand page. – páginas preliminares

FSI Abbreviation for *free-standing insert.*

f/stop Measure of aperture setting on a camera. Illustrated on page 228.

Large-numbered f/stops (f/16 or f/22 on a personal camera, f/90 or f/128 on a process camera) signify small apertures and are referred to as small f/stops; small-numbered f/stops (f/3.5 and f/1.9 on a personal camera, f/9 or f/11 on a process camera) indicate wide aperture openings, thus are called large f/stops.

Changing from a wide f/stop to the next smaller f/stop halves the amount of light that will reach the film. Changing from a small f/stop to the next wider f/stop doubles the amount of light. – paso de diafragma

fugitive color inks Inks that fade when exposed to light, as compared to light-fast inks. – tintas de colores incostantes

fulfillment Recording, packaging, and otherwise handling orders for products and subscriptions. Some types of printers, such as book and magazine printers, offer fulfillment services as well as printing and binding. – cumplimiento

full bound Book covered entirely with one material, as compared to half bound and quarter bound. Illustrated on page 23.
– encuadernacado total

full-coated carbon paper Carbon paper coated on both sides.

full-color printing Alternate term for *four-color process printing.*

full frame Photograph printed without cropping, showing the entire image area of the negative. Contact prints show full-frame images. – marco completo

full measure Maximum width of a column of type. A line of type that is four inches wide is set full measure in a column specified as a 4-inch column. That same 4-inch line appearing in a 5-inch column is not full measure. – anchura total

full-range black Alternate term for *full-scale black.* – negro de escala completa

full-range halftone Halftone ranging from 0% coverage in its highlights to 100% coverage in its shadows.
– mediotono de escala completa

full-scale black Black separation made to have dots throughout the entire tonal range of the image, as compared to half-scale black and skeleton black. Also called full-range black. – negro de escala completa

full-web press See *web press.*

furnish Mixture of fibers, water, dyes, and chemicals poured from the headbox onto the Fourdrinier wire of a papermaking machine. Also called slurry and stock.

Furnish becomes paper as the papermaking process removes approximately 95% of its water.
– pasta

G

G Abbreviation for giga, one billion (10 to the 9th).

galley 1) Tray used to hold metal type that is composed and ready to proof. 2) Column of photo or laser type ready for pasteup. – galera

galley proof Proof of type from any source, whether metal type or photo type. Also called checker and slip proof. – prueba de galera

gang 1) To halftone or separate more than one image in only one exposure or scan. Ganging photos is done to save time and money. By placing several images on the copyboard or scanner drum at once, all images are reduced, enlarged, or color corrected by the same amount and are halftoned simultaneously.
2) To reproduce two or more different printed products simultaneously on one sheet of paper during one press run. Ganging print jobs is done to save time and money and to use paper that might otherwise be wasted. Also called combination run. – 1 & 2, reproducir en combinación

gap Space between die-cut labels. Paper in the gaps is waste. – hueco

gate fold 1) Fold, running into the gutter, that opens like a gate. Illustrated on page 105.
2) Alternate term for *foldout*.
– 1, doblado de puerta

gathered Signatures assembled next to each other in the proper sequence for binding, as compared to nested. Perfect bound signatures are gathered. Illustrated on page 223. Also called stacked. In Great Britain called made up. – alzado

gauze Alternate term for *crash (1)*.

gazette Alternate term for *newspaper*.

gazetteer Index of geographical names. – diccionario geográfico

Gb Abbreviation for *gigabyte*.

GBC bind Brand name of plastic comb bind. – encuadernación GBC

GCR Abbreviation for *gray component replacement*.

generation Refers to number of steps that a reproduction is distant from the original.

A first generation image is the original; second generation is made from the original; third generation is made from the second generation. Technically speaking, this page is fifth generation: first was type; second was negative; third was plate; fourth was blanket; fifth is ink on paper.

Generation commonly refers to the number of times that film has been duplicated or an image has been photocopied. Three copies made from the same original are all second generation but three copies, each made using a preceding copy as an orginal are all different generations. – generación

genre Category of writing, such as romance, mystery, travelogue, or how-to. – genero

geometric printing Alternate term for *container printing*.

Gerber Brand name of machines that use computers to automate step-and-repeat and other stripping processes.

ghost halftone Normal halftone whose density has been reduced to produce a very faint image. Illustrated on page 219. – mediotono traspintado

ghosting 1) Phenomenon of a faint image appearing on a printed sheet where it was not intended to appear. Chemical ghosting refers to the transfer of the faint image from the front of one sheet to the back of another sheet. Mechanical ghosting refers to the faint image appearing as a repeat of an image on the same side of the sheet.

2) Phenomenon of a faint image appearing slightly out of register with the intended image. Also called fadeback.

3) Phenomenon of printed image appearing too light because of ink starvation.

4) Technique of screening back or reducing the dot size of an image to make it reproduce faintly.
– 1 & 2, fantasma; 3 & 4, traspintarse

ghost key Alternate term for *shadow black*. – plancha traspintada

ghost writer Professional who writes a book or article under contract with another person where the other person claims authorship.
– escritor fantasma

gigabyte One billion (1,000,000,000) bytes. – gigabyte

gilding Technique of making a book's pages look like they are covered with gold or silver when the book is closed.

Gilding is done by covering the edges of pages with very thin varnish, then dusting the sticky edges with powdered metal. The result looks lavish and prevents the edges from smudging. – bordes dorados

glassine Glossy, translucent or transparent paper used for windows in envelopes and as release paper for labels and decals. Also called pergamyn. – papel cristal

gloss Characteristic of paper, ink, or varnish that seems shiny because it reflects light well. – brillo

gloss art British term for *gloss coated paper.*

glossary Alphabetical list of words giving definitions relevant to a specific topic, such as this glossary of printing and publishing. – glosario

gloss-coated paper Paper with a coating that reflects light well, as compared to dull or matte coated paper. Illustrated on pages 31 and 202. Also called art paper, enamel paper, and slick paper. In Great Britain called art paper, gloss art, imitation art.

Gloss papers come in a variety of ratings determined by their brightness and opacity and, among the lower ratings, by the amount of groundwood pulp they contain. Ultra premium is the highest designation, followed by premium, then five grades numbered 1-5.
– papel glaseado, papel lustre

gloss ink Ink that dries to a finish that reflects light well, as compared to dull ink. – tinta brillante

gloss paper Alternate term for *coated paper.* – papel glaseado

gloss varnish Varnish that dries to a finish that reflects light well, as compared to dull varnish. – barniz brillante

glossy print Photography term for black-and-white print made on glossy paper. – fotografía brillante

glue bind Alternate term for *perfect bind.* – encuadernación engomado

Goldenrod 1) Brand name for orange masking paper used in film

assembly. **2)** The color of paper typically specified for the internal file copy in multipart business forms. **3)** Alternate term for *flat (1).*

gothic type Alternate term for *sans-serif type.* – letra gótica

grade General term used to distinguish between or among printing papers, but whose specific meaning depends on context. Grade can refer to the category, class, rating, finish, or brand of paper. All the following examples represent correct and common usage. In Great Britain called quality.

category One of the major groups of paper determined by how it is made. "I prefer groundwood grade for this job, not free sheet."

class One of the major classes of paper such as bond, uncoated book, coated book, text, cover, bristol, and board. "Bond is a better grade for letterhead than cover."

rating One of many ratings of paper, such as 100% cotton or #4 gloss. "Our separations look better on a #1 grade than a #4 grade."

finish One of several finishes such as wove or laid. "Which grade do you want, antique or vellum?"

brand One of thousands of brands of paper. "The mill makes 27 grades of paper, but SilkSmooth is most popular."

other Any paper that differs from any other paper in any one respect. "Grain long is a better grade for this job than grain short." – grado

gradient Alternate term for *graduated screen tint.* – gradiente

graduated screen tint Screen tint that changes density gradually and smoothly, not in distinct steps. Also called dégradé, gradient, ramped screen, and vignette. – gradiente

grain 1) In paper, the predominant direction of fibers. Illustrated on page 179. See also *grain direction.*

2) In photographic film, crystals of chemicals that make up the emulsion. Illustrated on page 228.

Fast films have larger crystals than slow films. Negatives, prints, or transparencies made from fast films may show more crystals, so appear 'grainy.' Enlarging any photographic image, regardless of the film used to photograph the original, may lead to a grainy appearance.

3) (verb) To roughen the surface of a lithogaphic plate so that it holds moisture better. – 1, fibra; 2, granular; 3, granear

grain direction Predominant direction in which fibers in paper become aligned during manufacturing. Illustrated on page 179. Also called machine direction.

Mills have several ways of indicating grain direction on labels and in swatchbooks and pricebooks. They print 'grain long' or 'grain short;' 'GL' or 'GS.' They underline the dimension parallel to the grain; for example, 11 x 17 means grain short. They write 'M' for 'machine direction' after the dimension parallel to the grain; for example, 890 x 1130 (M) means grain long.

Grain direction affects printing, folding, and binding.

printing Moisture in the air and in dampening solutions causes the fibers in paper to expand slightly. Fibers become much wider, but not much longer; a sheet expands a lot against the grain, but not very much with the grain. Printing that requires tight register is done on grain long paper so that fibers parallel the length of the cylinders, giving press operators maximum control over register as sheets expand.

folding Paper folds more easily and folds look cleaner with the grain than against it, especially with relatively thick paper.

binding Binding is strongest and smoothest with grain direction parallel to the binding edge. Leaves bound against their grain can become wavy at both the binding and the face of the publication as paper absorbs moisture. – dirección de la fibra

grained paper Paper embossed or printed to resemble material such as wood, leather, or marble. – papel granulado

grain long paper Paper whose fibers run parallel to the long dimension of the sheet. See *grain direction.* Also called long grain paper and narrow web paper. – papel con fibra a lo largo

grain short paper Paper whose fibers run parallel to the short dimension of the sheet. See *grain direction.* Also called short grain paper and wide web paper. – papel con fibra a lo corto

grainy Appearance of a photograph or halftone that has been enlarged so much that the pattern of crystals in the emulsion can be seen in the photo or its reproduction.
– granulado

grammage Basis weight of paper expressed in grams per square meter (gsm). Illustrated on page 115.

   Graphic arts professionals throughout the world, except in North America, use grammage to express basis weight. The grammage system does not involve the concepts of basic sizes or grade, so the basis weights of all papers can be compared without further interpretation. In the grammage, system a 100 gsm sheet weighs twice as much as a 50 gsm sheet of the same size and half as much as a 200 gsm sheet, regardless of whether the sheets are bond, offset, cover, or any other grade of paper — and regardless of whether the sheets being compared are all in one grade or are from different grades.
– gramaje

graphical user interface Refers to a computer that takes instructions from clicks on icons, as compared to character user interface. Abbreviated GUI. – interface gráfica con el usario

graphic arts The crafts, industries, and professions related to designing and printing on paper and other substrates. – artes gráficas

graphic arts camera Alternate term for *process camera*. – cámara de fotoreproducción

graphic arts film Film whose emulsion responds to light on an all-or-nothing principle to yield high contrast images suitable for reproduction by a printing press, as compared to continuous-tone film. Also called litho film and repro film.
– película para artes gráficas

graphic design Arrangement of type and visual elements along with specifications for paper, ink colors, and printing processes that, when combined, convey a visual message.

   Graphic design combines art, skill, and technology for purposes of communication. The designer imagines how a piece will look and perform, then plans how to get from vision to reality. At each step in the process the designer takes into account such factors as audience, budget, and capabilities of printing methods. – diseño gráfico

graphic designer Professional who designs, plans, and may coordinate production of a printed piece.
– diseñador gráfico

graphic papers Alternate term for *fine papers.*

graphics Visual elements that supplement type to make printed messages more clear or interesting.

   Graphics may be divided into three categories.

   design graphics Rules, screen tints, bleeds, and reverses used to organize layouts and highlight messages.

   info graphics Charts, tables, and maps used to convey information, such as statistics, visually instead of verbally.

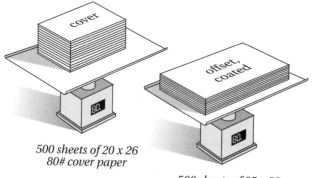

500 sheets of 20 x 26
80# cover paper

500 sheets of 25 x 38
80# book or text paper

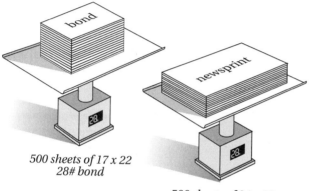

500 sheets of 17 x 22
28# bond

500 sheets of 24 x 36
28# newprint

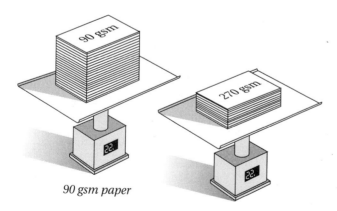

90 gsm paper

270 gsm paper

basis weight and basic sizes

grammage	basis weight
34	9# manifold
44	30# book
45	12# manifold
59	40# book
60	16# bond
67	45# book
74	50# book
75	20# bond
81	55# book
89	60# book
90	24#bond
104	70# book/text
105	28#ledger
118	80# book/text
120	32#ledger
135	36# ledger
147	67#bristol
148	100# book/text
150	40# ledger
162	60# cover
163	90# index
163	100# tag
176	65# cover
199	110# index
216	80# cover
218	125# tag
219	100# bristol
270	100#cover
352	130# cover

**comparison guide to
common basis weights**

art graphics Photographs, drawings, and illustrations used to convey information and feelings through images instead of words. – gráficos

graph paper 1) Paper printed with a grid of straight lines to aid drawing of charts and graphs. 2) Alternate term for *map paper*. – 1, papel cuadriculado

gravure Method of printing using metal cylinders etched with millions of tiny wells that hold ink. All images in products printed by gravure, including type, consist of dot patterns. Illustrated on page 117. See also *intaglio printing*.

Gravure 'plates' are cylinders, typically eight feet wide and almost two feet across that are relatively expensive to make and handle. The wide paper they can print yields 48-page signatures for 8½ x 11-inch publications and 96-page signatures for 5½ x 8½-inch publications.

The gravure process prints from plate directly to paper using relatively little pressure, so can run papers as light as 30# with high densities and minimal dot gain. Inks have almost no tack to ensure that they release easily from the well, so the process involves little risk of picking.

Because of its high prepress costs, gravure is best suited to long runs of magazines, catalogs, and inserts. The editorial portion of *National Geographic Magazine* is printed gravure. – huecograbado

gray balance Printed cyan, magenta, and yellow halftone dots that accurately reproduce a neutral gray image. Printers and color separators use gray balance as a starting point for achieving color balance in four-color process printing. – equilibrio del gris

gray component replacement Technique of replacing gray tones in the yellow, cyan, and magenta with black ink. Abbreviated GCR. Also called achromatic color removal. In Great Britain called complimentary colour removal.

GCR is done while making color separations. It reduces the amount of ink needed for four-color process printing, cuts drying time, makes it easier to maintain consistent color throughout the run, and may result in more pleasing reproductions.

Separators use percentages to express quantities of gray components replaced by black. A GCR of 50% uses black ink to replace half of the grey component of the chromatic color. – reemplasar el gris

gray levels Number of distinct gray tones that can be reproduced by a computer. Illustrated on page 215.

Relatively simple, 2-bit computers display 16 levels of gray. More complex 4-bit machines display 64 levels. Color scanners and 8-bit computers display 256 gray levels, the theoretical limit allowed by one byte of memory. Machines using 1.5 bytes – 12 bits – can produce 4,096 gray levels. – niveles del gris

gray scale Strip of gray values ranging from white to black. Used by process camera and scanner oper-

gravure

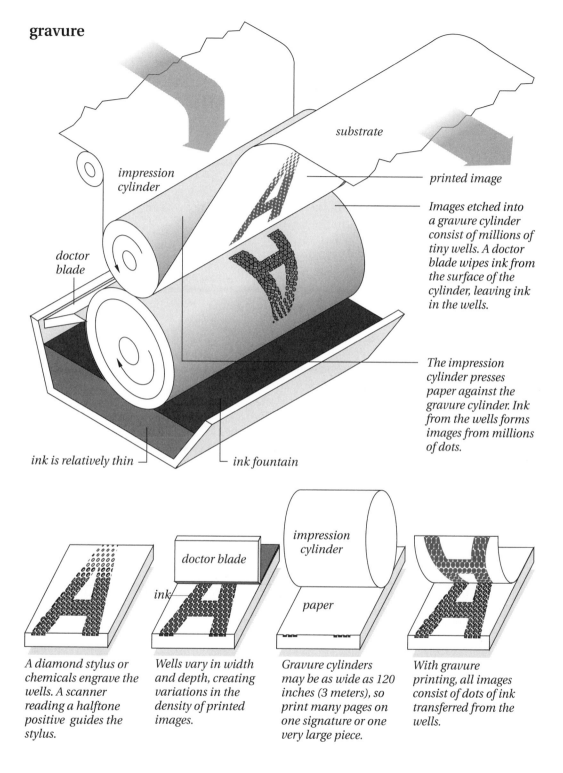

substrate

impression
cylinder

doctor
blade

printed image

Images etched into
a gravure cylinder
consist of millions of
tiny wells. A doctor
blade wipes ink from
the surface of the
cylinder, leaving ink
in the wells.

The impression
cylinder presses
paper against the
gravure cylinder. Ink
from the wells forms
images from millions
of dots.

ink is relatively thin

ink fountain

doctor blade

ink

impression
cylinder

paper

A diamond stylus or
chemicals engrave the
wells. A scanner
reading a halftone
positive guides the
stylus.

Wells vary in width
and depth, creating
variations in the
density of printed
images.

Gravure cylinders
may be as wide as 120
inches (3 meters), so
print many pages on
one signature or one
very large piece.

With gravure
printing, all images
consist of dots of ink
transferred from the
wells.

ators to calibrate exposure times for film and plates. Illustrated on page 215. Also called step wedge. – escala del gris

greeking Nonsense type, often in Latin, used on dummies.

Greeking simulates typography and typographic color without distracting viewers with messages they can read. The term may also be used to refer to blocks or shapes used in page assembly programs to simulate visuals to be inserted later. – texto simulado

green copy Magazine or catalog bound by hand and given to the customer to be checked for errors. A green copy has a corner cut off to distinguish it from production copies. – copia verde

green sheet Alternate term for *shopper*. – hoja verde

greeting card Folded heavyweight paper with printed message for events such as holidays and birthdays. – tarjeta de felicitaciones

grid 1) Pattern of lines representing the layout of a printed piece. A grid may be imaginary, or it may be printed on paper or displayed on a computer screen. 2) Pattern of non-printing guidelines on a pasteup board or computer screen. Grids help align and organize copy. – 1 & 2, cuadrícula

grind edge Alternate term for binding edge when referring to perfect bound products. – borde de encuadernación

grindoff Approximately ⅛ inch (3 mm) along the spine that is ground off gathered signatures before perfect binding. – amolado

grin through Loss of color density on screen printed fabics that occurs when fabrics are stretched so much that the color of the underlying fabric shows through the printing.

grip and grin Staged photograph of two people smiling and shaking hands at a ceremonial event. – sonriendo y dándose la mano

gripper edge Edge of a sheet held by grippers on a sheetfed press, thus the edge going first through the press. Also called feeding edge and leading edge. In Great Britain called pitch edge.

The gripper edge is a strip of paper between ⅛ inch (3 mm) and ¾ inch (19 mm), depending on the press. Presses cannot print paper held by the grippers. – borde de pinzas

grippers Mechanical fingers that hold a sheet of paper as it passes through a sheetfed press. – pinzas

grommet Large metal or plastic eyelet used to reinforce holes in banners, flags, and paper products such as sample books. – ojal

gross weight Weight of the contents plus weight of the wrapping, container, or vehicle. Gross weight equals net weight plus tare weight. – peso total

groundwood paper Newsprint and other inexpensive paper made from pulp created when wood chips are ground mechanically rather than refined chemically. Groundwood papers are relatively bulky and opaque. They retain the lignin found in wood, so deteriorate more rapidly than free sheets. In Great Britain called mechanical paper. – papel de pasta mecánica

groundwood pulp Pulp made by grinding wood chips into fibers without removing lignin, as compared to chemical pulp. Also called mechanical pulp. – pasta mecánica

guard Alternate term for *hanger.*

GUI Abbreviation for *graphical user interface.*

guide 1) Publication giving readers information such as geographical directions or instructions about using a product. 2) Template for design or imposition. – 1, guía; 2, plantilla

guillotine cutter Large cutting machine whose blade trims paper evenly across a stack of sheets. The blade is brought down from above, hence the term 'guillotine.' – guillotina

gummed paper Alternate term for *label paper.* – papel engomado

gusset Expandable bellows portion of a bag, file folder, or envelope. The capacity of the container is measured with the gusset open. – fondo de fuelle

gusset wrinkle Wrinkle on inside pages of a signature created during folding. Especially likely to occur with thick papers or when several sheets are folded at once.

gutter Line or fold at which facing pages meet. Illustrated on pages 23 and 165. In Great Britain called back margin. – medianil

gutter bleed/gutter jump Alternate term for *crossover.* – sangrado sobre el medianil

H

hairline Thinnest visible space or rule.

Because visibility is determined by factors such as contrast between ink and paper and eyesight of the viewer, hairline has no precise meaning. Hairlines exist in the eye of the beholder.

The US Postal Service defines a hairline as ½-point. Many printers and graphic designers define hairline as ¹⁄₁₀₀ inch. The Graphic Arts Technical Foundation defines hairline as ³⁄₁₀₀₀ inch. Most computer programs for the graphic arts define hairline as ¼ point. – rayita

hairline register Subjective term referring to very close register. The meaning depends entirely on who is using the term and in what circumstances.

Regarding four-color process printing, hairline register may mean register within one row of dots or half a row of dots, depending on the size of the dots. Regarding reverses or traps, the term may refer to an accurate choke or spread or may be an alternate term for butt register. – registro exacto

halation 1) Alternate term for *halo effect* on film. 2) Fuzzy or distorted images on a plate resulting from poor vacuum drawdown, thus uneven film contact, during plate-making. – 1, efecto halo; 2, borroso

half bound Book with its spine and corners covered in one material, frequently leather, and the rest of its sides covered in another, frequently cloth, as compared to full bound and quarter bound. Illustrated on page 23. – encuadernado a media piel

half scale black Black separation made to have dots only in the shadows and midtones, as compared to full scale black and skeleton black. – negro de escala media

half-sheet work British term for *work and turn.*

half title Book page showing the title only, not the subtitle or the names of author or publisher. Also called bastard title. – anteportada, portada falsa

halftone 1) (verb) To photograph or scan a continuous-tone image to convert the image into halftone dots. 2) (noun) A photograph or continuous-tone illustration that has been halftoned and appears on film, paper, printing plate, or the final printed product. Illustrated on page 215. – mediotono

halftone dots Thousands of dots that together create the illusion of shading or of a continuous-tone image. Illustrated on page 218.

Halftone dots come in many shapes. The most common are round, square, and elliptical (also known as chain). Each shape or pattern has slightly different advantages, depending on the nature of the image, printing method, and substrate.

In addition to having different shapes, halftone dots vary in size. Large dots cover a relatively high percentage of an area; small dots a relatively low percentage. Dots in the 70% to 100% range create shadow areas; dots between 40% and 60% create middle tones; dots below 25% have lots of paper showing around them, thus create highlights.

The terms 'halftone' and 'digital' have different meanings with respect to dots. Halftone dots vary in size; digital dots are all the same size. Computers use digital dots to create halftone dots, so halftone dots may consist of one or more digital dots. See also *screen ruling*. – puntos de mediotono

halftone gravure Gravure printing using cylinders made by scanning halftone positives and reproducing the dots by etching. – impresión grabado de mediotono

halftone negative Halftone showing a negative image. Halftone negatives are assumed to be on film for making lithographic plates. Illustrated on page 64. – negativo en medios tonos

halftone positive Halftone showing a positive image.

Halftone positives on paper, such as PMTs or Veloxes, are ready to add to mechanicals. They may also be used as proofs that show halftones more realistically than bluelines. Halftone positives on film are used by some printers to make plates. – positivo en medios tonos

halftone screen Piece of film or glass containing a grid of lines that breaks light into dots. Printers use halftone screens when making screen tints, halftones, duotones, and separations. Also called contact screen and screen. – trama para medios tonos

halftone with screen Alternate term for *fake duotone.* – bitono falso

half web press See *web press.*

halo effect 1) Faint shadow sometimes surrounding halftone dots when printed. When exposing film to make a halftone, some light may reflect from behind the dots in the screen back into the process camera. The shadow caused by the light makes the actual dot seem larger than it really is, so throws off densitometer readings and yields plates that print weak images. Also called halation. The halo itself is also called a fringe.

2) In screen printing, alternate term for *ghosting*.

3) In flexography, faint outline around images caused by using too much pressure to print. – 1 - 3, efecto halo

handbill Alternate term for *flier*.

handbook Reference book with many kinds of information related to a common theme, profession, or activity. – manual, guía

handout News release, booklet, questionnaire, or other item distributed to people attending a class or meeting. – hoja informativa

hand work Any work, such as repairing bindings or some collating jobs, that must be done by hand. – trabajo a mano

hanger Thin strip of paper near the binding edge of a publication. Illustrated on page 53. Also called flap, guard, and magna strip.

The hanger is used as a mount when a separate sheet, such as a map or insert, is tipped in. The hanger is the thin edge of a leaf wrapped around a signature or a strip tipped onto a signature. – suporte

hanging character Character that extends beyond the line measure at the beginning or end of the line. Illustrated on page 263. – carácter saliente

hanging columns Alternate term for *scalloped columns*. – columnas salientes

hanging indent Paragraph with first line set full measure and all remaining lines indented. This book is set with hanging indents. Illustrated on page 263. – sangria saliente

hanging paper Base stock used to make wallpaper. – papel para colgar

hanging punctuation Punctuation that extends slightly beyond the line measure. Hanging punctuation makes justified copy appear more evenly aligned. – puntuación saliente

hard bind Alternate term for *case bind*.

hard copy Copy on a substrate such as film or paper, as compared to soft copy. – copia impresa

hard cover Alternate term for *case bound*. – encuadernación con tapas rígidas

hard disk Computer storage built into computer, as compared to floppy disk. Also called rigid disk. – disco duro

hard dots Halftone dots with no halos or soft edges, as compared to *soft dots*. – puntos duros

hard mechanical Mechanical consisting of paper and/or acetate and made using pasteup techniques, as compared to electronic mechanical. – boceto final duro

hard proof Proof on paper or other substrate, as compared to a soft proof. – prueba dura

hard sized Paper treated with relatively large amount of size to make it especially water resistant, as compared to slack sized. – papel altamente encolado

hardware Keyboard, monitor, and other physical components of a computer system. – hardware

haze Alternate term for *scum.*

HDTV Abbreviation for *high definition television.*

HE Abbreviation for *house error.*

head Top of sheet or page. – cabeza

headband Small strip of decorative cloth at the top of the spine of a casebound book. Illustrated on page 23. – cabezada, cabecera

header Information, such as page number or chapter title, that appears at top of every page of a publication. Illustrated on page 163. – cabecera

headline Phrase in large type that draws attention to an advertisement or article in a periodical. Illustrated on page 162. – línea titular

headliner Machine that sets display type on paper so it is ready to paste up.

headline type Alternate term for *display type.* – tipo para título

head margin Margin at the top of a page or sheet. Illustrated on page 23. – margen superior

head-to-head Imposition with heads (tops) of pages facing each other. – de cabeza a cabeza

head-to-tail Imposition with heads (tops) of pages facing tails (bottoms) of other pages. – de cabeza a pie

head trim Trim taken off the tops of pages. – recorte de cabeza

heat-set ink Ink made to dry quickly by passing through a drying oven, as compared to cold-set ink. Heat-set ink uses solvents that dry quickly under intense heat. – tinta de secado por calor

heat-set roughening Alternate term for *fiber puff.*

heat-set web Web press equipped with an oven to dry ink, thus able to print coated paper.
   Uncoated paper absorbs ink quickly, but coatings prevent ink from drying quickly by absorption. Web presses without drying ovens are thus suited only to printing uncoated papers. Heat-set webs dry ink by evaporating its solvent when they pass paper through an oven the instant after printing it. – prensa de bobina con horno

heat stamp Alternate term for *foil emboss.* – estampación al caliente

hectography Alternate term for *spirit duplicate.* – hectografo

helio Short for the machine that makes gravure cylinders via HelioKlischography .

HelioKlischography Brand name of process of using lasers to scan copy for gravure printing, then using diamond cutters to engrave the cylinder. – helioklishografía

heliotype Alternate term for *collotype.* – fotogelatinografía

hickey Spot or imperfection in printing, most visible in areas of heavy ink coverage, caused by dirt on the plate or blanket. Also called bull's eye and fish eye. – mota

high-bulk paper Paper made relatively thick in proportion to its basis weight, thus yielding fewer pages per inch. High-bulk paper makes a book thicker than it would be if printed on lower-bulk paper. In Great Britain called bulky mechanical paper. – papel basto

high contrast Lacking tonal gradations between dark and light areas. Type is high contrast. – alto contraste

high fidelity color Color reproduced using six, eight, or twelve separations, as compared to four-color process. High fidelity color extends the tonal range that inks can reproduce closer to the range that the human eye can perceive. – color de alta fidelidad

high finish Paper finish relatively glossy, as compared to low finish. – acabado de alto brillo

high folio 1) Referring to a final product, a page with the odd numeral. The high folio page is the right hand page of any pair of open pages. 2) Referring to a signature, the highest page number on the printed sheet. – 1 & 2, folio alto

high key photo Photo whose most important details appear in the highlights. Illustrated on page 226. – fotografía clara

highlights Lightest portions of a photograph or halftone, as compared to midtones and shadows. Illustrated on pages 218 and 233. – zonas claras

hinge Crease at which cover and spine meet. Illustrated on page 23. Also called joint. – bisagra

hinged cover Perfect bound cover scored ⅛ inch (3 mm) from the spine so it folds at the hinge instead of along the edge of the spine, where folding might destroy the binding. – cubierta de bisagra

hit The printing of one ink color. For example, printing black ink twice to achieve greater density involves two hits of black, called a double hit or double bump. – pasada

HLS Abbreviation for hue, lightness, saturation, one of the color-control options often found in software for design and page assembly. Also called HVS. See also *color curves.*

holding lines Alternate term for *keylines.* – líneas guías

holdout Alternate term for *ink holdout.* – resistencia

holography Printing method using a laser to emboss images precisely overlaying each other on a thin piece of film. The resulting single image appears three-dimensional. – olografía

homespun finish Alternate term for *crash finish.*

horizontal bar code Bar code aligned parallel to the width of the product, such as the bar code at the bottom of an envelope. – código de barras horizontal

horizontal format Sideways orientation of paper, computer screen, or printed product, as compared to vertical format. Most computer screens are horizontal format. Illustrated on page 233. Also called album format, broadside format, downstairs, landscape format, lying pages, oblong format, and wide page. – formato horizontal

hot   Refers to ink color appearing too dense on a press sheet, as in "The magenta is running a little hot." – intenso

hot foil stamp   Alternate term for *foil stamp*. – estampación al caliente

hot spot   Printing defect resulting when a piece of dirt or an air bubble causes incomplete drawdown during contact platemaking, leaving an area of weak ink coverage or visible dot gain. –mancha defectuosa

hot type   Type made from metal, as compared to cold type. Used for letterpress printing. – tipo de metal

house error   Error resulting from an internal mistake, as compared to author error or customer error. Abbreviated HE.

house organ   Periodical, such as a newsletter, magazine, or tabloid, published for employees or members of an organization. – boletín interno

house sheet   Paper kept in stock by a printer and suitable for a variety of printing jobs. Customers usually pay less for the house sheet than for comparable paper because printers buy house sheets in large quantities. Also called floor sheet. – hoja de la casa

house style   Guidelines for grammar, typography, color, and other graphic features as adopted by a specific organization. A house style ensures consistency and good taste according to the standards of the organization. – estilo de la casa

how-to book   Trade book explaining and illustrating how to perform tasks such as household repairs or gardening. – libro instructivo

hue   A specific color such as yellow or green. Burgundy, crimson, cardinal, rose, rubine, and rhodamine are all red hues. Illustrated on page 79. – matiz

hundredweight   100 pounds in North America, 112 pounds in the United Kingdom. Abbreviated CWT. Paper in the US or Canada that costs $90 CWT costs $90 for 100 pounds. – cien libras

HVS   Abbreviation for hue, value, saturation, an alternate term for HLS. See also *color curves*.

hydrotype   Alternate term for *collotype*. – hidrótipo

hyphen   Short dash that divides a word at the end of a line or connects some words into compounds. – guión

hypo   Alternate term for *fixer*. – fijador

I

icon Small illustration, on a computer screen, that represents a file or function.

illustration Artwork used to describe, explain, or attract attention. – ilustración

image Type, illustration, or other original as it has been reproduced on computer screen, film, printing plate, or paper. – imagen

image area 1) Portion of a plate, stencil, or other printing master containing the copy. Also called copy area. In Great Britain called inclusive type area. 2) Portion of paper on which printing appears. – área de la imagen

image assembly Alternate term for *strip.* – montaje de imagenes

image carrier Film, plate, cylinder, screen, or other medium that holds an image. – porta imagen

image processing Creating, changing, and printing out type, graphics, photos, and other digital information that can be displayed on a computer screen. – procesamiento de imagenes

imagesetter Laser output device using photosensitive paper or film. Imagesetters have higher resolutions than laser printers because they create dots from chemical crystals in emulsions instead of from toner. – productora de imagenes

imitation art British term for *gloss coated paper.*

impact paper Alternate term for *carbonless paper.* – papel autocopiante

impact printer Printer using needles, a daisy wheel, or other device that presses a ribbon into direct contact with paper, as compared to non-impact laser and ink jet printers. Typewriters and dot-matrix computer printers are examples of impact printers. – impresora de impacto

imposed colour proofs British term for *composite proof.*

imposition Arrangement of pages on mechanicals or flats so they will appear in proper sequence after press sheets are folded and bound. Imposition varies according to number of pages, sheet size, printing technique, binding method, and other factors. In Great Britain called planning. – imposición

imposition proof Alternate term for *composite proof.* – prueba de imposición

impression 1) Referring to printing, one impression equals one press sheet passing once through a printing unit. For example, a press sheet printed four-color process has four impressions. A plate with a life of 100,000 impressions prints one color on approximately 100,000 press sheets.

2) Referring to the speed of a press, one impression equals one press sheet passing once through the press. For example, a two-color press running at 10,000 impressions per hour yields 10,000 press sheets in one hour.

3) Refers to pressure applied to substrate by a press. In letterpress and flexography, impression targets reveal whether there is the correct amount of pressure.

4) British term for printing when referring to publishing. For example, "The book is in its second impression" (second printing).
– 1 - 3, impresión

impression cylinder Cylinder, on a press, that pushes paper against the plate or blanket, thus creating the pressure needed to transfer the image. Illustrated on pages 101 and 167. Also called impression roller.
– cilindro impresor

impression roller Alternate term for *impression cylinder.*

impressions per hour Measure of the speed of a printing press. Abbreviated iph.

A relatively fast sheet fed press runs 12,000 to 15,000 impressions per hour; a web press may run 50,000 impressions per hour (although web speeds are usually expressed in feet per minute or meters per second). – impresiones por hora

impression target Quality control image used to evaluate whether a letterpress or flexographic press is using the correct amount of pressure. – blanco de impresión

imprimatur Symbol printed on a publication showing that an organization authorized or endorsed it. A book with the imprimatur of a church conforms to doctrine of that church. – imprimátur

imprint 1) (verb) To print new copy on a previously printed sheet, such as imprinting an employee's name on business cards. Also called surprint.

2) (noun) The name of a category of books produced by one publisher. "Young Reader Series is an imprint of Popular Publishing Company."

3) (noun) The name of a book's owner stamped on its cover.
– 1, sobreimprimir 2 & 3, marca de imprenta

incandescent Refers to light emitted by bulbs, as compared to fluorescent. Illustrated on page 79. Also called tungsten. Incandescent light is considered warm and may produce a yellow cast on color photos. – luz incidente

incident light Light falling directly from its source onto a subject or scene, as compared to reflected light. – luz incidente

inclusive type area British term for *image area (1)*.

indelible ink Ink that withstands repeated laundering of the fabric on which it is printed. – tinta indeleble

indent Space at the left of the first line of most paragraphs to signal readers that a new paragraph is starting. – sangria

index Alphabetical list of topics mentioned in the text of a publication telling the page numbers on which each may be found. Illustrated on pages 160 and 162. – índice

index board British term for *index bristol*.

index bristol Bristol paper made for products such as index cards and file folders. In Great Britain called index board. – papel bristol

india paper Alternate term for *bible paper*. – papel india

indicia Postal permit information printed on objects to be mailed and accepted by US Postal Service in place of stamps. Illustrated on page 163. – permiso postal

industrial papers Alternate term for *coarse papers*. – papeles industriales

industrial screen printing Printing logos, signs, and instructions on items such as machines and cables. – impresión serigráfica industrial

inferior character Alternate term for *subscript*. – subíndices

infographics Charts, graphs, tables, and other visual representations of ideas and statistical information. Also called business graphics and management graphics. Illustrated on pages 129 and 160. – información gráfica

in house Refers to an activity, such as graphic design, photography, or printing, performed within an organization, not purchased from outside organizations. – uso propio

ink Liquid used to print images on paper and other substrates. Ink comes in a wide variety of colors, viscosities, and formulas suited to various printing methods, designs, and products. – tinta

ink balance Relationship of the densities and dot gains of process inks to each other and to a standard density of neutral gray. Whether inks are balanced or not balanced depends on color requirements of the particular printing job. – balance de la tinta

ink fountain Reservoir, on a printing press, that holds ink. Illustrated on page 117. – tintero

ink gloss Sheen that some inks have when dry. – brillo de la tinta

ink holdout Characteristic of paper that prevents it from absorbing ink, thus allowing ink to dry on the surface of the paper. Illustrated on page 202. Also called holdout.
  Ink holdout is affected by paper characteristics, such as calendering,

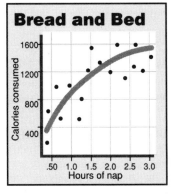

scattergram

map

Travers Stakes champs
Jockeys who have won the
Travers Stakes the most times:

pictograph

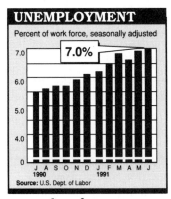

bar chart

organizational chart

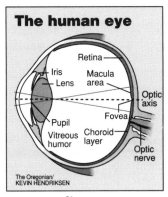

diagram

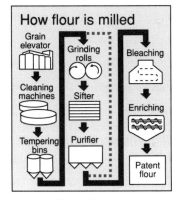

flow chart

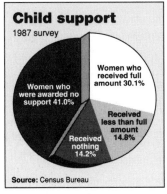

pie chart

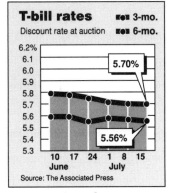

line chart

coating, and formation, and by ink characteristics such as tack and viscosity. Good holdout makes ink look glossy and affects image sharpness, color saturation, drying time, and many other factors. – resistencia a la tinta

in-house printer Alternate term for *in-plant printer*. – imprenta de la casa

ink jet printing Method of printing by spraying droplets of ink through computer-controlled nozzles. Illustrated on page 246. Also called jet printing.

Ink jet printing is used in a wide range of situations, from making proofs to personalizing and addressing large mailings. Ink jet printing may be done by machines that are also performing binding tasks, such as inserting coupons, or mailing tasks, such as sealing envelopes. – impresción por chorro de tinta

ink rollers Cylinders that transmit ink from the ink fountain to the plate cylinder of a printing press. Illustrated on page 167. In Great Britain called distributing rollers. – rodillos entintadores

ink set-off British term for *setoff*.

ink starvation Printing defect of images on one area of the press sheet appearing washed out because images printed ahead require so much ink that rollers cannot resupply fast enough. One cause of ghosting. – deficiencia de tinta

ink station Alternate term for *printing unit*. – mecanismo entintador

ink trap Alternate term for *trap*.

ink/water balance Correct relationship between water and ink on a lithographic plate. – balance entre tinta y agua

in line 1) Process that occurs as part of a sequence, as compared to off line. A press equipped to apply UV coating in the same pass as printing inks applies the coating in line.

2) Images lying within a strip, or channel, of a press sheet that responds to changes in ink flow controlled by one fountain key. Conflict between images in line may cause ghosting. – 1 & 2, en línea

inline British term for *outline (1)*.

inner form Form (side of the press sheet) whose images all appear inside the folded signature, as compared to outer form. – forma interior

in-plant printer Department of an agency, business, or association that does printing for its parent organization. Also called captive printer and in-house printer. – imprenta de la casa

in print Publication that a publisher has available and expects to continue selling, as compared to a publication that is out of print. – publicación disponible

input Information entered into a computer via a device such as a keyboard, scanner, or light pen. – entrada

insert 1) Flier, BRC, or other item put between the pages of a book,

magazine, or newspaper, as compared to a wraparound. Illustrated on page 53. Also called inset.
2) Piece of film to be patched in during stripping. – 1 & 2, inserción

insertion date Date on which an insert will be distributed, the issue date of its host publication. – fecha de distribución

inset Alternate term for *insert (1)* and *nested.* – inserción

inspection copy Alternate term for *examination copy.* – copia para inspección

inspection drawing Alternate term for *dimension drawing.*

instant lettering Alternate term for *dry transfer lettering.* – letras transferibles

intaglio printing Printing method whose image carriers are surfaces with two levels, having inked areas lower than non-inked areas. Also called recess printing.

Images for intaglio printing are cut below the surface of the plate. After ink fills the recessed images, a doctor blade wipes excess ink from the surface of the plate. Gravure and engraving are the most common forms of intaglio.

The ability to cut portions of the image to various depths into the plate gives intaglio the ability to print a wide range of tones because the plate can deliver different amounts of ink to different parts of an image. – impresión en hueco

integral proof Color proof of separations shown on one piece of proofing paper, as compared to an overlay proof. Also called composition proof, laminate proof, plastic proof, and single-sheet proof.

There are two types of integral proofs: proofs made from film separations and digital proofs made from computer files. Proofs from separations are made by contact printing sets of film in register on one piece of paper. Digital proofs are made by output from computers without first making separation films. – prueba integral

intensity Alternate term for *chroma.* – intensidad

interface 1) Connection between two or more systems or machines that allows them to communicate.
2) Point or area at which two surfaces meet. – 1 & 2, interface

interleaf Alternate term for *slip sheet.*

interleaves British term for *slip sheets.*

interline spacing Alternate term for *leading.* – espaciado entre líneas

intermediates British term for *working film.*

International Organization for Standardization Worldwide organization that sets standards to promote commerce and research. Abbreviated ISO.

ANSI, DIN, BSI, and other national standards organizations use ISO meetings to negotiate international standards.

international paper sizes Alternate term for *ISO paper sizes.*

internegative Negative made from a transparency (which is a positive) for the purpose of making photographic prints. Prints made from internegatives are usually higher quality than prints made directly from transparencies, but lower quality than prints made from a first generation negative.
– internegativo

interword spacing British term for *word spacing*.

introduction Comments, written by the author, giving background about a book. – introducción

invoice List of goods or services provided, what they cost, and the terms of sale. Also called bill. – factura

iph Abbreviation for *impressions per hour*, a measure of the speed of sheetfed presses.

IR coating Liquid plastic coating bonded and cured using infrared light. IR coating goes on after printing to protect ink and give it a high sheen. – baño infrarojo

ISBN Abbreviation for International Standard Book Number.
An ISBN is a ten-digit numeral unique to each edition or version of a book. The ISBN identifies the country of origin, publisher, and title. Libraries and book sellers rely on ISBNs to ensure efficient ordering and accurate cataloging or inventory control.
In the US, the ISBN system is administered by the R R Bowker Company in New York City. Canada has two ISBN agencies, one for publications in English, at the National Library in Ottawa, and one for publications in French, at the Bibliotheque Nationale in Montreal. ISBNs in the United Kingdom are assigned by Jay Whittaker Ltd, in London. ISBNs in Mexico are assigned by Centro Nacionál de Información in Mexico City.

island rack Display fixture designed to hold publications or products and stand in the middle of an aisle so viewers can walk around it.
– estante de isla

ISO Abbreviation for *International Organization for Standardization.*

ISO envelope sizes Sizes for envelopes made to hold products printed on sheets using ISO paper sizes.
ISO envelope sizes coordinate with ISO sheet sizes. For example, a C4 envelope holds an A4 sheet flat, an A3 sheet folded once, or an A2 sheet folded twice. – tamaños de sobres ISO

ISO film speed See *film speed.*

ISO paper sizes Sizes for printing papers designated by the International Organization for Standardization and used throughout the world except in the US and Canada. Illustrated on page 178. Also called international paper sizes. Compare to *North American paper sizes.*
The ISO system of paper sizes applies to all grades of paper and paper board and expresses sizes in millimeters. The system has five series of sizes: A, RA, SRA, B, and C.

Within each series, each sheet is twice the size of the next smaller sheet and half the size of the next larger sheet.

A sizes For standard trim sizes on products that don't involve bleeds or trimming outside edges.

RA sizes Sheets about 2% bigger than A sizes to allow for bleeds, small trims, and narrow color bars.

SRA sizes Sheets about 10% bigger than A sizes to allow for bleeds, large trims, wide color bars, and binding laps.

B sizes Sheets about 18% bigger than A sizes for printing large items such as charts, maps, and posters.

C sizes Sheets with correct dimensions to make folders and envelopes for products trimmed to A sizes. – tamaños de papeles ISO

ISSN Abbreviation for International Standard Serial Number.

An ISSN is assigned to magazines, newsletters, and other serials requesting one. Libraries, book sellers, and news dealers rely on ISSNs to ensure efficient ordering and accurate cataloging or inventory control.

In most countries, ISSNs are assigned by the national library. In the US they are assigned by the Library of Congress.

issue 1) All copies of a periodical having content related to one theme, such as the 10th Anniversary issue, or location, such as western issue. 2) All copies of a periodical published on the same date, such as the September issue.
– 1 & 2, edición

issue date Year, month, or date on which a publication was mailed or released. – fecha de publicación

italic type Type slanted to the right to resemble handwriting, as compared to roman type. Italic type is a separate font related by design to a roman counterpart, not merely roman set at an angle. Illustrated on page 255. – tipo itálico

ivory bristol Uncoated, smooth bristol used mainly for business cards. – bristol marfíl

J

jacket 1) Alternate term for *dust cover* and *album cover*. 2) Large envelope holding mechanicals and other art for a job. Also called job jacket. – 1, sobrecubierta; 2, sobretrabajo

jaggies Ragged edges on slanted or curved lines, or on boundaries between colors, made using a computer. Also called *aliasing* and *sawtoothing*.

Jaggies result from the fact that raster-based imagesetters can only draw horizontal and vertical lines. These lines form tiny squares which are the pixels. Low resolution machines create relatively large pixels—large enough to seem ragged along the edges of slanted and curved lines.

Jaggies are made less visible by using an output device with higher resolution or by anti-aliasing. – perfil dentado

J card Printed and folded card inside the clear plastic box holding a cassette tape or compact disk. The J card, meaning 'jacket card,' serves as both decorative cover and location for business and artist information. Also called cassette cover (for tapes) and liner (for CDs). – tarjeta del cassette

jet printing Alternate term for *ink jet printing*. – impresión a chorro de tinta

jobber Alternate term for *broker* and *distributor*. – distribuidor

job jacket Alternate term for *jacket (2)*. – carpeta de trabajo

job lot merchant Paper merchant who sells job lot paper. Also called clearance merchant and seconds merchant. – vendedor de papel de segunda

job lot paper Paper that didn't meet specifications when produced, has been discontinued, or for other reasons is no longer considered first quality. Job lot paper does not carry the brand name assigned by the mill that made it and costs less than first quality paper. In Great Britain called retree. – papel de segunda

job printer Alternate term for *commercial printer*.

job ticket Form used by service bureaus, separators, and printers to specify the production schedule of a job and the materials it needs. Also called docket, production order, and work order. – orden de trabajo

jog To straighten or align sheets or signatures in a stack. In Great Britain called knock up. – alineación

joint Alternate term for *hinge*. – bisagra

Joint Photographic Experts Group Organization of companies that develops international standards for compression of digital photographic images. Abbreviated JPEG.

journal Periodical specializing in articles of interest to members of a trade association, scholarly organization, or special interest group. From a production standpoint, most journals are saddle stitched or perfect bound and resemble magazines or books. Some newspapers are called journals, such as *The Wall Street Journal* and many local journals of commerce. – revista

JPEG Abbreviation for *Joint Photographic Experts Group*.

jumbo roll Alternate term for *reel*.

jump Point at which text moves from one page to another. When the second page does not immediately follow the first, a jump is indicated with 'continued on p.__.' Illustrated on page 160. – saltar

jumpover Type that continues from above a photo or illustration to below it, so the reader's eyes must jump over the visual to continue reading the copy.

junior carton Case of five, eight, or ten reams of cut size paper. Junior cartons weigh approximately 50 pounds. – cartón tamaño mediano

junior page Half the page size of the host publication. In North America, a junior page in an 8½ x 11-inch publication is 5½ x 8½ inches and a display ad made for a junior page in a tabloid is 8½ x 11 inches. In the ISO system, a junior page in a A4 book is A5. – media página

justified type Type set flush right and left. Illustrated on page 270. – texto justificado

jute board Strong, durable paperboard with good bending abilities. Also called kraft board. – cartón de yute

K

K 1) Abbreviation for kilo, one thousand (1,000). In computer terminology, K refers to the number 1024 (2 to the 8th power). A 2K file has 2048 bytes. In practice, however, the world of computers thinks of K as 1,000 because 1,000 is easier to imagine and multiply than 1,024.
2) Abbreviation for black or key (authorities disagree which) in four-color process printing. Hence the 'K' in CMYK.

Kelvin scale Measurement system used to express the color temperature of light. Standard viewing condition of 5000 degrees is expressed using the Kelvin scale. – escala Kelvin

kenaf Small, fast-growing tropical tree sometimes used to make pulp for newsprint. – kenaf

kern To reduce space between two or three characters so those characters appear better fitted together. Illustrated on page 263.
Kerning is different from tracking and changing letter spacing, each of which adjusts the distance between all selected characters. – acoplar

key 1) (noun) The screw that controls ink flow from the ink fountain of a printing press.
2) (verb) To relate loose pieces of copy to their positions on a layout or mechanical using a system of numbers or letters. 3) (noun) Alternate term for *legend*. 4) (adjective) Alternate term for the color black, as in 'key plate.' 5) British term for *keyboard (1)*. – 1, tecla; 2, identificar; 3, leyenda; 4, clave

keyboard 1) (verb) To write, enter data, or give commands using a keyboard on a typewriter or computer. In Great Britain called key. 2) (noun) The array of keys used to enter information and instructions. – 1, teclar; 2, teclado

key forme British term for *key negative*.

keyline Type at the bottom of pages of a reference book that explains symbols used in the text. – leyenda

keylines Lines on a mechanical or negative showing the exact size, shape, and location of photographs or other graphic elements. Illustrated on page 162. Also called holding lines.

Keylines may be printed or not printed, according to instructions on the mechanical. Keylines not intended for printing are referred to as FPO, meaning for position only. – líneas guías

key negative In a set of separations, the negative used to make the key (black) plate. In Great Britain called key forme. – negativo clave

key number Numeral on items such as advertising inserts and address labels that allows the sender to control production and monitor response. – número clave

key plate Plate that prints the most detail, thus whose image guides the register of images from other plates. In four-color process printing, the black plate is usually the key plate. Also called key printer. – plancha clave

key printer Alternate term for *key plate*. – plancha clave

kicker Small, secondary headline, placed above a primary headline to lead into the primary headline. Illustrated on page 164. – subtítulo

kid finish Vellum finish on a soft bond paper made to feel like soft leather. – acabado imitación cabritilla

kiosk Large, often permanent, island rack made to display items such as posters and rack brochures. – quiosco

kiss die cut To die cut the top layer, but not the backing layer, of self-adhesive paper. Also called face cut. – troquelar kiss

kiss impression Lightest possible impression that will transfer ink to a substrate. – impresión kiss

kiss plate Alternate term for *touch plate*. – plancha kiss

kiss register Alternate term for *butt register*. – registro kiss

Kivar Brand name of a pyroxylin-coated paper.

Kleenstick Brand name of a pressure-sensitive label paper.

Klischography Process of using a diamond stylus to etch wells in a cylinder for gravure printing. See also HelioKlischography.

knife coating Alternate term for *blade coating*. – estucado de cuchilla

knockout 1) Alternate term for *mask*. 2) Alternate term for *reverse*. Often abbreviated as K/O.

knockout film Alternate term for *masking material* and *positive film*.

knockout halftone Alternate term for *outline halftone*. – mediotono perfilado

knock up British term for *jog*.

K/O Abbreviation for *knockout*.

Kodachrome Brand name of a transparency film.

kraft paper 1) Strong paper used for wrapping and to make grocery bags and large envelopes. 2) Alternate term for *sulphate paper*. – 1, papel kraft

Kromecote Brand name of a cast-coated paper.

L

label Piece of paper or cloth attached to an object to explain contents, give directions, or state ownership. – etiqueta

label holder Transparent pocket on a ring binder or other product to hold a label. – bolsa para etiqueta

label paper Paper made to meet labeling requirements such as die cutting and application to irregular surfaces.

Some mills make label paper for specific industries. For example, paper for products, such as wine bottles, that will be stored under moist conditions has additives that prevent absorption and staining.

Label paper may have an adhesive coating. Dry labels are activated by moisture, pressure-sensitive labels by peeling away from a waxed backing, and heat-sensitive labels by applying heat. Each variety is designed for specific conditions and products. – papel para etiquetas

lacquer British term for *varnish*.

ladder code Alternate term for *vertical bar code*.

laid finish Finish on bond or text paper on which grids of parallel lines simulate the surface of handmade paper. Laid lines are close together and run against the grain, as compared to chain lines. – acabado verjurado

laid lines Closely spaced lines running across the grain on laid paper, as compared to chain lines. – líneas verjuradas

laminate To bond plastic film to paper, or to glue paper to chipboard or corrugated cardboard. Laminating increases caliper, gloss, and, depending on the materials used, protects paper from grease, water, light, and other environmental influences. – laminar

laminate proof Alternate term for *integral proof*. – prueba integral

landscape format Alternate term for *horizontal format*. – formato apaisado

landscape printing Sheetfed printing using a press that feeds paper with its long edge parallel to the cylinders.

Landscape printing minimizes tail whip and ghosting, and promotes accurate, consistent register. Most presses at commercial printers use landscape printing. – impresión apaisada

lap 1) Edge of a signature that a machine grips during binding operations. Signatures are printed and folded slightly off center to create a lap. Also called binding lap, feed lap, folio lap, lip, and pickup lap. **2)** Abbreviation for *overlap*. **3)** Partially dried paper pulp in the form of a large sheet made for convenient storage and shipping. Lap is approximately ⅛ inch (3 mm) thick with dimensions of 40 x 40 inches (1 x 1 meter). – 1, orilla doblada

lap line Line at which inks or substrates overlap, as compared to butt line. – línea de superposición

lap mark In screen printing, the slight ridge often resulting from overlapping inks. – marca de superposición

lap register Register where ink colors overlap slightly, as compared to butt register. A lap register ensures that ink colors appear to touch with no white space between them. – registro de superposición

large-format camera Camera using sheet film 4 x 5 inches (102 x 126 mm) or larger. – cámara de formato grande

large print Subjective term referring to large type for children and people with impaired vision. The text type in large-print books is at least 14 point. – letras grandes

laser Acronym for light amplification by stimulated emission of radiation, very intense light that can be precisely focused to make tiny dots.

Computer printers and image-setters using lasers create type and graphics from millions of dots of light. Lasers are also used in the graphic arts for making halftones, color separations, and plates, and for perforating and die cutting elaborate patterns. – láser

laser bond Bond paper made especially to run well through laser printers.

Laser bond is smoother and brighter than xerographic or DP bond and has a low moisture content. Some laser bonds also have coatings on the non-printing side to prevent wax bleed through when they are used for pasteup. Most, however, are designed to use as stationery and for publication pages reproduced by a laser printer or photocopier. – papel bond para láser

laser engraving Using laser light to engrave a printing die or plate. – grabado a láser

laser-imprintable ink Ink that will not fade or blister as the paper on which it is printed is used in a laser printer.

laser printer Device using a laser beam and xerography to reproduce type and graphics.

Laser printers have lower resolutions than imagesetters because they create dots by xerography instead of photography. Most laser printers have a resolution of 300 dpi. More costly machines have resolutions of 600 dpi, 1,000 dpi, or more.

Laser printed images look best on smooth, uncoated paper. Toner does not stick as well to coated paper and the image may not seem sharp when printed on a rough or textured surface. – impresora láser

laser scanner Scanner using laser beams to record images on film. – scanner láser

laser type Type made using a laser printer. Imagesetters also use lasers to make type, but the term 'laser type' refers to type produced by toner on plain paper. – tipo láser

last color down Final ink color printed on a sheet. – último color a imprimir

latent image Image on film, plate, or stencil whose emulsion has been exposed but not yet developed. – imagen latente

lateral reverse British term for *flop*.

laydown sequence Alternate term for *color sequence.* – secuencia de impresión

layer Electronic overlay in computer software for design or drawing. For example, when creating a map, land could be one layer and water another layer. Roads, buildings, and other features could each have their own layer. The map maker could make all layers appear at the same time on the screen or display any combination of layers. When printing out the map, or when making mechanicals, film, or plates

for offset printing, layers and combinations of layers could be assigned different colors. – capa

layered proof Alternate term for *overlay proof.* – prueba de superpuestas

layout 1) Sketch or plan of how a page or sheet will look when printed. In Great Britain called scamp. 2) Alternate term for *ruleup*. – 1, trazado; 2, maqueta de imposición

layout sheet Master guide showing imposition for all forms for a specific printing job. – bosquejo, croquis

lc Abbreviation for lower case, used as a proofreader's instruction to change a character from capital to lower case.

LCL Abbreviation for *less than carload.*

lead 1) Main story in a periodical. 2) First paragraph in a news story. Pronounced "leed." 3) Metal strip, one or two points thick, used to add space between lines of metal type. Pronounced "led." – 1 & 2, editorial; 3, interlinear

leaders Dots, dashes, or other symbols which guide the eye from one item to another, as in a table of contents. Pronounced "leeder" because the term refers to the verb 'to lead.'

True leaders are pi characters designed for the purpose, not merely periods or hyphens. – puntos conductores

lead-free ink Ink for use on toys and packaging where lead might harm the consumer. In the US, lead-free ink must contain less than .06% lead by weight. Pronounced "led-free." – tinta sin plomo

leading Space between lines of type expressed as the distance between baselines. Pronounced "ledding" because the term originally referred to strips of metal (lead) used to separate lines of metal type. Illustrated on page 259. Also called interline spacing and line spacing. – interlineado

leading edge 1) In sheetfed printing, alternate term for *gripper edge.* Pronounced "leeding" because the term refers to the verb 'to lead.' 2) In web printing, the first edge of the form to go through the press. – 1& 2, borde frontal

leaf One sheet of paper in a publication. Each side of a leaf is one page. – hoja

leaflet Alternate term for *flier.*

leave edge Alternate term for *trailing edge.* – orilla posterior

ledger paper Strong, smooth bond paper used for keeping business records. Ledger paper is usually basis 28 or 32. Also called record paper. – papel ledger

left-hand page Page on the left when a publication lies open. Also called verso page. Because it is closest to the front, so has the lower page number, the left-hand page is also called the low-folio page. – página izquierda

left justified Alternate term for *flush left.* – justificado por la izquierda

legal paper North American term for 8/ x 14-inch bond paper. – papel bond legal

legend 1) Caption or sidebar that explains symbols used in a map or illustration. Also called key. 2) Alternate term for *caption.* – 1& 2, leyenda

legible Referring to type that has sufficient contrast with its background that readers can easily perceive the characters, as compared to readable.
Legibility affects how quickly and accurately readers recognize type. It is determined by typographic features such as typeface, size, letter spacing, line length and leading, by color and surface of paper, and by color and density of ink. – legible

lens One or more pieces of clear glass or plastic designed to focus light. – lente

lens speed Refers to the greatest amount of light that a camera lens can admit and still focus sharply. Lens speeds are expressed as f/stops. A fast lens such as an f/1.9 admits much more light than a relatively slow lens such as an f/5.6. See also *f/stop.* – velocidad del lente

less carton Alternate term for *broken carton.* – cartón incompleto

less than carload Amount of paper weighing less than one carload. Abbreviated LCL.

Letraset Brand name for dry transfer type, screen tints, computer software, and other graphic supplies.

letter US Postal Service term for a piece of mail whose height is between 3½ and 6⅛ inches and length between 5 and 11½ inches, as compared to a flat which has larger dimensions. – carta

letter-fit British term for *letter spacing.*

letter fold Two folds creating three panels that allow a sheet of letter-head to fit a business envelope. Illustrated on page 105. Also called barrel fold and wrap around fold. – doblado carta

letterhead 1) Logo and information printed on letter paper. 2) The stationery itself. – 1, logotipo; 2, membrete

letter paper In North America, sheets that are 8½ x 11 inches. In Europe, A4 sheets. – papel carta

letterpress Method of printing from raised surfaces, either metal type or plates whose surfaces have been etched away from image areas. Ink is applied to the raised printing surface and transferred to the paper under pressure from the press. Illustrated on page 246. Also called block printing.

Letterpress was the primary method of printing for 500 years until eclipsed by offset lithography in the 1960s. It is a printing method that requires no fluids other than ink and which wastes little paper. Presses, however, run relatively slowly and prepress costs are higher than with offset.

Because letterpress is easy to set up for jobs involving a small amount of type, it is commonly used to imprint information on short runs of products that have been produced in a longer run by another printing process. For example, an organization might print 10,000 business cards using offset, then use letterpress to print the name of an individual employee on 500 cards at a time.

Letterpress is used for numbering products such as tickets and forms because numbers can be made to change with each impression. US currency is engraved, then imprinted and numbered using letterpress.

Machines used for letterpress printing push raised surfaces into paper, so they are used extensively for die cutting, embossing, foil stamping, debossing, scoring, and perforating. – impresora tipográfica

letter-quality type Type of the quality produced by a typewriter or by a computer printer using a daisy wheel, as compared to near letter quality.

letterset Printing method using a relief plate that transfers ink to a blanket. Letterset printing does not require water, but its plates are difficult to make. It was a transition technology between letterpress and offset. Also called dry offset printing. – offset seco

lettershop Alternate term for *mailing service.* – servicio de correos

letter spacing Amount of space between all characters. Illustrated on page 270. Also called character spacing. In Great Britain called character fit, letter-fit.

Computers and typesetters can reduce or increase letter spacing in uniform increments. Letter spacing can only be adjusted on typewriters by changing the pitch.

Changing letter spacing not the same as kerning, which reduces the distance between two or three specific characters. – espacio entre entre caracteres

lexicon Alternate term for *dictionary*.

library binding Case binding to standards set by the American Library Association, including round corners, four-cord thread, and reinforced end signatures. – encuadernación de biblioteca

lick-coated paper British term for *film coated paper*.

lie flat bind Method of perfect binding that allows a publication to lie fully open. Illustrated on page 16. – encuadernación tendida

lift 1) The number of sheets that a worker can conveniently pick up or handle at one time. 2) British term for *pick up*.

lifter Plastic bar at the front or back of a ring binder to help sheets move freely on the rings.

liftout Alternate term for *reverse*.

ligature Two letters that, because of their design, are typeset as one character. The letters 'f' and 'i' form a ligature in many typefaces. Ligatures are treated as one character by computer programs doing kerning, tracking, or letterspacing. Illustrated on page 263. – ligadura

light box 1) Enclosure with proper viewing conditions for evaluating photos, swatches, proofs, and press sheets. 2) Alternate term for *light table*. – 1, caja para observación

lighten Technique of using a computer to increase shadow detail in an image appearing on a screen, as compared to darken.

When photographic techniques are used in a darkroom to increase shadow detail, it's called dodging. – iluminar

light fast Characteristic of paper or ink that resists fading under long exposure to light. – resistencia a la luz

lightfast ink British term for *fast color ink*.

lighting standards Alternate term for *standard viewing conditions*.

light meter Instrument used in photography to measure intensity of light and calculate the correct f/stop and shutter speed. Also called exposure meter. – fotómetro

lightness Alternate term for *value* of color. – valor

light printer Film or plate with the highlights and lighter middle tones for a duotone. – plancha clara

light table Translucent glass surface lit from below. Photographers, production artists, and strippers view their work on light tables because the backlighting shows through overlays and film. Also called light box and stripping table. – mesa luminosa

light type Type with relatively thin strokes. Illustrated on page 255. – letras finas

lightweight paper Book paper with basis weight less than 40# (60 gsm). Used to reduce weight and bulk, thus keep postage and space to a minimum.

Both coated and uncoated papers are available in light weights. Coated lightweights are for catalogs, free standing inserts, and other publications printed in color. Uncoated lightweights are for products such as prospectuses, statement stuffers, and package inserts. – papel ligero

lignin Substance in trees that holds cellulose fibers together. If not removed from pulp, lignin causes paper to discolor and deteriorate rapidly. Free sheet has most lignin removed; groundwood paper contains lignin. – lignina

limited edition Relatively short print run of a book or art reproduction. Publishers of limited editions hope that scarcity will build demand. Items in limited editions are sometimes signed and numbered. – edición limitada

limp binding British term for *perfect binding.*

line 1) One row of type, usually the width of a column. 2) British term for *rule, line copy.* – 1, línea

lineale British term for *sans-serif type.*

line art Alternate term for *line copy.*

line chart Chart using lines to show numerical or statistical relationships. Illustrated on page 129. – gráfico de líneas

line copy Any high-contrast image, including type, as compared to continuous-tone copy. Line copy is usually a black image against a white background, but could be created using any color, such as red, that yields high-contrast when photographed using graphic arts film. Also called line art and line work. – original de líneas

line count 1) Number of lines in a column or on a page or proof. 2) Alternate term for *screen ruling.* – 1, recuento de líneas; 2, lineatura de la trama

line edit Alternate term for *copy edit.*

line feed Space between lines of type when typography is described in metric units. A line feed might be 1 mm. – línea aumentada

line gauge Device used to measure typographic features such as type size and leading. Also called pica pole. In Great Britain called type gauge. – lineómetro

line measure Alternate term for *measure.* – medida tipográfica

line mechanical British term for *camera-ready copy.*

line negative Negative made from line copy. Illustrated on page 64. – negativo de línea

linen finish 1) Embossed finish on text paper simulating the pattern of linen cloth. 2) Finish of book cloth not completely saturated with ink so that some white of the threads gives the cloth a slightly two tone appearance. – 1 & 2, acabado lino

linen screen One of many special effect screens. – trama de lino

linen tester Alternate term for *loupe.* – cuentahilos

liner Alternate term for *flute, J card,* and *release paper.*

liner notes Background information about recorded music and printed inside the cover of the record, tape, or CD. – notas del forro

line screen Alternate term for *straight line screen.* – trama de lino

line spacing Alternate term for *leading.* – espaciado entre líneas

lines per centimeter Linear measure of screen ruling expressing how many lines of dots there are per centimeter in a screen tint, halftone, or separation. – líneas por centímetro

lines per inch Linear measure of screen ruling expressing how many lines of dots there are per inch in a screen tint, halftone, or separation. Abbreviated lpi.

Lines per inch is different from dots per inch, the measure of digital resolution. One halftone dot consists of more than one digital dot, depending on the size of each variety of dot. See also *screen ruling.* – líneas por pulgada

lines per minute Measure of output speed of a computer printer or typesetter. – líneas por minuto

lineup board Alternate term for *pasteup board.* – cartulina de alineación

lineup table Light table with built-in devices that help precise pasteup and stripping. – mesa de alineación

line work Alternate term for *line copy.* – original de línea

Linotronic Brand name of an imagesetter using PostScript.

Linotype Brand name of machine that sets lines of metal type for letterpress printing.

lint Fibers not securely bonded to paper, thus liable to come off during printing and cause hickies. – pelusa del papel

lip Alternate term for *feed lap.*

liquid laminate Plastic applied as a liquid to paper, then bonded and cured into a hard, glossy finish. – laminante líquido

list Books produced by a specific publisher, thus that publisher's list. See also *back list* and *front list.* – lista de publicaciones

list house Business that maintains and prints out mailing lists for periodicals and direct mailings. – servicio de listas

literal British term for *typographical error.*

litho film Alternate term for *graphic arts film.* – película litho

lithography Method of printing using plates whose image areas attract ink and whose non-image areas repel ink. Non-image areas may be coated with water to repel the oily ink or may have a surface, such as silicon, that repels ink.

Illustrated on page 167. See also *offset printing*.

Lithographic plates can be made quickly using either photographic techniques to reproduce camera-ready copy or digital techniques to reproduce computer files. They carry fine detail, such as halftone dots, and are easy to prepare and mount on press.

Lithography was first developed as an artistic medium using limestone as the substrate. The prefix 'litho,' from the Greek 'lithos' for 'stone,' survived as the technique evolved into a method for efficient commercial printing. – litografía

litho prep British term for *prepress*.

live area Area on a mechanical within which images will print.

Type appears within the live area, crop marks outside of it. Printing outside the live area might be trimmed away or covered during binding. Also called safe area. In Great Britain called type area. – área activa

live matter Images in forms or on plates ready for printing, as compared to dead matter. – composición válida

lock up 1) To tighten hot type assembed in the chase so it stays in place during printing. 2) To take the last steps getting a publication, such as a book, ready to print. 3) Final step in mounting a plate securely on a press. – 1 – 3, fijar

log Alternate term for *reel*.

logo Abbreviation for logotype, an artistic assembly of type and art into a distinctive symbol unique to an organization, business, or product. Illustrated on pages 160 and 163. Also called emblem. – logotipo

long-grain paper Alternate term for *grain-long paper*. – papel con fibra a lo largo

long ink Relatively thin ink that flows easily because it has low viscosity, as compared to short ink. When long ink is poured from a can, the strands are relatively long before splitting. – tinta fluida

long lens Alternate term for *telephoto lens*. – lente telefoto

long run Relatively large quantity to print in relation to the size and speed of press used.

A long run of fliers at a quick print shop might be any quantity more than 3,000, whereas a long run of books might be any quantity more than 10,000. A printing of 200,000 booklets could be a long run on a half web press, depending on trim size and number of pages. – tiraje grande

long ton 2,240 pounds, as compared to a short ton of 2,000 pounds. In the US, a ton refers to 2,000 pounds. – tonelada

look through British term for *formation*.

loop stitch To bind using staples through the spine that also form loops that slip over rings of binders.

loose-leaf binder Binder using rings, posts, springs, or other devices to hold sheets that can then be added or taken away individually. – carpeta de hojas sueltas

loose proof 1) Proof of a halftone or color separation that is not assembled with other elements from a page, as compared to composite proof. Also called first proof, random proof, scatter proof, and show-color proof. One piece of proofing paper may contain several images as loose proofs. 2) British term for *progressive proof.* – 1, prueba suelta

loose ring Single ring used to fasten punched sheets, usually at a corner. – anillo suelto

loose sketch Sketch on a tissue overlay attached to a mechanical showing size and/or position of loose art. Also called loosie. – bosquejo suelto

loosie Alternate term for *loose sketch.*

loupe Lens built into a small stand. Used to inspect copy, film, proofs, plates, and printing. Also called glass and linen tester. – lupa

lowercase letters Letters that are not capitals. Also called minuscule letters. Called lowercase because of the way that metal type was arranged in cases (trays). The lower case contained small letters, the upper case contained capital letters. Illustrated on page 259. – letras minúsculas

low finish Paper finish that is relatively dull, as compared to high finish. Matte paper has a low finish. Also called flat finish. – acabado mate

low folio page 1) The lowest page number of any given signature. 2) Alternate term for *left-hand page* in a finished publication. – 1, primera página

low key photo Photo whose most important details appear in the shadows. Illustrated on page 226. – fotografía oscura

lpc Abbreviation for *lines per centimeter.*

lpi Abbreviation for *lines per inch.*

lucy Short for *camera lucida.*

Ludlow Brand name for a machine that casts display sizes of hot type.

lying pages Alternate term for *horizontal format.* – formato horizontal

M

M Roman numeral for 1,000. In paper terminology refers to 1,000 sheets.

machine direction Alternate term for *grain direction.* – dirección de máquina

machine finish 1) General term referring to paper finishes produced on the Fourdrinier machine, as compared to finishes produced off-machine. 2) British term for *smooth finish.* – 1, acabado de máquina

machine glazed British term for *cast coated.*

machine proof Proof made on a printing press. – prueba de máquina

macro lens Camera lens capable of focusing at distances from six inches to two feet away from the camera. Also called close-up lens. – lente macro

magalog Consumer catalog that contains editorial matter, such as feature articles, as well as advertising. The term blends the words 'catalog' and 'magazine.'

magapaper Periodical with a cover like a magazine and page format and size like a tabloid newspaper.

magazine Periodical publication. Magazines usually are plus cover and are saddle stitched or perfect bound. – revista

magazine format Alternate term for *vertical format.*

magenta One of the four process colors. Illustrated on pages 72 and 78. – magenta

magenta printer Flat, plate, or ink station that controls printing of the magenta ink. Illustrated on page 72. – plancha magenta

magnetic ink Ink containing traces of metal that can be magnetized after printing. Magnetic inks allow printed images, such as checking account numbers, to be read by electronic devices. – tinta magnética

magnetic ink character recognition Electronic method of reading characters, such as account numbers on checks, printed in magnetic ink. Abbreviated MICR. – reconocimiento magnético de caracteres

mailing service Business specializing in addressing and mailing large quantities of printed pieces. Also called lettershop. – servicio de correos

main exposure Initial exposure made by a process camera during halftoning. The main exposure converts the continuous-tone image to a halftone before it is enhanced, if necessary, by the flash and bump exposures.
– exposición principal

majuscule letters Alternate term for *capital letters.* – letras mayúsculas

makegood Advertisement given at no cost by a publication to an advertiser because of a printing error on a prior ad.

makeover 1) New design replacing an old design. 2) Printing job done over again—made over without changes—because of unacceptable flaws in the previous run. – 1, diseño modificado; 2, hacer de nuevo

makeready 1) All activities required to prepare a press or other machine to function for a specific printing or bindery job, as compared to production run. Press makeready takes the press up to the point of producing a satisfactory press sheet. It includes mounting plates, loading inks, and running preparatory sheets. Bindery makeready includes such activities as loading pockets and adjusting fold bars. Also called setup.

2) Paper used in the makeready process at any stage in production. Makeready paper is part of waste.
– 1 & 2, arreglos

make up 1) To arrange type and

graphics into their proper pattern according to the layout for the job. 2) Alternate term for *presort.* 3) British term for *gather.*
– 1, montar, arreglar

making order Order for paper that a mill makes to the customer's specifications, as compared to a mill order or stock order. Making orders typically require large minimums and long lead times.
– orden para hacer

male die Die that applies pressure during embossing or debossing. Illustrated on page 247. Also called force card. – contramatriz

manifold bond Alternate term for *onionskin.* – papel cebolla

manila paper Strong, light brown paper used to make envelopes and file folders. – papel manila

manual Book of instructions for using a system or device, or giving techniques for performing a function. Also called technical manual and user guide. – manual

manuscript Typed, handwritten, or computer printed copy in some stage of preparation for final output or reproduction. – manuscrito

map Printed sheet showing roads, cities, and other geographic or demographic features. Illustrated on page 129. – mapa

map paper Rag-content bond on which to print charts and maps that must be very durable. Also called chart paper and graph paper.
– papel para mapas

marble finish Finish on paper resembling the pattern of marble. – acabado mármol

margin Space forming the unprinted border of a page or sheet. – margen

marking Alternate term for *tracking*.

mark up To write on a manuscript or proof instructions about matters such as typesetting, color correcting, or printing. – preparación tipográfica

markup Amount of money that one supplier adds to the price of goods or services secured for a customer from another supplier. For example, printers may mark up the cost of paper, separations, and binding.

Markup is different from profit, which is considerably lower. Money generated by markups pays many expenses associated with the purchase, such as shipping, handling, accounting, and storage, before some of it becomes profit. – aumento de precio

marry Alternate term for *associate*.

mask To prevent light from reaching part of an image, therefore isolating the remaining part.

A printer might mask light from part of a flat or plate so the remaining portion could be exposed. A computer or scanner operator might use masking to isolate part of an image before retouching it. Also called knock out. In Great Britain called stop out. – máscara

masking material Opaque paper or plastic used to prevent light from reaching selected areas of film or a printing plate. When used to make windows on mechanicals, masking material creates open areas on film for inserting photos or other graphics. Also called knockout film.

Masking material is often referred to by brand names such as Goldenrod and Rubylith. These names are often abbreviated and their abbreviations are used as synonyms for 'mask.' For example, 'rubies on a mechanical' refers to 'masks on a mechanical, cut from Rubylith.' – material para enmascarar

mass market book Perfect bound book printed inexpensively on high-bulk groundwood paper for sale in supermarkets, variety stores, and newsstands as well as in book stores. Many novels and self-help guides are mass market books. – libro para el mercado en general

master 1) Paper or plastic plate used on a duplicator press. 2) Paper plate for a spirit duplicator. 3) Final copy on which all changes have been made. 4) Any guide used in all situations, such as a master overlay. – 1 & 2, plancha; 3 & 4, patrón

master art Original image that a printer will reproduce in several different sizes and perhaps different colors on different printing jobs. Camera work for each job begins with the master art. – imagen original

master film Composed negatives or other film ready for step-and-repeat or to be duplicated for more than one printing job. – película patrón

master page Page with headers, rules, or other elements that repeat on all pages of a document. Also called underlying page. – página patrón

masthead Block of information in a periodical that identifies its publisher and editor, and tells about advertising and subscribing. Illustrated on page 162. – tope

mat Abbreviation for *matrix (1)*.

match color To duplicate with printing ink a specified color. The color to be matched is either supplied to the printer or, more commonly, specified using a numeral in a color matching system.

Whether a printer can match a color depends on the color, the matching technique (four-color or flat color), the paper being used, and many other factors. Some colors are more easily reproduced than others, and some papers make even an approximate reproduction impossible. – igualación del color

Matchprint Brand name for integral proof.

mathematical signs Typographic symbols such as = (equals), + (plus), and – (minus). – símbolos matemáticos

matrice Alternate spelling of *matrix*.

matrix 1) Mold used to make metal type for letterpress or a rubber plate for flexography. Abbreviated mat. 2) Grid pattern of lines for framing information, as in a spread sheet created by a computer. – 1 & 2, matriz

matrix board Soft, high-bulk paperboard. Matrix board is used to make molds for relief printing plates by pressing the board into metal type, halftones, and other engravings.

matte finish Flat (not glossy) finish on photographic paper or coated printing paper. Illustrated on pages 31 and 202. – acabado mate

matte ink Alternate term for *dull ink*.

matte varnish Alternate term for *dull varnish*. – barniz mate

mature Alternate term for *condition*.

maximum density Alternate term for *total area coverage*. – densidad máxima

Mb Abbreviation for *megabyte*.

mealy Alternate term for *mottle*.

measure Width of a column of type. With justified type, all lines have the same measure. With ragged type, measure equals the longest possible line. Also called line measure. – medida

measured photography Technique of making photographs with tonal ranges that a printing press can reproduce. See also *four-stop photography* and *tone compression*.

In measured photography, lighting is controlled to produce a photo whose critical details fall within the range of f/stops that can be most faithfully reproduced using the paper and printing method planned for the job. In addition to ensuring more predictable results on press, the technique eliminates bracketing and produces consistent photos that can be gang scanned. – fotografía medida

mechanical Camera-ready assembly of type, graphics, and other copy complete with instructions to the printer. Illustrated on page 64.

A hard mechanical consists of paper and/or acetate, is made using pasteup techniques, and may also be called an artboard, board, or pasteup. A soft mechanical, also called an electronic mechanical, exists as a file of type and other images assembled using computers. – boceto

mechanical artist Alternate term for *production artist.* – artista de bocetos finales

mechanical bind To bind using a comb, coil, ring binder, post, or any other technique not requiring gluing, sewing, or stitching. – encuadernación mecánica

mechanical dot gain Dot gain caused by press pressures and ink absorption, as compared to optical dot gain. See also *dot gain.* – ganancia mecánica de puntos

mechanical paper British term for *groundwood paper.*

mechanical pulp Alternate term for *groundwood pulp.* – pasta mecánica

mechanical separation Color breaks made on the mechanical using a separate overlay for each color to be printed.
    Mechanical separations refer to graphic elements, such as type and rules, designed to print in different flat ink colors. They are not related to color separations for four-color process printing. – separación de colores en superpuestas

media 1) All forms of publication, such as newspapers, magazines, books, and newsletters. Media include broadcast publishing via radio and TV. 2) All forms of computer information storage methods, such as disks, paper, and cassettes. – 1, media; 2, almacenes de memoria

media kit Alternate term for *press kit.*

medium format camera Camera using roll film sizes such as 2¼ x 2¼-inch and 6 x 7 cm. – cámara de formato mediano

medium screen Screen with ruling of 120, 133, or 150 lines per inch (48, 54, or 60 lines per centimeter). – trama mediana

meg Abbreviation for *megabyte.*

megabyte 1,048,576 bytes or 1,000 K. A 10-Mb disk holds 10,485,760 bytes. Abbreviated Mb and meg. – megabyte

memo book Small ring binder for carrying in a briefcase or purse. – libro de notas, carpeta

memoirs Alternate term for *autobiography.* – autobiografía

memory 1) Ability of a computer to retain information as measured in bytes. Memory exists in RAM, which is active only when the machine is turned on, and on disks that store data. 2) Ability of any flexible material to return to its original shape after being bent or compressed. – 1 & 2, memoria

menu 1) In a computer, the list of operations that a program can perform, usually displayed on the screen. 2) As a product, the list of foods and prices at a restaurant. – 1 & 2, menú

merchant brand Brand name of a paper assigned by a merchant, as compared to a mill brand. Also called private brand.

Several paper merchants may buy the same paper from the same mill, but give it their own brand names. For that reason, merchant brands that appear to be different papers can be identical sheets. – marca de vendedor

merge To combine two or more databases, such as two lists of addresses, into one database. – unir, combinar

merge/purge To combine two or more databases (merge), then eliminate duplicate records (purge). Merge/purge usually refers to a function performed by a list house on address lists before mailing. – combinar/depurar

mesh Pattern of threads making up a fabric such as a screen for screen printing. – malla

mesh count Alternate term for *mesh number.*

mesh marks Fine pattern left by threads of a screen printing stencil after printing with ink that didn't flow together properly. – marcas de la malla

mesh number Number of apertures per linear inch or centimeter in a fabric. Also called mesh count. – número de mallas

mesh opening area Alternate term for *aperture percentage.*

metallic ink Ink containing powdered metal or pigments that simulate metal. When dry, the ink looks like metal. – tinta metálica

metallic paper Paper coated with a thin film of plastic or pigment whose color and gloss simulate metal. Some metallic paper is coated with a thin film of metal. – papel metálico

metal plate Printing plate made of metal, usually aluminum. Commercial offset printers typically use metal plates, as compared to the paper or plastic plates used most often by quick printers.

Metal plates last longer, hold finer detail, and allow tighter register than paper or plastic plates. Most are exposed using film rather than camera-ready copy, so cost more and require more time to make. Some imagesetters make metal plates using lasers or electric sparks. – plancha de metal

metameric Refers to traits that seem similar under some conditions and seem different under other conditions.

In the graphic arts, a patch of metameric magenta is used to signal standard lighting conditions. When the patch is viewed under 5000° lighting, its color looks uniform. When the patch is viewed under any other lighting conditions, the patch shows broad stripes of dark and light magenta. – metamérico

meters per second Metric measurement of rate at which paper passes through a web press or at which a machine makes paper. Abbreviated m/sec. – metros por segundo

mezzotint screen One of many special effect screens. Illustrated on page 218. – trama mezzotinto

mic 1) (verb) To measure thicknesses of materials such as paper, blankets, and plates using a micrometer. Pronouced "mike." 2) Alternate term for *micrometer*. – 1, espesor

MICR Abbreviation for magnetic ink character recognition.

microline Pattern of thin parallel lines used in color control bars to ensure that films, proofs, and plates have been correctly exposed. The width of the bars and distance between them is measured in microns. Exposure affects bar width and distance between bars, allowing visual inspection of the effect of the exposure. – microlínea

micrometer Instrument for measuring thickness in microns. Also called mike. – micrómetro

micron One millionth ($\frac{1}{1,000,000}$) of a meter.
Microns are used to express the height and width of gravure cells, and the thickness of electroplatings. 25.4 microns equal one thousandth ($\frac{1}{1,000}$) of an inch. – micrón

midtones In a photograph or illustration, tones created by dots between 30% and 70% of coverage, as compared to highlights and shadows. Midtones are half way between the lightest and darkest areas of the typical halftone. Illustrated on pages 218 and 233. – medios tonos

mil One thousandth ($\frac{1}{1,000}$) of an inch.
The thickness of plastic films as printing substrates is expressed in mils. Graphic arts films for halftones and flats come in several thicknesses, with 4 mil (.004 inch) and 7 mil (.007 inch) being the most common. In metric countries, bar code widths are expressed in mils. – mil

mill brand Brand name of paper assigned by a mill, as compared to merchant brand. – marca de la papelera

mill order Order for paper that will be filled from inventory at a mill, not inventory at a paper merchant. Mill orders ensure supply and often reduce unit costs. They may require a large minimum amount, depending on the paper being ordered.
A mill order may be placed by a merchant on behalf of a customer or by the customer dealing directly with the mill. – orden a la papelera

mill swatch Sample of paper supplied by a mill. – muestra de la papelera

Mimeograph Brand name for stencil printing machine. – mimeógrafo

Mimeograph bond Highly absorbent paper made for stencil printing. – bond para mimeógrafo

miniskid Term used in the US and Canada referring to a pallet with dimensions of 100 x 60 cm. Miniskids conveniently hold 25 x 38-inch sheets of paper and, because they are half of standard size, still fit efficiently into standard containers. – paleta pequeña

miniweb press See *web press.*

minuscule letters Alternate term for *lowercase letters.* – letras minúsculas

misprint Alternate term for *typographical error* once it is printed.

misregister Alternate term for *out of register.* – fuera de registro

misting Phenomenon of droplets of ink being thrown off the roller train. Severe misting can result in random ink spots on the sheets being printed. Also called flying ink. – nube de tinta

mobile Display consisting of several or numerous parts suspended from wires or strings such that each part moves on a current of air. – móvil

mockup Alternate term for *dummy.* – maqueta

modem Acronym for modulator/demodulator, a device that converts digital signals to analog tones and vice versa so that computers (digital) can communicate over telephone lines (analog). Regardless of their baud rates, all modems use a common language, simplifying telecommunication between a wide range of devices. – modem

modular design Layout technique using rules, tints, colors, and white space to place items related to each other within a visual group. For example, the front page of a newspaper might have several modules, each consisting of a headline, story, and infographic. – diseño modular

moiré 1) Undesirable pattern resulting when halftones and screen tints are made with improperly aligned screens, or when a pattern

in a photo, such as a plaid, interferes with a halftone dot pattern. A moiré may also occur in screen printing when a halftone and the printing screen are improperly aligned. Pronounced "mor-ay." Illustrated on page 81. In Great Britain called screen clash.
   2) Wavy pattern on cloth sometimes specified for case binding. – 1 & 2, muaré

moisture content Amount of moisture in paper. Moisture content is expressed as a percentage of weight and is usually between 5% and 7%. – contenido de humedad

monarch Paper size (7 x 10 inches) and envelope shape often used for personal stationery. Illustrated on page 209. – monarca

monochrome Having only one color. A black-and-white photo or an amber computer screen are both monochrome. – monocromo

monograph Short, scholarly book about a highly specialized topic. Usually has only one author. – monografía

monospacing Alternate term for *equal spacing.* – espaciado fijo

montage Image created when similar elements, such as several photos, are assembled into one visual whole. Illustrated on page 156. – montaje

morgue Alternate term for *archive.*

mortice Block containing type or a visual that overlaps into another block, such as a photo. – mortaja

mottle Spotty, uneven ink absorption. Also called sinkage. A mottled

montage

collage

image may be called mealy.

Mottling is especially noticeable in large solids or screen tints. It can result from poor formation or uneven coating of paper, uneven distribution of ink on the plate, and several other causes. – moteado

mounting board Any thick, smooth piece of paper used to paste up copy or mount photographs. Boards especially made for mounting are coated, free from curl, and sometimes printed with grid patterns in non-reproducing blue. – cartulina para montaje

mouse Device containing a tracking ball which, when rolled over a smooth surface, moves a cursor on a computer screen. – ratón

mouse pad Piece of foam rubber that makes it easy to roll the track ball in a mouse. – cojinete para el ratón

ms Abbreviation for *manuscript.*

mug shot Photograph showing only a person's face. – fotografía de cabeza

mull Alternate term for *crash (1).*

Mullen test Standard test for bursting strength of paper. Also called pop test. – prueba Mullen

multicolor printing Printing in more than one ink color (but not four-color process). Also called polychrome printing. – impresión policroma

Multilith Brand name for a small offset printing press.

Munsell color system System of describing colors according to the three characteristics of hue, value, and chroma. 'Hue' refers to the color itself, 'value' to its relative lightness or darkness, and chroma to its 'density.' See also *color, language of.*

The Munsell system was developed in the early 20th Century to organize colors into logical relationships. Its concepts and language are widely used by both scientists and artists. The system is also used by the US National Bureau of Standards, American Optical Society, British Standards Institution, and many other national agencies and organizations. – sistema de color Munsell

music Sheets or books with printed notes showing what to play or sing. The standard size of sheet music in North America is 9 x 12 inches. – música

muslin screen One of many special effect screens. – trama muselina

mutt Alternate term for *em.*

M weight Weight of 1,000 sheets of paper in any specific size. – peso M

Mylar Brand name for clear polyester used as a stable base in stripping and to make film. Mylar is also used to make overlays and to reinforce tabs of file folders and spines of sheets for ring binding.

N

nailhead Defect in perfect binding where the spine is thicker than the pages, giving the product the shape of a nail when viewed from the head or foot. – cabeza de clavo

nameplate 1) Printed piece of metal, glass, or plastic on a machine that gives information such as its brand name and model number. **2**) Portion of the front page of a newsletter that graphically presents its name, subtitle, and date line. Illustrated on page 162. – 1 & 2, cabecera

nametag Printed piece of paper, often enclosed or laminated in clear plastic, that identifies a person or personal belongings. – etiqueta

narrow web paper Alternate term for *grain long paper*, referring to a sheet cut from the web with the grain. – papel de bobina angosta

natural color Very light brown color of paper. Natural paper has relatively little glare, making it appropriate for products, such as books, that will be read for long periods at a time. May also be called antique, cream, ivory, mellow white, or off-white. – color natural

natural spread Alternate term for *center spread.*

NCR paper Abbreviation for No Carbon Required paper, a brand name. – papel NCR

needle printer Alternate term for *pin printer.*

negative assembly British term for *strip (1).*

negative film Photographic film for making prints, as compared to reversal film. – película negativa

negative image Image on film, plate, or paper in which solids in the original subject are white or clear in the negative and clear areas in the original are black or opaque, as compared to positive image.
Negative images typically appear on film, hence the film itself is called a negative. – imagen negativa

negative-positive print British term for *C print.*

negative space Alternate term for *white space.* – espacio negativo

negative-working plate Printing plate made by exposing it to film carrying a negative image. – plancha negativa

nested Signatures assembled inside one another in the proper sequence for binding, as compared to gathered. Saddle-stitched signatures are nested. Illustrated on page 223. Also called inset. – encajado

net weight Weight of the contents of a container or vehicle. Net weight plus tare weight equal gross weight. – peso neto

neutral gray Gray with no hue or cast.
  The tone of neutral gray can range from light to dark. Neutral grays of specific brightnesses are used to calibrate instruments and set standards of illumination. Photographic light meters are calibrated to 18% brightness. The gray walls of standard viewing areas are 60% brightness. – gris neutro

neutral pH paper Alternate term for *acid-free paper.* – papel sin ácido

newsletter Short, usually informal periodical presenting specialized information to a limited audience. – boletín

newspaper Daily or weekly periodical printed on newsprint. – periódico

newsprint Grade of lightweight, uncoated groundwood paper made primarily for newspapers. Illustrated on pages 115 and 202. – papel de periódico

Newton ring Flaw in a photograph or halftone that looks like a drop of oil on water.

Newton rings appear when air is trapped between surfaces that should be in perfect contact, such as between film and paper during contact printing, under the glass of a vacuum frame during platemaking, or between the cylinder of a scanner and a transparency during scanning. The trapped air forms a crude lens, causing light to refract unevenly. – anillo de Newton

nip Line of contact between two rollers or cylinders. – línea de contacto

NIP Abbreviation for *non impact printer.*

nominal basis weight Basis weight of a specific paper as advertised or specified, which may differ from its actual basis weight. – peso base nominal

non-heat-set ink Ink made to dry without passing through a drying oven, as compared to heat-set ink. – tinta para prensa de bobina sin horno

non-heat-set web Web press without a drying oven, thus not able to print on coated paper. Also called coldset web and open web. – prensa de bobina sin horno

non-image area Portion of mechanical, negative, or plate that is not intended to carry an image. – área sin imagen

non-impact printing Printing using lasers, ions, ink jets, or heat to transfer images to paper. Abbreviated NIP.
  Non-impact printing does not require a plate. It is controlled by

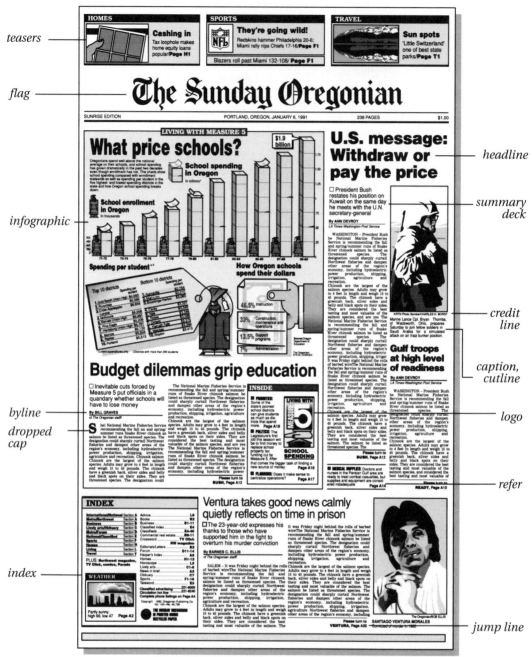

teasers

Cashing in
Tax loophole makes home equity loans popular/**Page H1**

SPORTS

They're going wild!
Redskins hammer Philadelphia 20-6;
Miami rally nips Chiefs 17-16/**Page F1**

Blazers roll past Miami 132-108/ **Page F1**

TRAVEL

Sun spots
'Little Switzerland' one of best state parks/**Page T1**

flag

The Sunday Oregonian

SUNRISE EDITION   PORTLAND, OREGON, JANUARY 6, 1991   238 PAGES $1.00

LIVING WITH MEASURE 5

What price schools?

$1.9 billion

Oregonians spend well above the national average on their schools, and school spending has grown dramatically in the past two decades even though enrollment has not. The charts show school spending compared with enrollment statewide as well as spending per student in the five highest and lowest-spending districts in the state and how Oregon school spending breaks down.

School spending in Oregon
In billions*

School enrollment in Oregon
In thousands

71-72 73-74 75-76 77-78 79-80 81-82 83-84 85-86 87-88 89-90

Spending per student

infographic

How Oregon schools spend their dollars

46.5% Instruction
33% Construction, maintenance and operations
13.5% Support programs
7% Administration

Source: Oregon Department of Education

The Oregonian/STEVE COWDEN

Budget dilemmas grip education

□ Inevitable cuts forced by Measure 5 put officials in a quandary whether schools will have to lose money

byline

By BILL GRAVES
Of The Oregonian staff

dropped cap

Shei National Marine Fisheries Service is recommending the fall and spring/summer runs Snake River chinook are listed as threatened species. The designation could sharply curtail Northwest fisheries and dampen other areas of the region's economy, including hydroelectric power production, shipping, irrigation, agriculture and recreation. Chinook are the largest of the salmon species. Adults may grow to 4 feet in length and weigh 15 to 45 pounds. The chinook have a greenish back, silver sides and belly and black spots on their sides. They are considered the best tasting and most valuable of the salmon species. The designation could

The National Marine Fisheries Service is recommending the fall and spring/summer runs of Snake River chinook salmon be listed as threatened species. The designation could sharply curtail Northwest fisheries and dampen other areas of the region's economy, including hydroelectric power production, shipping, irrigation, agriculture and recreation. Chinook are the largest of the salmon species. Adults may grow to 4 feet in length and weigh 15 to 45 pounds. The chinook have a greenish back, silver sides and belly and black spots on their sides. They are considered the best and most valuable of the salmon species. The National Marine Fisheries Service is recommending the fall and spring/summer runs of Snake River chinook salmon be listed as threatened species. The designation could sharply curtail Northwest fisheries and dampen other areas of the region's economy, including hydroelectric power

INSIDE

■ **PRIORITIES:** Some of the state's poorest school districts can give students as much as districts that spend more. **Page A18**

■ **POLITICS:** The Legislature's first job this season will be to find money to replace school property tax funding cut by Measure 5. After that comes the bigger task of finding a new source of money. **Page A18**

■ **PLANNING:** Does it make sense to centralize operations? **Page A17**

Please turn to BUSH, Page A12

U.S. message: Withdraw or pay the price

headline

□ President Bush restates his position on Kuwait on the same day he meets with the U.N. secretary-general

summary deck

By ANN DEVROY
LA Times-Washington Post Service

WASHINGTON – President Bush he National Marine Fisheries Service is recommending the fall and spring/summer runs of Snake River chinook salmon be listed as threatened species. The designation could sharply curtail Northwest fisheries and dampen other areas of the region's economy, including hydroelectric power production, shipping, irrigation, agriculture and recreation. Chinook are the largest of the salmon species. Adults may grow to 4 feet in length and weigh 15 to 45 pounds. The chinook have a greenish back, silver sides and belly and black spots on their sides. They are considered the best tasting and most valuable of the salmon species, and are yes The National Marine Fisheries Service is recommending the fall and spring/summer runs of Snake River chinook salmon be listed as threatened species. The designation could sharply curtail Northwest fisheries and dampen other areas of the region's economy, including hydroelectric power production, shipping, irrigat It was Friday night behind the rolls of barbed wireThe National Marine Fisheries Service is recommending the fall and spring/summer runs of Snake River chinook salmon be listed as threatened species. The designation

KRTN Photo Service/CHARLES H. BORST

credit line

Marine Lance Cpl. Bryan Thombs, of Wadsworth, Ohio, prepares Saturday to join fellow soldiers in Saudi Arabia for a simulated attack on an Iraqi bunker position.

caption, cutline

Gulf troops at high level of readiness

By ANN DEVROY
LA Times-Washington Post Service

WASHINGTON – President Bush he National Marine Fisheries Service is recommending the fall and spring/summer runs of Snake River chinook salmon be listed as threatened species. The designation could sharply curtail Northwest fisheries and dampen other areas of the region's economy, including hydroelectric power production, shipping, irrigation, agriculture and recreation. Chinook are the largest of the salmon species. Adults may grow to 4 feet in length and weigh 15 to 45 pounds. The chinook have a greenish back, silver sides and belly and black spots on their sides. They are considered the best tasting and most valuable of the salmon species, and considered the best tasting and most valuable of

Please turn to READY, Page A15

logo

LIVING WITH

5

SCHOOL SPENDING

refer

■ **MEDICAL SUPPLIES:** Doctors and nurses in the Persian Gulf area are ready to treat combat casualties, but supplies and equipment are considered inadequate. **Page A14**

Please turn to BUSH, Page A12

INDEX

index

WEATHER

Partly sunny; high 66; low 47   **Page A2**

THE SUNDAY OREGONIAN
IS PRINTED USING
RECYCLED PAPER

Copyright 1991, Oregonian Publishing Co.
Vol. 140—No. 46,739

Ventura takes good news calmly quietly reflects on time in prison

□ The 23-year-old expresses his thanks to those who have supported him in the fight to overturn his murder conviction

By BARNES C. ELLIS
Of The Oregonian staff

SALEM – It was Friday night behind the rolls of barbed wireThe National Marine Fisheries Service is recommending the fall and spring/summer runs of Snake River chinook salmon be listed as threatened species. The designation could sharply curtail Northwest fisheries and dampen other areas of the region's economy, including hydroelectric power production, shipping, irrigation, agriculture and recreation. Chinook are the largest of the salmon species. Adults may grow to 4 feet in length and weigh 15 to 45 pounds. The chinook have a greenish back, silver sides and belly and black spots on their sides. They are considered the best tasting and most valuable of the salmon. The

It was Friday night behind the rolls of barbed wireThe National Marine Fisheries Service is recommending the fall and spring/summer runs of Snake River chinook salmon be listed as threatened species. The designation could sharply curtail Northwest fisheries and dampen other areas of the region's economy, including hydroelectric power production, shipping, irrigation, agriculture and recreation. Chinook are the largest of the salmon species. Adults may grow to 4 feet in length and weigh 15 to 45 pounds. The chinook have a greenish back, silver sides and belly and black spots on their sides. They are considered the best tasting and most valuable of the salmon. The designation could sharply curtail Northwest fisheries and dampen other areas of the region's economy, including

Please turn to VENTURA, Page A20

jump line

The Oregonian/BOB ELLIS

SANTIAGO VENTURA MORALES
—Convicted of murder in 1986

Copyright 1991 © Oregonian Publishing Co.

elements of a newspaper

computer files linked directly to the output device. Laser printers, thermal printers, and photocopy machines are non-impact printers. – impresión sin impacto

non-reproducible colors Colors, such as certain light tones of blue, that do not reproduce when photographed using graphic arts film or during photocopying. – colores no reproducibles

non-reproducing blue Light blue color that does not record on graphic arts film, therefore may be used to preprint layout grids and write instructions on mechanicals. Also called blue pencil, drop-out blue, fade-out blue, and non-repro blue.

Although non-repro blue does not record using lights and film, it may record using a scanner. – azul no reproducible

non-repro pencil Alternate term for *blue pencil.* – lápiz azul

North American envelope sizes Sizes for envelopes made to hold products printed on sheets using North American paper sizes. The envelope sizes coordinate with the sheet sizes. For example, a #10 business envelope holds a piece of 8½ x 11-inch letterhead folded twice. – tamaños de sobres norteamericanos

North American paper sizes Paper sizes used in the US and Canada. Illustrated on page 178.

The North American system of paper sizes, expressed in inches, includes dozens of sheet sizes. There are no official standards, but tradition and convenience have made 8½ x 11 inches the norm on which other dimensions are based. The most common sizes are:
• 11 x 17 (279 x 432 mm) sheets used to print jobs such as letterhead two-up, 4-page newsletters, and saddle-stitched covers for 8½ x 11 booklets.
• 17 x 22 sheets (432 x 559 mm) used to print jobs such as letterhead four-up, 8-page newsletters, and brochures.
• 23 x 35 sheets (584 x 889 mm) used to print jobs such as 16-page signatures requiring no bleeds, small trims, and narrow color bars.
• 25 x 38 sheets (635 x 965 mm) used to print 16-page signatures and other products requiring bleeds, large trims, wide color bars, and bindery laps.

These sheet sizes also dictate the width of rolls typically ordered for web printing. See *web press.* – tamaños de papeles norteamericanos

no-screen bump Alternate term for *bump exposure.* – exposición sin plantalla

notch bind Alternate term for *burst perfect bind.* – encuadernación a la americana ranurada

novel paper Alternate term for *bulking book paper.*

novelty printing Printing on products such as coasters, pencils, balloons, golf balls, and ashtrays, known as advertising specialties or premiums. – impresión de novedades

nutt Alternate term for *en.*

nameplate

dateline

index

subtitle

issue number

headline

summary
deck

mug shot

caption

drop
shadow

Fish Wrap

A fresh look at paper recycling

Volume IV Number 3

Summer 1995

Red Herring invites quick solution

Understanding the basics of papermaking helps you choose papers best suited to your printing jobs.

Mills make paper from cellulose fibers, most of which come from trees. A few mills also make paper using cotton fibers.

Fibers from softwood trees such as pine are long, producing strong, relatively rough paper; amachinery. Bleaching makes pulp more white and chemically stable. White pulp yields white paper and is easily dyed for colored papers.

After bleaching, pulp may go directly into the papermaking machine or may be stored for shipment or later use. When stored, pulp is pressed and dried into large sheets that look and feel like paper used for egg cartons.

The papermaking process begins with beating, refining, and dyeing to prepare pulp for the kind of paper desired. After preparation, pulp is mixed with water in the headbox. The mixture is called furnish and is 99% water.

Furnish flows onto a Fourdrinier

wire, a wide loop of material similar to fine-mesh window screening. As the wire moves continuously in the direction shown by the arrows, it catches fibers, but allows water to fall through. When fibers reach the end of the loop 20 or 30 feet away, they contain about 90% water and will support their own weight. They have become paper.

The press and drier sections

DD Perkins

Pepper Mache installed as director for remaining board term ending in December. Ms Mache was formerly vice president at Excelsior industries.

Inside

Waste collection....2
Building from trash....3
Community compost....3

remove more water, make the paper smooth, and may impose patterns in its surface. Later in that sequence, mills may apply coatings that make the surface stronger and improve ink holdout.The press and drier sections remove more water, make the paper smooth, and may impose patterns in its surface. Later in that sequence, mills may apply coatings that make the surface stronger and improve ink holdout.The press and.drier sections remove more water, make the paper smooth, and may impose patterns in its surface. Later in that sequence, mills may apply coatings that make the surface stronger and improve ink holdout.

As steel rollers in the calender section press paper, it becomes smoother, thinner, and more

Fish Wrap is published quarterly by the Use & Reuse Institute, PO Box 19 Neahkahnie, OR 97130

Publisher
Charlie Tuna
Editor
Red Snapper

Subscriptions are free to members of the pulp and paper industry. Foreign subscriptions are $25.00 (US) per year.

Submissions should be sent to Editor at the above address. All published work is uncompensated. No part of this journal may be reproduced without the prior written approval of the publisher.

screen tint

keyline

credit line

masthead

elements of a newsletter
cover

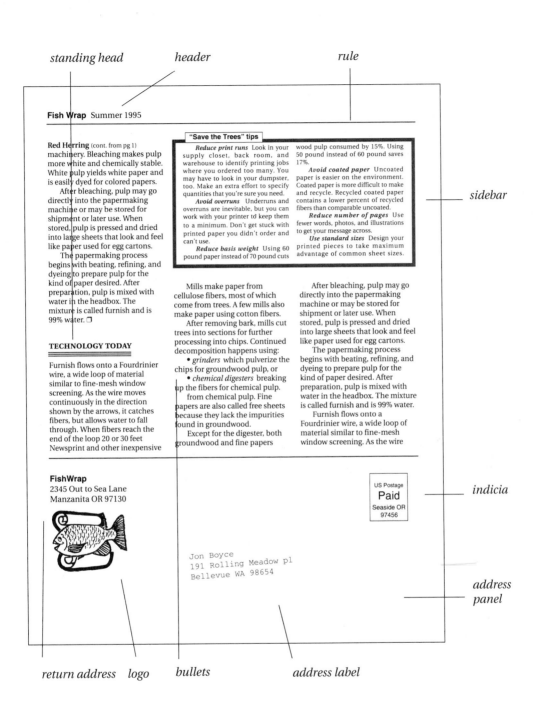

standing head   header   rule

Fish Wrap Summer 1995

Red Herring (cont. from pg 1) machinery. Bleaching makes pulp more white and chemically stable. White pulp yields white paper and is easily dyed for colored papers.

After bleaching, pulp may go directly into the papermaking machine or may be stored for shipment or later use. When stored, pulp is pressed and dried into large sheets that look and feel like paper used for egg cartons.

The papermaking process begins with beating, refining, and dyeing to prepare pulp for the kind of paper desired. After preparation, pulp is mixed with water in the headbox. The mixture is called furnish and is 99% water. ❑

TECHNOLOGY TODAY

Furnish flows onto a Fourdrinier wire, a wide loop of material similar to fine-mesh window screening. As the wire moves continuously in the direction shown by the arrows, it catches fibers, but allows water to fall through. When fibers reach the end of the loop 20 or 30 feet Newsprint and other inexpensive

"Save the Trees" tips

Reduce print runs Look in your supply closet, back room, and warehouse to identify printing jobs where you ordered too many. You may have to look in your dumpster, too. Make an extra effort to specify quantities that you're sure you need.

Avoid overruns Underruns and overruns are inevitable, but you can work with your printer to keep them to a minimum. Don't get stuck with printed paper you didn't order and can't use.

Reduce basis weight Using 60 pound paper instead of 70 pound cuts wood pulp consumed by 15%. Using 50 pound instead of 60 pound saves 17%.

Avoid coated paper Uncoated paper is easier on the environment. Coated paper is more difficult to make and recycle. Recycled coated paper contains a lower percent of recycled fibers than comparable uncoated.

Reduce number of pages Use fewer words, photos, and illustrations to get your message across.

Use standard sizes Design your printed pieces to take maximum advantage of common sheet sizes.

Mills make paper from cellulose fibers, most of which come from trees. A few mills also make paper using cotton fibers.

After removing bark, mills cut trees into sections for further processing into chips. Continued decomposition happens using:
• *grinders* which pulverize the chips for groundwood pulp, or
• *chemical digesters* breaking up the fibers for chemical pulp. Fine papers are also called free sheets because they lack the impurities found in groundwood.

Except for the digester, both groundwood and fine papers

After bleaching, pulp may go directly into the papermaking machine or may be stored for shipment or later use. When stored, pulp is pressed and dried into large sheets that look and feel like paper used for egg cartons.

The papermaking process begins with beating, refining, and dyeing to prepare pulp for the kind of paper desired. After preparation, pulp is mixed with water in the headbox. The mixture is called furnish and is 99% water.

Furnish flows onto a Fourdrinier wire, a wide loop of material similar to fine-mesh window screening. As the wire

sidebar

FishWrap
2345 Out to Sea Lane
Manzanita OR 97130

US Postage
Paid
Seaside OR
97456

indicia

Jon Boyce
191 Rolling Meadow pl
Bellevue WA 98654

address panel

return address   logo   bullets   address label

elements of a newsletter
back page

kicker

Fish Wrap Summer 1995

body copy

subhead

Stale news barged downriver

Waste collection station open to recyclers

Understanding the basics of papermaking helps you choose papers best suited to your printing jobs.

Mills make paper from cellulose fibers, most of which come from trees. A few mills also make paper using cotton fibers.

Fibers from softwood trees such as pine are long, producing strong, relatively rough paper; those from hardwoods such as maple are short, yielding weak, relatively smooth paper. Most printing papers contain a blend of softwood and hardwood. Papers made with long, supple cotton fibers are durable and smooth.

Small fee for trunk load

After removing bark, mills cut trees into chips. Mechanical grinders pulverize the chips for groundwood pulp, or chemical digesters (as illustrated) break up the fibers for chemical pulp.

Newsprint and other inexpensive papers such as tissue, called coarse papers, come from groundwood. Printing and writing papers, called fine papers, come from chemical pulp. Fine papers are also called free sheets because they lack the impurities found in groundwood.

Except for the digester, both groundwood and fine papers come from the same raw materials, processes, and machinery. Bleaching makes pulp more white and chemically stable. White pulp yields white paper and is easily dyed for colored papers.

After bleaching, pulp may go directly into the papermaking

After removing bark, mills cut trees into chips. Mechanical grinders pulverize the chips for groundwood pulp, or chemical digesters (as illustrated) break up the fibers for chemical pulp.

Newsprint and other inexpensive papers such as tissue, called coarse papers, come from groundwood. Printing and writing papers, called fine papers, come from chemical pulp. Fine papers are also called free sheets because they lack the impurities found in

> *"Our plant has an agreement with two major east coast publishers to have their mass market returns come directly to our recycling center"*

Except for the digester, both groundwood and fine papers come from the same raw materials, processes, and machinery. Bleaching makes pulp more white and chemically stable. White pulp yields white paper and is easily dyed for colored papers.

After bleaching, pulp may go directly into the papermaking machine or may be stored for shipment or later use. When stored, pulp is pressed and dried into large sheets that look and feel like paper used for egg cartons.

The papermaking process begins with beating, refining, and dyeing to prepare pulp for the kind of paper desired. After preparation, pulp is mixed with

Understanding the basics of papermaking helps you choose papers best suited to your printing jobs.

Mills make paper from cellulose fibers, most of which come from trees. A few mills also make paper using cotton fibers.

Plastics create confusion

Fibers from softwood trees such as pine are long, producing strong, relatively rough paper; those from hardwoods such as maple are short, yielding weak, relatively smooth paper. Most printing papers contain a blend of softwood and hardwood. Papers made with long, supple cotton fibers are durable and smooth.

After removing bark, mills cut trees into chips. Mechanical grinders pulverize the chips for groundwood pulp, or chemical digesters (as illustrated) break up the fibers for chemical pulp.

Newsprint and other inexpensive papers such as tissue, called coarse papers, come from groundwood. Printing and writing papers, called fine papers, come from chemical pulp. Fine papers are also called free sheets because they lack the impurities found in groundwood. ❑

Newspaper logs exported for fuel

Except for the digester, both groundwood and fine papers come from the same raw materials, processes, and machinery. Bleaching makes pulp more white and chemically stable. White pulp yields white paper and is easily dyed for colored papers.

After bleaching, pulp may go directly into the papermaking

2

alley   *pull quote*   *column*

elements of a newsletter
low-folio inside spread

Understanding the basics of papermaking helps you choose papers best suited to your printing jobs.

Mills make paper from cellulose fibers, most of which come from trees. A few mills also make paper using cotton fibers. Fibers from softwood trees. ❐

State number one in non toxic waste

Pine fibers are long, producing strong, relatively rough paper; those from hardwoods such as maple are short, yielding weak, relatively smooth paper. Most printing papers contain a blend of softwood and hardwood. Papers made with long, supple cotton fibers are durable and smooth.

After removing bark, mills cut trees into chips. Mechanical grinders pulverize the chips for groundwood pulp, or chemical digesters (as illustrated) break up the fibers for chemical pulp.

Newsprint and other inexpensive papers such as tissue, are called coarse papers.

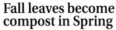

Fall leaves become compost in Spring

After removing bark, mills cut trees into chips. Mechanical grinders pulverize the chips for groundwood pulp, or chemical digesters (as illustrated) break up the fibers for chemical pulp.

Newsprint and other inexpensive papers such as tissue, called coarse papers, come from groundwood. Printing and writing papers, called fine papers, come from chemical pulp. Fine papers are also called free sheets because they lack the impurities found in groundwood.

those from hardwoods such as maple are short, yielding weak, relatively smooth paper. Most printing papers contain a blend of softwood and hardwood. Papers made with long, supple cotton fibers are durable and smooth.After removing bark, mills cut trees into chips. Mechanical grinders pulverize the chips for groundwood pulp, or chemical digesters (as illustrated) break up the fibers for chemical pulp.

Newsprint and other inexpensive papers such as tissue, called coarse papers, come from groundwood. Printing and writing papers, called fine papers. ❐

Building bricks made from resins and the *Sunday Times*

Machine pulp may be stored for shipment or later use. When stored, pulp is pressed and dried into large sheets that look and feel like paper used for egg cartons. The papermaking process begins with beating, refining, and dyeing to prepare pulp for the kind of paper desired. After preparation, pulp is mixed with water in the headbox. The mixture is called furnish and is 99% water.

Furnish flows onto a Fourdrinier wire, a wide loop of material similar to fine-mesh window screening. As the wire moves continuously in the direction shown by the arrows, it catches fibers, but allows water to fall through. When fibers reach the end of the loop 20 or 30 feet Newsprint and other inexpensive papers such as tissue, papers, called fine papers, come Except for the

from chemical pulp. Fine papers are also called free sheets because they lack the impurities found in groundwood.

Except for the digester, both groundwood and fine papers come from the same raw materials, processes, and   Mills make paper from cellulose fibers, most of which come from trees. A few mills also make paper using cotton fibers.

Fibers from softwood trees such as pine are long, producing strong, relatively rough paper; those from hardwoods such as maple are short, yielding weak, relatively smooth paper. Most printing papers contain a blend of softwood and hardwood. Papers made with long, supple cotton fibers are durable and smooth.Mills make paper from cellulose fibers, most of which come from trees.

3

oblique Slanted to the right. Oblique type appears italic, but is only the vertical font with an electronic slant. True italic type is a separate font. – oblicuo

oblong format Alternate term for *horizontal format.* – formato horizontal

OCR Abbreviation for *optical character recognition.*

octavo **1**) Sheet folded three times, making pages ⅛ the size of the original. An octavo makes a 16-page signature. **2**) Book made from octavo sheets and traditionally measuring about 6 x 9 inches. – 1 & 2, octavo

off-color Not matching the color specified or on the sample. – fuera del color

official envelope Alternate term for *business envelope.* – sobre oficio

off line **1**) Process occurring separately, not as an integral part of one sequence. For example, die cutting takes place off line from offset printing. **2**) Machine not ready to operate, such as a broken folding machine or a computer printer out of paper. – 1 & 2, fuera de línea

off-press proof Alternate term for *prepress proof.*

offprint Deliberate overrun of a chapter or article, usually bound as a booklet and shipped along with the order for the main publication. Also called separate. – sobretiraje separado

offset Alternate term for *setoff.*

offset lithography Lithography using the offset printing technique. – litografía offset

offset paper Alternate term for *uncoated paper.* – papel offset

offset powder Alternate term for *anti-offset powder.* – polvo offset

offset printing Printing technique that transfers ink from a plate to a blanket to paper instead of directly from a plate to paper. Illustrated on page 167.

Offset printing is the most popular method of commercial printing because it produces excellent results quickly while using inexpensive materials and processes. Transferring the image from plate to blanket keeps water away from

offset lithography

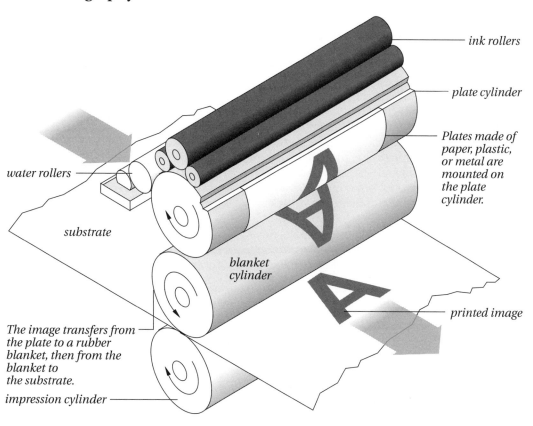

ink rollers

plate cylinder

Plates made of paper, plastic, or metal are mounted on the plate cylinder.

water rollers

substrate

blanket cylinder

printed image

The image transfers from the plate to a rubber blanket, then from the blanket to the substrate.

impression cylinder

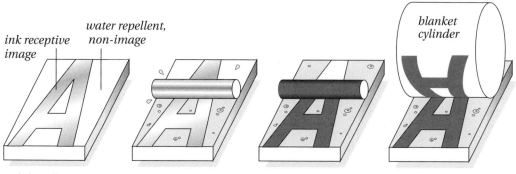

ink receptive image

water repellent, non-image

blanket cylinder

Ink for offset printing is slightly oily. It does not stick to the areas of plates that have no images.

Some plates use water to repel ink. Other types of plates have a smooth surface that keeps ink away from non-image areas.

Ink from the inking roller sticks only to image areas on the plate. The inked image offsets from plate to blanket.

The impression cylinder presses the substrate into the blanket, causing the ink to transfer.

the paper, reduces plate wear, and means plates are right reading. In addition, the relatively soft blanket prints finer detail on a greater variety of surfaces than does the relatively hard plate.

The offset technique is most commonly used in combination with lithography, thus the word 'offset' usually refers to offset lithography. Offset presses range from small duplicators at quick print shops to huge web presses able to print millions of magazines in a few days. See also *printing presses.* – impresión offset

off-shore sheet Term used in the US and Canada for paper made overseas, not in North America. – papel importado

off-square sheet Paper whose corners are not 90° angles. Such sheets do not feed or register properly. – hoja no cuadrada

oil-based inks Inks that must be washed up using solvents, as compared to water-based inks. – tintas con base de aceite

oil mount To coat a transparency thinly with light oil before scanning. Oil mounting helps prevent Newton rings, eliminates fine scratches and fingerprints, and keeps out dust. – montar con aceite

OK sheet Printed sheet approved and signed by the customer at a press check. Also called color guide.

The OK sheet represents the final inking and register adjustments made before the formal production run begins. After the customer

approves an OK sheet, the press crew tries to match that sheet throughout the press run. – pliego autorizado

omnibus Alternate term for *anthology.* – antología

one-point perspective Three-dimensional objects illustrated such that all lines seem to converge at one point in the distance. Illustrated on page 195. – perspectiva de un punto

one-sided art British term for *C1S paper.*

onionskin Lightweight (9# or 11#) bond made for carbon copies. Also called manifold bond. In Great Britain called bank. – papel cebolla

on lay Alternate term for *tip in.*

on line Alternate term for in-line, although 'in-line' typically refers to a manufacturing process such as printing and 'on-line' typically refers to an electronic process such as imagesetting. – en línea

opacity 1) Characteristic of paper or other substrate that prevents printing on one side from showing through to the other.

Opacity is expressed as a contrast ratio, the percentage of light that a sheet reflects with a white backing as compared to a black backing. If the reflectance drops by 10% using the black backing, the sheet has a 90% opacity rating.

Generally speaking, thick paper is more opaque than thin, coated paper more opaque than uncoated, rough paper more opaque than smooth, colored paper more

opaque than white, and ground-wood more opaque than free sheet.
2) Characteristic of ink that prevents substrate from showing through. In Great Britain called covering power. – 1 & 2, opacidad

opaque 1) (adjective) Not transparent. 2) (verb) To cover flaws in negatives with tape or opaquing paint. Also called block out and spot. – 1, opaco; 2, opacar

opaque ink Heavily pigmented ink that prevents the color of underlying ink or paper from showing through. – tinta opaca

opaquing paint Fluid used by strippers to cover flaws in film so they will not transfer as images to the printing plate. – pintura para opacar

open prepress interface Hardware and software that link desktop publishing systems with color electronic prepress systems. Abbreviated OPI. – interface abierto de preimpresión

open up 1) To make a layout seem less crowded by adding white space. 2) To dodge or use other techniques to reveal more detail in shadow areas of a photo, halftone, or separation. 3) To reduce ink densities to diminish the effects of dot gain. – 1 - 3, abrir

open web Alternate term *non-heat-set web.* – prensa de bobina sin horno

optical center Point within a photo, illustration, or page that appears to be its center. For most images, the optical center is slightly above the geometric center. – centro óptico

optical character recognition Method of reading type or bar codes by scanning. Abbreviated OCR. – reconocimiento óptico de caracteres

optical disc Disc on which a laser reads and writes data, as compared to magnetic disk. – disco óptico

optical dot gain Dot gain that occurs because of how the internal structure of the sheet affects the appearance of dots printed on its surface by reflecting or refracting light, as compared to mechanical dot gain. See also *dot gain.* – ganancia óptica de puntos

orange peel Defect of screen printed ink, IR or UV coating, or thermography resin that cracked or wrinkled as it dried, so resembles the rind of an orange. – cáscara de naranja

organization chart Diagram showing titles and responsibilities of people and departments and their relationship to each other. Illustrated on page 129. – organigrama

orientation Alignment of an image or page, as in vertical (portrait) orientation or horizontal (landscape) orientation. – orientación

original art Initial photo or illustration prepared for reproduction.
Original art may be in the form created by the artist, such as a photographic print, or may be in a form such as a halftone or PMT. From the standpoint of the prepress service or printer, 'original' means the starting point for making film or plates. – arte original

origination British term for *prepress.*

orphan Single word or line of type appearing alone. Also called widow.
Authorities disagree about the precise meanings of 'orphan' and 'widow.' Some use the terms as synonyms. Some claim an orphan has several words, whereas a widow is only one word or a partial word. Some distinguish by location rather than amount, saying that widows appear at ends of paragraphs and columns, and orphans at beginnings. Some argue that the meanings are identical, but that widows happen by accident, thus are not wanted, whereas orphans are planned to attract readers to the next column or page. – huérfano

orthochromatic Referring to film that is sensitive to blue and green, as compared to panchromatic. Most litho films are orthochromatic.
– ortocromático

Otabind Brand name for a method of lie-flat binding.

outer form Form (side of a press sheet) containing images for the first and last pages of the folded signature—its outside pages—as compared to inner form. – forma exterior

outline 1) Line marking the outer edges of an image. In Great Britain called inline. 2) List of main points or subjects in a manuscript, in the order in which they occur.
– 1, perfilar; 2, lista de hechos

outline halftone Halftone in which background has been removed or replaced to silhouette the image. Illustrated on page 219. Also called knockout halftone and silhouette halftone. – mediotono perfilado

outline type Type represented only by lines along the edges of letterforms. Illustrated on page 255.
– tipo perfilado

out of print Publication that a publisher no longer has available and does not plan to reprint.
– publicación agotada

out of register Characteristic of an image not printed in register. Also called misregister. Illustrated on page 67. See also *register.*
– fuera de registro

outpush Alternate term for *creep.*

output Material or results produced by an electronic device such as an imagesetter or scanner. – salida

output device Mechanism that prints images created using a computer.
– dispositivo de salida

output house Alternate term for *service bureau.* – servicio de preimpresión

outsert 1) Printed sheet included loose with another publication, in a polybag. 2) Alternate term for *cover wrap* and *wraparound.*

outsource To buy a service from an outside vendor rather than performing the service in house.
– subcontratar

out-turn sheet British term for *advance sheet.*

outwork British term for *buyout.*

overdevelop To leave film, photo paper, or a printing plate in developing chemicals too long. – sobrerevelar

overexpose To allow too much light to reach film, photo paper, or a printing plate. Illustrated on pages 82 and 226. – sobreexponer

overhang cover Cover larger than the trim size of the inside pages, as compared to flush cover. Case-bound books have covers that overhang. – cubierta sobresaliente

overlay Layer of material taped to a mechanical, photo, or proof. An overlay has the same dimensions as the mounting board that it covers. There are two types of overlays:
Acetate overlays are used to separate colors by having some type or art on them instead of on the mounting board. They are registered to the base art, thus are camera-ready. – superpuesta de acetato
Tissue overlays are used to carry instructions about the underlying copy and to protect the base art. – superpuesta de papel mantequilla

overlay proof Color proof consisting of polyesther sheets laid on top of each other with their images in register, as compared to integral proof. Each sheet represents the image to be printed in one color. For example, an overlay proof for a map to be printed in five ink colors would have five sheets. Also called celluloid proof and layered proof. In Great Britain called acetate proof, colour overleaf proof. – prueba de superpuestas

overprint To print one image over a previously printed image, such as printing type over a screen tint. Illustrated on page 213. Also called surprint. – sobreimprimir

overrun Number of pieces printed or paper made in excess of the quantity ordered.
Printing trade customs offer a guideline for specific amounts of allowable overrun or underrun, depending on the quantity ordered. Overrun tolerances are also usually specified in contracts from printers and paper mills. See also *trade tolerance.* – sobre tiraje

overs Printed pieces in an overrun. – sobres

overset copy Type that has been copyedited and proofread as final copy, but exceeds the space available in the current issue of a publication. Overset copy, in the form of a chapter or article, is typically saved for a later publication. In Great Britain called overmatter. – copia sobrecompuesta

oversize book Book that is larger than 9 x 12 inches, the largest size that fits conveniently on most book shelves. Also called folio size. – libro de tamaño excesivo

overspray Phenomenon of flecks of toner from laser printers appearing in non-image areas, thus confusing scanners and making them reproduce the flecks on flats and printing plates. – manchas de toner

ozalid Alternate term for *blueline.*

P

package 1) (verb) To wrap or enclose an item. 2) (noun) Box, bag, or other materials used to wrap or enclose. 3) US Postal Service designation for a group of printed pieces secured together as one unit for bulk mailing. Also called bundle. – 1, empaquetar; 2 & 3, paquete

packaging paper 1) Printing paper made for specific packaging applications, such as food packages whose papers must meet government standards. 2) Coarse and other inexpensive paper suitable for wrapping packages. 3) Board used to make folding cartons and boxes. – 1 & 2, papel para empaquetar; 3, cartulina

packing Very thin sheets of paper or plastic placed under plates or blankets on presses. Press operators use packing to adjust plate or blanket pressure, thus control ink transfer. – revestimiento

packing schedule Chart showing sizes, weights, and number of sheets in cartons, skids, and other units used for shipping and selling paper. – tabla del empaquetado

pad 1) (verb) To bind by applying glue along one edge of a stack of sheets. 2) (noun) Stack of small sheets, usually with a chipboard backing, bound by glue on one edge. Also called tablet. – 2, bloc de hojas

padfolio Sturdy folded cover with a clip mounted inside for holding a pad of paper.

pad printing Printing technique using a spongy rubber pad that transfers a relief image onto irregular surfaces such as golf balls.

page One side of a leaf in a publication.
One leaf has two pages. One sheet folded in half yields four pages. A 16-page signature has eight pages printed on each side of the sheet. Pages in publications often have specific names, such as title page or sports page. – página

page count Total number of pages that a publication has. The page count includes blank pages and printed pages without numbers. Also called extent. – número de páginas

page description language Computer program built into laser printers and imagesetters that assembles text and graphics into a single image. PostScript is a page description language. Abbreviated PDL. – lenguaje de descripción de la página

page makeup Arrangement of type and graphics, during prepress, into final form ready for printing. – compaginación

page proof Proof of type and graphics as they will look on the finished page complete with elements such as headings, rules, and folios. – prueba de página

pages per inch Expression of the caliper of paper that is used to estimate the thickness of a bound publication. Abbreviated ppi. – páginas por pulgada

pages per minute Measurement of output speed of a laser printer or imagesetter. Abbreviated ppm.
Pages per minute refers to multiple copies of a single page, not to many different pages. New pages require machine time to compose, so make output much slower. – páginas por minuto

pages to view Number of pages printed on one side of a press sheet. A 16-page signature has eight pages to view. – páginas para observar

pagination Assembly of type with other copy into page format. When done by hand, pagination is called make up or paste up; when done electronically, it is called computer aided pagination (CAP). – paginación

painted sheet Sheet printed with ink edge to edge, as compared to spot color.
The 'painted sheet' refers to the final product, not the press sheet, and means that 100% coverage results from bleeds off all four sides. – hoja pintada

palette Selection of colors available from any one source, such as a computer program or ink company. – paleta

pallet Portable platform used as a base for handling, storing, and transporting materials and products. Pallets are made of wood, plastic, and various composites. Also called skid and stillage.
In the United States and Canada, pallets measure 48 x 40 inches or 48 x 48 inches and hold 1,500-3,000 pounds, depending on what they contain and how high they are loaded. The US Postal Service standard pallet measures 48 x 40 inches (1,220 x 1,016mm). The European standard pallet measures 1,220 x 965mm (48 x 38 inches) and is usually specified not to exceed 1220 mm (4 feet) in height.
The words 'skid' and 'pallet' are often used as synonyms, with 'pallet' used more commonly. Warehouses have pallet racks, not skid racks. Companies that manufacture the platforms make pallets, not skids. Some paper merchants call the platforms pallets when loaded with cartons and skids when loaded with sheets not in cartons, but the distinction is not consistent throughout the industry. – paleta

palletization Stacking and shipping items, such as mail, on pallets.
– almacenar en paletas

pallet knife Knife with a flat, flexible blade made for mixing and spreading ink by hand. – espatula para tintas

pamphlet Publication ranging from four to 16 pages, usually paste bound and printed on inexpensive paper. – panfleto

pamphlet stitch Alternate term for *saddle stitch*. – engrapado al lomo

panchromatic Referring to film that is sensitive to all colors, as compared to orthochromatic. – pancromático

panel 1) One page of a brochure, such as one panel of a rack brochure. One panel is on one side of the paper. A letter-folded sheet has six panels, not three. 2) Portion of a product reserved for a specific use, such as the address panel. 3) One frame of a comic strip. 4) British term for *display board*. – 1 - 3, panel

Pantone Colors Brand name of colors in the Pantone Matching System. – colores Pantone

Pantone Matching System Brand name for a system of identifying and communicating color.

The Pantone Matching System helps professionals at every stage of the production process communicate clearly what colors they want to appear on printed products and ensures that printers can match colors that printing buyers specify.

To meet these goals, the system has four groups of components:

design aids Art supply stores sell marking pens, papers, and overlay materials made by several companies using Pantone Colors. Software publishers produce desktop publishing software that simulates Pantone Colors on computer screens.

specifying aids Books printed by the Pantone Company show several thousand solid and four-color process colors. Each color is identified by number so it can be clearly specified.

proofing aids Several companies that manufacture thermal printers, integral proofing systems, and other proofing devices and materials, have agreements allowing reproduction of Pantone Colors.

color formulas Pantone books tell computer and scanner operators, printers, and ink manufacturers how to produce the colors shown. Printers try to match colors either by mixing inks or by using four-color process printing. The books also tell desktop publishers how to simulate colors on computer screens.

The Pantone Company does not make ink. It licenses ink companies to make ink identified by Pantone Colors. – sistema de igualación Pantone

paper Substrate for printing and writing that is made of cellulose fibers from trees or other plants.

Paper for printed products is called printing and writing paper. It is also called fine paper to distinguish it from paper for industrial and sanitary uses, which is called coarse paper. Printing paper is divided into many categories, such as bond, off-set, and newsprint. Each category has subcategories defined by characteristics such as quality and surface. – papel

paper, selling units Printing paper is sold either in rolls or sheets, depending on the kind of press used to print it.

Rolls for web presses are sold by weight, either in pounds or kilos. The buyer specifies total weight, not number of rolls. Buyer and seller know that total weight yields a specific number of rolls.

Sheets for sheetfed presses are sold in many units, including:
- package = 250 sheets
- ream = 500 sheets
- broken carton = any number less than a full carton
- case = 10 reams
- carton = approximately 150 pounds (60 kilos). A carton can contain anywhere from 500 to 5,000 sheets, depending on their size and basis weight.
- miniskid = approximately 500 kilos (1,100 pounds). A miniskid can contain anywhere from 4,000 to 30,000 sheets, depending on their size and basis weight. Mini-skids are standard dimensions to fit into shipping containers.
- skid = 2,500 pounds (1,136 kilos). A skid can contain anywhere from 8,000 to 75,000 sheets, depending on their size and basis weight.
- carload = anywhere between 20,000 pounds (9,090 kilos) and 100,000 pounds (45,450 kilos), depending on who is buying or selling.

paperback Book bound using perfect binding or burst perfect binding.
– libro en rústica

paper bind Alternate term for *perfect bind.* – encuadernación perfecta

paperboard Alternate term for *board.* – cartulina

paper distributor Merchant selling paper wholesale to printers and other buyers of large quantities.
– distribuidor de papel

paper dummy Unprinted sample of a proposed printed piece, which has been trimmed, folded, and bound using the paper specified for the printing job. – muestra de papel

paper mill Facility that makes paper. Paper mills are large industrial complexes that produce millions of tons per year. One paper company may own many mills. Each mill specializes in a category of paper, such as newsprint. – papelera

paper surface efficiency British term for *printability.*

papeterie 1) Soft, high-quality bond paper that accepts handwriting well, packaged in small quantities for sale as social stationery. 2) Store selling such paper. 3) Stiff paper used for greeting cards.
– 1 & 2, papelería

papyrus Name for a large grass that grew in ancient Egypt, and for the paper made from that plant. – papiro

parallel fold Any fold where the creases run parallel to each other. Illustrated on page 105. – doblado paralelo

parallel perspective Objects having three dimensions and illustrated so that opposite lines are equal distances from each other. – perspectiva paralela

parchment paper Paper that simulates writing surfaces of paper formerly made from animal skins. Also called diploma paper. – papel pergamino

parent sheet Any sheet larger than 11 x 17 inches or A3. The smallest common parent sheets are 17 x 22 inches or A2. Large sheets are called 'parents' because they can be trimmed into cut sizes. In Great Britain called broadside. – hoja madre

parent size Referring to the size of paper, any size large enough to be called a parent sheet. Also called folio size. – tamaño madre

pass One complete sequence of activities, such as a pass through a manuscript to check spelling or a pass through a press to lay down varnish. A sheet to be printed four-color process requires one pass through a four-color press, two passes through a two-color press, and four passes through a one-color press. Also called working. – pasada

PASS Abbreviation for Package and Sack Sequencing for Publications and Catalog Mailings, a set of guidelines and procedures for mail makeup developed by the Graphic Communications Association.

passive white space White space, such as in the margin, that frames copy, as compared to active white space. – espacio en blanco pasivo

paste To fasten copy to a mechanical using rubber cement, mounting spray, or wax. – pegar

paste bind To bind by fastening sheets with glue along the fold of the spine. Paste binding is done with self-cover pamphlets and other inexpensive products. – encuadernación engomada

pasteboard Chipboard with another paper pasted to it. The second paper is usually a coated paper and the resulting pasteboard is used to make products such as matchbook covers. – cartulina pegada

pastedown Alternate term for *end sheet.*

pastel colors Relatively soft, light colors created by adding white to darker tones of the same hues. Pink is a pastel of red; lavender is a pastel of purple. – colores pasteles

paste up To paste copy to mounting boards and, if necessary, to overlays so it is assembled into a camera-ready mechanical. The mechanical produced is often called a pasteup. – montar

pasteup Alternate term for *mechanical.* – boceto final

pasteup artist Alternate term for *production artist.* – artista de boceto final

pasteup board Any piece of paper or board used as the base for a mech-anical. Also called lineup board. – cartulina para boceto final

pasteup knife Alternate term for *art knife.* – cuchilla para montaje

patch correction A few words or lines of type pasted over an incorrect passage on a mechanical, as compared to correcting the error by printing out an entire page of new type. – corrección con parche

patent bind Alternate term for *perfect bind.* – encuadernación perfecta

path Series of lines and points created using computer drawing software.

PC Abbreviation for *personal computer.*

PDL Abbreviation for *page description language.*

PE Proofreader mark meaning printer error and showing a mistake by a typesetter, prepress service, or printer, as compared to an error by the customer.

PEs are corrected at no charge by the business that made the errors, as compared to alterations that are billed to the customer.

peaking Alternate term for *unsharp masking.* – enmascar para mejorar la nitidez

peculiars British term for *pi characters.*

peel-off label Label with adhesive backing that removes easily from a release paper. Peel-off address labels come on rolls, continuous forms, and on sheets. Also called pressure-sensitive label and self-adhesive label. – etiqueta autoadhesiva

pel Alternate term for *pixel.*

penalty stock Paper having some unusual characteristic, such as being extra thick or extra thin, that causes problems on press, making the printer charge extra to print it.

peninsula display Display fixture designed to hold publications or products and stand at the end of an aisle so viewers see three sides of it.

pennant Small flag made of felt or other sturdy cloth and printed with the logo of a school or athletic team. – banderola

pennysaver Alternate term for *shopper.* – revista publicitaria

percentage wheel Alternate term for *proportional scale.* – scala de proporción

perf Abbreviation for perforation and perforate. – perforación

perfect bind To bind sheets that have been ground at the spine and are held to the cover by glue. Perfect binding creates the common paperback book. Illustrated on page 16. Also called adhesive bind, cut-back bind, glue bind, paper bind, patent bind, soft bind, and soft cover. In Great Britain called drawn-on cover, limp binding, thermoplastic binding, threadless binding. – encuadernación perfecta

perfecting press Press capable of printing both sides of the paper during a single pass. Also called duplex press and perfector. There are two styles of perfecting press:

22×34
$= 8\left(8\tfrac{1}{2} \times 11\right)$

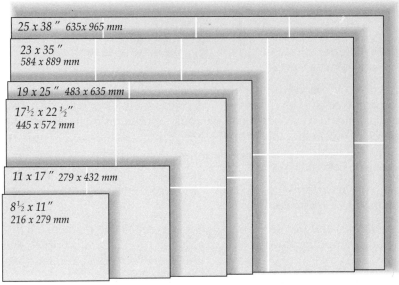

25 x 38 " 635x 965 mm

23 x 35 " 584 x 889 mm

19 x 25 " 483 x 635 mm

17½ x 22 ½" 445 x 572 mm

11 x 17 " 279 x 432 mm

8½ x 11" 216 x 279 mm

North American sheet sizes

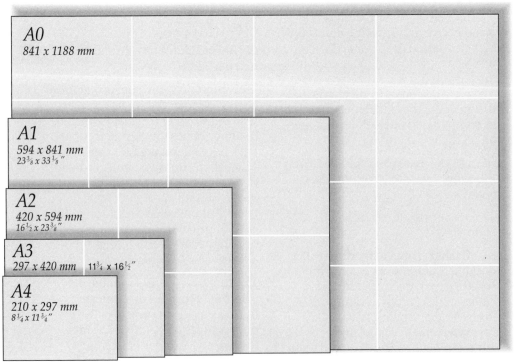

A0 841 x 1188 mm

A1 594 x 841 mm 23⅜ x 33⅛ "

A2 420 x 594 mm 16½ x 23⅜ "

A3 297 x 420 mm 11¾ x 16½"

A4 210 x 297 mm 8¼ x 11¾"

ISO sheet sizes

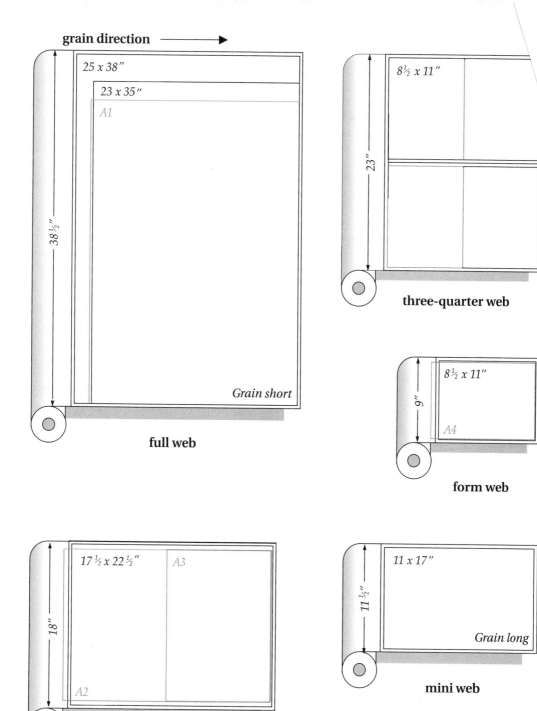

grain direction ⟶

25 x 38"

23 x 35"

A1

Grain short

full web

8½ x 11"

23"

three-quarter web

8½ x 11"

9"

A4

form web

17½ x 22½"   A3

18"

A2

half web

11 x 17"

11½"

Grain long

mini web

179

blanket-to-blanket Opposing blanket cylinders print both sides of the paper at once as it passes between them. Most web presses use this technique.

mechanical Special equipment turns the paper over. Sheetfed perfectors use special grippers to flip the sheet over. Web presses pass the web over an angle bar to present the second surface for printing.

Most sheetfed perfecting presses can be switched from printing on two sides to printing on one side, then back to two sides again, according to the needs of the job. These are sometimes called convertable presses.

Like one-side-only presses, perfectors can be described by their number of ink stations. A two-color perfector can print two colors on one side of a sheet or one color on each side. A six color perfector might be set up in a variety of ways, such as 6/0 (six colors on one side and none on the second side) and 4/2 (four colors on one side and two on the second side). – prensa de retiración

perfector Alternate term for *perfecting press.* – prensa de retiración

perforate To punch a line of small holes or incisions into paper along a straight line. Some perforating can be done in-line on an offset press. Perforating can also be done off-line by letterpress. Illustrated page 247.

Perforation makes it easy to tear paper along the line, as with removing coupons from advertisements. Printers also perforate the fold lines

of signatures to allow air to escape during folding, thereby reducing the possibility of gusset wrinkles. Abbreviated perf. – perforar

pergamyn Alternate term for *glassine.* – pergamino

periodical Publication issued on a regular schedule, such as every week or month. Also called serial.

Magazines, newsletters, and journals are periodicals. The term is not usually applied to newspapers or yearbooks, although each appear on a regular schedule and are technically periodicals. – periódico

peripherals Hardware connected to a computer system for additional input, output, or memory. Printers, scanners, and modems are peripherals. – periféricos

permanent inks British term for *fade-resistant inks.*

permanent paper Alternate term for *acid-free paper.* – papel sin ácido

personal computer 1) Alternate term for *microcomputer.* 2) May refer as a class to microcomputers made by or compatible with IBM machines. Abbreviated PC. – computadora personal

PGS Abbreviation for publication groundwood specialties, guidelines for heatset web printing on uncoated premium groundwood papers used for publications.

photocopier Alternate term for *photocopy machine.*

photocopy Method of printing that transfers images electrostatically and reproduces them with powder (toner) bonded to paper by heat. Also called electrostatic printing and xerography.

Photocopy is one of the technical bases for printing on demand because laser beams can be controlled by computers. – fotocopia

photoengraving Engraving done using photochemistry.

Photoengraving may be used to make plates for relief printing by letterpress or engraving. It may also refer to making metal plates for offset lithography. – fotograbado

photogram Photographic print made by placing an object on photographic paper and exposing it to light. Photograms may not involve a camera or enlarger. – fotogramo

photographic film Film made to produce continuous-tone images, as compared to graphic arts film – película fotográfica

photomechanical British term for *flat (1)*.

Photomechanical transfer Brand name for a diffusion transfer process used to make positive paper prints of line copy and halftones. Often used as alternate term for Photostat. Also called *blackprint*.

photo resist Resist created photographically, as compared to stencil resist. – fotoresistente

photosensitive Characteristic of paper, film, and printing plates coated with chemicals that react to light. – fotosensible

Photostat Brand name for a diffusion transfer process used to make positive paper prints of line copy and halftones. Often used as alternate term for PMT. Also called *blackprint*.

phototype Type created by projecting light onto photosensitive paper. – fototipia

pica Anglo-American unit of typographic measure equal to .166 inch (4.218mm). One pica has 12 points. Illustrated on page 259.

Picas are used to express the width of columns and margins. The term is also used to express the size of standard typewriter type, called pica type. – pica

pica pole Alternate term for *line gauge*. – lineómetro

pica type Larger of the two standard typewriter typefaces, being 12 point size and usually set in ten pitch. – tipo pica

pi characters Math symbols, dingbats, and other characters for special typographic needs. Also called sorts. Most fonts include some pi characters, but there are also special fonts consisting exclusively of pi characters. In Great Britain called peculiars. – caracteres pi

picking 1) Phenomenon of ink pulling bits of coating or fiber away from the surface of paper as it travels through the press, thus leaving unprinted spots in the image area. Picking results from ink being too tacky or paper surface lacking strength to withstand printing forces. It is most likely to occur near the trailing edge of a press sheet, where tension between sheet and blanket are greatest.

2) In gravure printing, white spots called picking can occur because of poor ink transfer or shallow cells. – 1 & 2, repelado

pick up To take art or text from a previous job to use in the current job. For example, a stripper might say, "I picked up the logo from last month's brochure." In Great Britain called lift. – escoger

pickup art Artwork, used in a previous job, to be incorporated in a current job. Pickup art could include type, halftones, and even film from old jobs. It could also include images stored digitally in computer files for previous jobs. – arte escogida

pickup lap Alternate term for *lap.*

pictograph Chart or diagram that includes drawings. Illustrated on page 129. – pictografía

pie chart Circular chart divided into wedges like pieces of a pie. Each wedge represents a percentage of the whole. Illustrated on page 129. Also called circle chart. – gráfica circular

pigment Tiny particles that give color and opacity to ink or paper. – pigmento

piling Buildup of dirt, lint, powder, or dried ink on a blanket, plate, or cylinder of an offset press. Piling results in uneven ink coverage. – apilamiento

pin feed paper Paper with rows of holes along both sides or in the middle, designed for continuous feeding with computer printers. Also called sprocket feed paper. – papel de arrastre por espigas

pinholes 1) Tiny holes in the emulsion of negatives. Pin holes represent dust or spots on mechanicals and, if not opaqued out, reproduce as dark dots in the printed image. 2) Tiny holes in printed surfaces due to incomplete ink coverage. – 1 & 2, puntos de aguja

pin printer Dot-matrix computer printer that creates images from dots made when pins strike an inked ribbon held over paper. Dot matrix printers have either 9-pin or 24-pin print heads. Also called needle printer, stylus printer, and wire printer. – impresora por puntos

pin register Technique of registering separations, flats, and printing plates by using small holes, at the edges of both flats and plates. The holes fit over pins that stick up from the edge of a light table or platemaker, ensuring precise positioning at all stages of prepress production. – registro por clavija

pitch Number of characters per inch produced by a typewriter or computer printer. Common pitches are 10 (pica), 12 (elite), and 15. – paso

pitch edge British term for *gripper edge.*

pixel Short for picture element, a dot made by a computer, scanner, or other digital device. Also called pel.

A pixel is the smallest point that the user can control on a screen. The number of pixels a computer will display determines screen resolution; more pixels means better resolution. A 72 dpi computer screen shows 72 pixels per linear inch and 5,184 pixels per square inch. A 300 dpi laser printer prints 300 pixels per linear inch and 90,000 pixels per square inch. – pixel

pixel editing Adding or deleting individual pixels on a computer screen. Editing may involve color correcting, sharpening, removing blemishes, or any other changes to the images. – editado de pixel

plain type Alternate term for *roman type (2)*. – tipo sencillo

planning British term for *imposition*.

planographic printing Printing method whose image carriers are level surfaces with inked areas separated from non-inked areas by chemical means. Planographic printing includes lithography, offset lithography, and spirit duplicating. – impresión planográfica

plastic bind Alternate term for *comb bind*. – encuadernación plástica

plastic grip bind To bind sliding a plastic sleeve over a small stack of paper. Illustrated on page 16. – encuadernación con manga plástica

plastic proof Alternate term for *integral proof*. – prueba integral

plastic wrap British term for *polybag*.

plate 1) Piece of paper, metal, plastic, or rubber carrying an image

to be reproduced using a printing press. Technically speaking, a gravure cylinder and a screen printing frame are also plates.

2) General term sometimes applied to film negatives and positives, flats, cabriolets, screens, and other image carriers.

3) Piece of glass or film coated with photosensitive emulsion and used as the image receiver in a view camera.

4) Page of a book showing illustrations or photos in color and printed on higher quality paper than used for the text. – 1 - 3, plancha; 4, chapa

plate cylinder Cylinder on a printing press on which the plate is mounted. Illustrated on page 167. – cilindro de plancha

plate finish Very smooth, hard finish on bond, cover, or bristol paper similar to supercalendered finish on book or cover papers. – acabado de plato

platemaker 1) In quick printing, a process camera that makes plates automatically from mechanicals.

2) In commercial lithography, a machine with a vacuum frame used to expose plates through film.

3) Person who makes plates. A person who makes plates may also be called an engraver, an historical reference to letterpress technology, and making the plates may also be called engraving. – 1 & 2, constructura de planchas; 3, planchista

platen 1) Rubber cylinder that lies under the paper and receives the impact of the keys on a typewriter. 2) On a letterpress, a flat surface that holds the paper. A platen on a letterpress functions similarly to an impression cylinder on a rotary press. – 1 & 2, platina

platen press Any press that uses a platen. Platen presses are letterpresses that open and close like a clamshell. Illustrated on page 246. – prensa platina

plate-ready film Stripped negatives or positives fully prepared for platemaking. – película lista para plancha

platesunk British term for *deboss*.

pleasing color Color that the customer considers satisfactory even though it may not precisely match original samples, scenes, or objects. – color satisfactorio

plugged up Undesirable characteristic of printing when halftone dots in the midtones or shadows have spread to touch each other, causing loss of detail. Also called filled in. – tapado

plus cover Printed product with a cover printed on paper different from the paper used for the text, as compared to self cover. A book is plus cover. Illustrated on page 53. – cubierta plus

ply One of the layers of paper used to make duplex paper or cardboard. – capa

PMS Obsolete reference to *Pantone Matching System*. The correct trade name of the colors in the Pantone Matching System is Pantone Colors, not PMS Colors.

PMT Abbreviation for *Photomechanical transfer.*

pocket 1) Enclosure to hold items, such as pockets in a presentation folder that hold brochures or pockets on a binding machine that hold signatures. 2) Alternate term for *ink fountain.* – 1, bolsillo; 2, tintero

point 1) Regarding paper, a unit of thickness equaling $1/1000$ inch. The thickness of 8-point paper is $8/1000$ (.008) inch. In North America, cover paper is usually described in points, with 8 point, 10 point, and 12 point being the most popular calipers.

2) Regarding type, a unit of measure used to express size (height) of type, distance between lines (leading), and thickness of rules. In the Anglo-American type system, one point equals $1/12$ pica and .013875 inch (.351mm). In the Didot type system, one point equals .0148 inch (.3759 mm). Illustrated on page 259.

Desktop publishing software defines a type point as $1/72$ inch, not $1/12$ pica. In decimal terms, $1/72$ inch equals .0138 inch and $1/12$ pica equals .01384 inch. The difference rarely has any practical significance. – 1 & 2, punto

point of purchase display Exhibit on a counter, floor, or other location where a consumer might buy something. Abbreviated pop. Also called counter display and point of sale display. – exhibición en el lugar de compra

184

point of sale display Alternate term for *point of purchase display.*

point size The height of a typeface, measured in points. Illustrated on page 259. – cuerpo tipográfico

polarizing filter Filter that reduces glare and increases contrast of light before it passes through the lens. Polarizing filters are used in cameras, imagesetters, and some densitometers.

policy envelope Long, relatively thin envelope with the flap on the short dimension. Policy envelopes are used to hold insurance policies and legal documents. – sobre para pólizas

polybag Transparent plastic bag used to enclose a publication and, sometimes, additional materials, such as brochures or catalogs. Polybags protect their contents in the mail and achieve single-piece mail rate for an entire package. Also called polywrap. In Great Britain called plastic wrap. – bolsa plástica transparente

polychrome printing Alternate term for *multicolor printing.*

polywrap Alternate term for *polybag.*

pop 1) (verb) alternate term for *vibration.* 2) (noun) Acronym for *point of purchase.*

pop strength Alternate term for *bursting strength.* – resistencia a la ruptura

pop test Alternate term for *Mullen test.* – prueba Mullen

porosity Degree to which paper allows liquid or gas to pass through

it. Porosity is an important consideration regarding papers used for packaging. – porosidad

port Connecting point for cables that connect computers with peripherals. – puerta

portfolio 1) Collection of the best work by an artist, photographer, or designer for showing to prospective clients. Also called book. 2) Alternate term for both *expansion envelope* and *presentation folder.* – 1, portafolio

portrait format Alternate term for *vertical format.* – fomato vertical

portrait lens Camera lens that is slightly longer than a normal lens for the format being used. A portrait lens for a 35mm camera has a focal length between 80mm and 105mm. – lente para retratos

position marks Alternate term for *register marks.* – marcas de posición

position proof Any proof used only to show position of elements such as photos and headlines. Bluelines are typically used as position proofs. – prueba de posición

position stat Photocopy or PMT of a photo or illustration made to size and affixed to a mechanical. Position stats show proper cropping, scaling, and positioning. They are not intended for reproduction, thus are marked 'for position only.' – fotoestática para posición

positive film Film that prevents light from passing through images, as compared to negative film. Positive film produces a negative image on a negative plate, thus is used to make reverses. Also called knockout film. – película positiva

positive image Image on film, plate, or paper in which solids in the original subject are black or opaque and clear areas in the original are white or clear, as compared to a negative image. – imagen positiva

postal code Numeric or alphanumeric sequence telling postal officials the destination of an item. In the US, the ZIP code is the postal code. – código postal

post bind To bind using a screw and post inserted through a hole in a pile of loose sheets. – encuadernación con tornillo

post card Small card designed as a self-mailer. Post cards must conform to specific aspect ratios and calipers, depending on postal regulations in the country of origin. – tarjeta postal

poster 1) Large advertisement or notice, printed on one side of durable paper suitable for mounting on a bulletin board or wall. Also called bill. 2) Large, inexpensive reproduction of an image, used for decoration. 3) Alternate term for *billboard*. – 1 & 2, cartel

poster board Cardboard whose caliper is over .024 inches and usually having a laminated, coated surface. Also called showcard. – cartulina para carteles

posterization Line reproduction of a continuous-tone image. Illustrated on page 60.

poster paper Paper treated to resist water. Available in large sheets slightly rough on one side to enhance pasting to other surfaces. – papel para carteles

POSTNET Acronym for postal numeric encoding technique, the bar code that the US Postal Service uses for letters.

PostScript Brand name for a page description language used in laser printers and imagesetters.

powder Alternate term for *anti-offset powder.* – polvo secador

ppi Abbreviation for *pages per inch.*

ppm Abbreviation for *pages per minute.*

precedence code Alternate term for *delimiter.*

précis Alternate term for *abstract.*

preface Short statement by an author explaining the purpose of a book. – introducción

prekissing British term for *doubling.*

preliminaries Alternate term for *front matter.* – páginas preliminares

premium paper Paper considered by its manufacturers to be better than #1 paper. – papel de lujo

premiums Alternate term for *advertising specialties.*

preparation Alternate term for *prepress.* – preparación

preparation service Alternate term for *camera service, color separator,* and *service bureau.* – servicio de preparación

prepress Camera work, color separating, stripping, platemaking, and other prepress functions performed by a printer, separator, or a service bureau prior to printing. Also called preparation. In Great Britain called litho prep, origination. – preimpresión

prepress proof Any color proof made using ink jet, toner, dyes, or overlays, as compared to a press proof printed using ink. Also called dry proof and off-press proof. – prueba de preimpresión

preprint 1) (verb) To print portions of sheets that will be used for later imprinting. Business cards are often preprinted with organizational information, then later imprinted with the names and titles of individual employees.
2) (noun) Selection from a book that is distributed before publication of the book. Preprints may be used to alert the market to a forthcoming book. – 1, preimprimir; 2, preimpresión

prescan analysis Evaluation, made by a scanner service and customer, of images to be scanned. The analysis is part subjective judgment and part technical readout from the scanner with the goal of making satisfactory separations with the first scan. – análisis de preexploración

presentation folder Folder used to enclose materials handed out at events such as conventions, press conferences, and workshops. Also called folio and portfolio.
    Presentation folders are commonly made of heavy, high-quality text paper and are often foil stamped or embossed. They have pockets, flaps, slits, and other devices to hold materials. – carpeta de presentación

presentation graphics Charts, graphs, and other data on transparencies, posters, and other visual media. Presentation graphics are used to supplement and reinforce information presented in speeches and workshops. – gráficos para presentaciones

presentation wallet Open-ended envelope used to enclose small brochures. – cartera de presentación

preseparated art Alternate term for *separated art.*

presort To separate mail into categories, such as postal codes, before mailing it. Presorting reduces postage and speeds delivery because it speeds handling by the postal service. Also called make up. – preseparar

press check Event at which make-ready sheets from the press are examined before authorizing full production to begin.
    Press checks take place either at the delivery end of a press or in a special room near the press. They are meetings that can include customers, graphic designers, printers, and others involved in a printing job. Press checks occur while operators run the press at

slow speeds and make final adjustments while waiting for approval. – inspección de los pliegos

press gain Alternate term for *dot gain*. – ganancia de puntos

press kit Collection of brochures, news releases, and other publicity materials about a product, service, or cause. Press kits are prepared for journalists—members of the press— who might write articles about topics explained by materials in the kit. Also called media kit. – paquete para la prensa

press layout Alternate term for *ruleup*. – maqueta de imposición

press-on type Alternate term for *dry transfer lettering*. – letras transferibles

press proof Proof made on press using the plates, ink, and paper specified for the job. A press proof could be a sheet from a progressive proof or a fully-printed sheet approved at a press check. Also called strike off and trial proof. – prueba de prensa

press run 1) The number of pieces printed. "Our press run was 20,000." 2) Alternate term for *edition*. "We finally finished the November press run." 3) Alternate term for *press time (1)*. "Our press run took four hours." – 1, tiraje; 2, edición

press sheet One sheet as it comes off the press. Also called form. – pliego de prensa

press time 1) Amount of time that one printing job spends on press, including time required for make-ready. A job might require three hours of press time. 2) Time of day at which a printing job goes on press. Press time for a job might be 8:00 AM. – 1, tiempo de impresión; 2, empiezo de la impresión

pressure sensitive paper Paper with an adhesive backing to make it stick to other surfaces. Also called *label paper*. – papel sensible a la presión

presystem ink Ink made to withstand the heat of laser printers and photocopy machines.

price break Quantity at which unit cost of paper or printing drops. In the US and Canada, price breaks for paper are typically at four cartons, 16 cartons, 5,000 pounds, and 20,000 pounds. Price breaks on printing jobs vary, depending on specifications. – descuento en volumen

primary colors See *additive primary colors* and *subtractive primary colors*.

prime coat Coating of ink applied as a base to enhance the density and gloss of subsequent printing. – capa de fondo

primer Textbook teaching first rules or basic principles. – cartilla

print 1) (verb) To reproduce by any printing process. 2) (noun) One copy, such as a print of a photograph or lithograph. – 1, imprimir; 2, copia

printability Subjective term referring to how well paper or other substrate accepts an image. Printability depends on ink color, tack, and coverage, paper caliper and surface, pressroom conditions, and many other factors. In Great Britain called paper surface efficiency.

print and tumble Alternate for *work and tumble.* – imprimir y a lo largo

print and turn Alternate for *work and turn.* – imprimir y voltear a lo ancho

print and twist Alternate for *work and twist.*– imprimir y girar

print contrast Quantitative measure of shadow detail on a printed piece. Print contrast is computed using the following formula:
- PC = ([Ds -D75] ÷ Ds) x 100.
- Ds means density of a solid.
- D75 means density of an area with a 75% dot.

Many publishers and printers use a print contrast of 25% as a quality guideline. – contraste de impresión

printer 1) One of the separation films used for four-color process printing, as in "the cyan printer is out of register." 2) Person who owns or manages a print shop or operates a printing press. 3) Company or organization that does printing. 4) Device that prints out copy from a computer. 5) Alternate term for *printing unit.* – 1, plancha; 2, impresor, 3, imprenta; 4, impresora

printer error See *PE.*

printer font Type font that a printer can output, as compared to a screen font.

printer marks Register marks, center lines, and other guides on mech-

anicals and film that help a printer produce a job correctly. – marcas para el impresor

printer's layout Alternate term for *ruleup.* – boceto de impresor

printer spreads Mechanicals made so they are imposed for printing, as compared to reader spreads. For example, an 11 x 17 mechanical for an eight-page newsletter would have pages 2 and 7 opposite each other. See also *imposition.*

print farmer British term for *broker.*

print in Alternate term for *burn in.*

printing 1) Any process that transfers to paper or another substrate an image from an original such as a film negative or positive, electronic memory, stencil, die, or plate. 2) One complete press run, such as the first printing of a book. – 1, impresión; 2, tiraje

printing plate Surface carrying an image to be printed. Quick printing uses paper or plastic plates; letterpress, engraving, and commercial lithography use metal plates; flexography uses rubber or soft plastic plates. Gravure printing uses a cylinder. Photocopy uses a drum. The screen in screen printing is also called a plate. Also called form. – plancha de impresión

printing press Machine used for printing with ink. Printing presses are categorized in five major ways.
method of image transfer The major methods of printing with ink are planography (collotype, lithography, offset lithography, and

spirit duplicating), relief (letterpress, flexography, and pad), intaglio (engraving and gravure), and serigraphy (stencil and screen). (Ink jet printing also uses ink, but doesn't use a press.)

mechanism for printing Platen presses hold the substrate flat while making an impression; flatbed rotary presses have the plate wrapped around a cylinder that rolls across the substrate; cylinder rotary presses have both the image carrier and the substrate mounted on a cylinder.

format of substrate Paper, and most other substrates, comes in either sheets or rolls. Presses that feed individual sheets are sheetfed presses; presses that feed from a roll are web presses. Most engraving presses are sheetfed. Most flexography and gravure presses are web presses. Both sheetfed and web are used for letterpress and lithography. Most screen printing presses operate on the sheetfed principle of printing one item at a time.

size of substrate Press size is expressed as the width of substrate the press will print. A 40-inch sheetfed press will print sheets narrower than 40 inches, but not wider. A half-meter web prints a roll 500 cm wide. Small presses for quick printing are not rated by this size system, but typically handle sheets up to 12 x 18 inches.

number of ink stations Presses range from one ink station to eight or more. A press with six ink stations is called a six-color, six-station, or six-unit press. Sheetfed presses typically offer one, two, four, five, or six unit configurations. Web presses typically offer two, four, six, or eight ink stations. – prensa para impresión

printing sequence British term for *color sequence.*

printing trade customs See *trade customs.*

printing unit Assembly of fountain, rollers, and cylinders that will print one ink color. Also called color station, deck, ink station, printer, station, and tower. – unidad impresora

printout Output from a computer printer. – impresión de salida

print wheel Alternate term for *daisy wheel.*

private brand Alternate term for *merchant brand.* – marca particular

privately printed Alternate term for *self-published.* – impresión privada

process black Black ink formulated for four-color process printing. Process black is slightly less dense than black used to print type. As a practical matter, most printers use the same black ink and plate for both type and the black separation when printing four-color process. – negro de proceso

process camera Camera used to photograph mechanicals and other camera-ready copy. Also called copy camera and graphic arts camera. A small, simple process camera may be called a stat camera. – cámara de fotoreproducción

process colors The colors used for four-color process printing: cyan, magenta, yellow and black. Abbreviated, CMYK.

Although the process colors have identical names everywhere in the world, they do not have identical hues. The yellow and cyan used in North America have slightly less chroma than the yellow and cyan used elsewhere. There are three hues called magenta—one common in North American, the second in Europe, and the third elsewhere in the world. European cyan is slightly greener than cyan in North America.

Local preferences and variations among ink companies make the range of process hues even wider than described above. – colores de cuatricromia

process printing Alternate term for *four-color process printing* – cuatricromía

process yellow Specific yellow used for four-color process printing. – amarillo de proceso

production artist Person who does pasteup. Also called mechanical artist and pasteup artist. – artista de arte final

production copy Printed piece taken at random from the production run, as compared to green copy. A production copy represents all copies in the run. – copia de producción

production manager Person who coordinates work flow to ensure that jobs get done efficiently and profitably. – 1 & 2, gerente de producción

production order Alternate term for *job ticket.* – pedido de producción

production run Press run intended to manufacture products as specified, as compared to makeready. – tiraje de producción

product match Separations or printing made to match the colors in an original product. – igualación de producto

prog Abbreviation for *progressive proof.*

program 1) Booklet or pamphlet describing performers and the sequence of activities at theatrical, athletic, and other events. 2) Alternate term for *computer software.* – 1, programa

progressive margins Alternate term *shingling (1).* – márgenes progresivos

progressive proof Press proof showing each color of a four-color process job separately and the colors in combinations. The typical set of progressives includes nine sheets: one for each process color and one each for various combinations of colors. Progressive proofs require setting up a press to production conditions. Also called prog. In Great Britain called bastard progressives and loose proofs. – pruebas progresivas

promotional kit Collection of displays and fliers provided to retailers to help them sell a product. – estuche de promoción

proof Test sheet made to reveal errors or flaws, predict results on press, and record how a printing job is intended to appear when finished. Illustrated on pages 68 and 69. – prueba

Proofs come in many forms, depending on the goals and complexity of the job.

type proofs Output from a type-setter, computer printer, or image-setter and also called galley proofs or page proofs, depending on the system used and what is considered camera-ready copy. – pruebas de texto

photo proofs Contact sheets showing all images shot on rolls of negative film (black-and-white film or color print film). Transparencies are positive images, so are examined directly rather than being printed. – pruebas de fotografías

photocopies Proofs for quick printing jobs. Photocopies of mechanicals may simulate the final product of a black-only job. – fotocopias

laser prints & thermal proofs Proofs of pages assembled in desk-top publishing systems, but not yet transferred for high-resolution output. – pruebas electrónicas

bluelines Proofs for commercial printing jobs. Bluelines show position of type and visuals and reveal any errors in stripping. They are contact prints of stripped film and are known by many other names, such as brownline, Dylux, ozalid, silverprint, and VanDyke. – pruebas azules

overlay proofs For multicolor jobs. Overlay proofs verify that elements appear in the correct colors and positions. They are known by several brand names, such as Color Key and Transfer Key. – pruebas de superpuestas

integral proofs For four-color process jobs. Integral proofs show register of separations and show how colors will reproduce on press. They are known by several brand names, such as Agfaproof, Cromalin, Fujiproof, Matchprint, Pressmatch, and Signature. – pruebas integrales

press proofs For jobs where the customer and/or printer want to ensure that all quality standards have been met. Press proofs show how the job will print using the same paper, ink, and press as the production run. They are also known as progressive proofs and press sheets. – pruebas de prensa

bindery proofs For jobs involving complex bindery procedures. They confirm correct folding, gathering, and trimming. Bindery proofs are also known as book proofs.

Some professionals distinguish between preproofs and proofs. In their view, a pre-proof is created directly from a computer and a proof is created using film. – pruebas de encuadernación

proofing paper Paper used to make press proofs.

For sheetfed jobs, the proofing paper is the same as the stock specified for the production run. Proofs for many web jobs are made using sheetfed presses. In those cases, printers use a proofing paper as close as possible to the production stock.

SWOP guidelines call for a 60# proofing paper of 70 brightness that simulates the #5 groundwood used by many publications. – papel para prueba

proof OK Signature from customer approving a proof and authorizing the job to advance to the next stage. – firma de autorización

proofread To examine a manuscript or proof for errors in writing or typesetting. – corregir

proofreader marks Symbols and abbreviations used to mark up manuscripts and proofs. Most dictionaries and style manuals include charts of proofreader marks. Also called correction marks. – marcas de corrección

proof sheet 1) Photographic term for sheet of images made by contact printing negatives. Also called contact sheet. 2) Printing term for any proof or press sheet used as a proof. – hoja de prueba

property release Contract that authorizes commercial use of a photograph that includes an image of private property. Also called release. – autorización

proportional spacing Typographic system of allocating spaces to characters according to their width, as compared to equal spacing. In proportional spacing, 'i' gets less space than 'p,' while 'w' gets more space than 'a.' – espaciado proporcional

proportion dial Alternate term for *proportion scale.* – escala proporcional

proportion scale Round device used to calculate percent that an original image must be reduced or enlarged to yield a specific reproduction size. Designers, production artists, and printers use proportion scales to plan layouts and specify sizes for type, halftones, and separations. Also called percentage wheel, proportion dial, proportion wheel, and scaling wheel. – escala proporcional

proportion wheel Alternate term for *proportion scale.* – escala proporcional

prospectus Small booklet, usually printed on lightweight paper, containing financial and business information about a specific company or investment opportunity. – prospecto

protective paper Alternate term for *safety paper.* – papel protector

protocol Codes that control a computer's internal functions and its interface with other devices. – protocolo

publication Any product reproduced with a message for an audience. Brochures, books, newsletters, magazines, musical scores, maps, and video tapes are all publications. This glossary deals only with printed publications. – publicación

publication date Date, announced by the publisher, that buyers or users can expect to find a publication readily available. In the case of a newsletter, publication date and press date may be identical. In the case of a book, however, publication date may be two or

three months after press date.
– fecha de publicación

publication printer Printing company specializing in magazines, catalogs, and other products that are typically web printed. – imprenta de publicaciones

publish To produce and sell or otherwise make publications available to an audience. – publicar

publisher 1) Person or organization that coordinates creation, design, production, and distribution of publications. 2) Chief executive officer or owner of a publishing company. – 1 & 2, editor

publishing paper Paper made in weights, colors, and surfaces suited to books, magazines, catalogs, and free-standing inserts.

Publishing papers are typically available only in rolls. Uncoated stock tends to be bulky, come in weights such as 50#, 55#, and 60#, and have off-white colors such as natural. Coated papers are typically white, available only with gloss surfaces, and come in weights such as 40# and 45#. – papel para publicaciones

pull Alternate term for *proof.*

pulldown Alternate term for *drawdown.*

pullout Alternate term for *foldout.*

pull quote Words from an article or book printed in large type and inserted in the page like an illustration. Illustrated on page 164. Also called callout. – cita

pulp Mixture of wood and/or cotton fibers, chemicals, and water from which mills make paper. – pulpa, pasta

pulp magazine Magazine printed on very inexpensive, uncoated groundwood paper, as compared to a slick. – revista en papel de pulpa

punch 1) (verb) To use a die to bore or cut holes in paper. 2) (adjective) Refers to printed image with high contrast and/or bright colors.
– 1, perforar

punctuation marks Typographic symbols such as the comma (,), colon (:), and period (.). – signos de puntuación

purity Alternate term for *chroma.*

push 1) To develop film longer than normal and thus compensate for under exposure. 2) To print a form with a relatively large (dense) amount of ink. A printer might push a form to darken halftones or because the paper was especially absorbent. – 1 & 2, empujar

pushout Alternate term for *creep (1).*

put to bed Newspaper term for completing all editorial and prepress steps needed before printing begins.

pyroxylin Plastic used to coat or impregnate paper. Pyroxylin holds very bright colors, including metallics and fluorescents, and is available in a variety of embossed finishes. It is commonly used to protect covers of casebound books.
– piroxilina

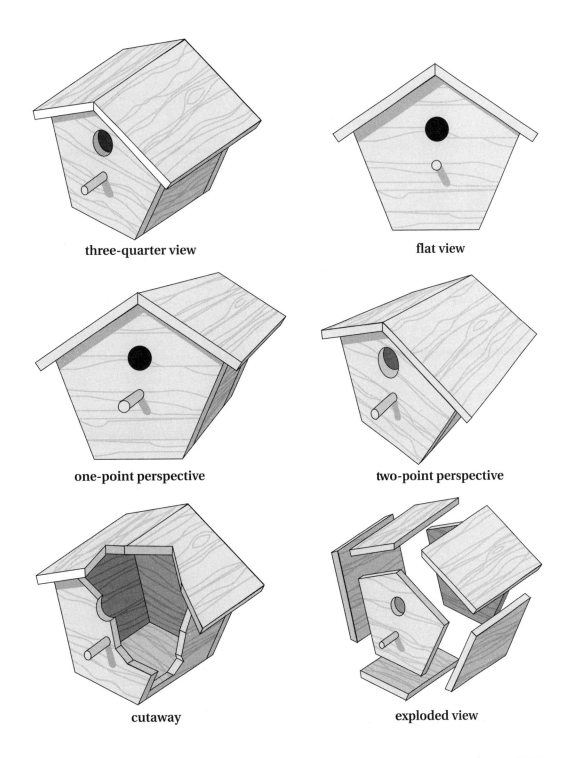

three-quarter view

flat view

one-point perspective

two-point perspective

cutaway

exploded view

quad Square piece of metal used to add space to a line of foundry type. Quads are expressed in point sizes. For example, a 12-point quad measures 12 points x 12 points.
– cuadrado

quad centre British term for *centered text.*

quad left British term for *flush left.*

quad right British term for *flush right.*

quad press Printing press large enough to print a 40 x 56 inch sheet (1010 x 1400mm), known as a quad sheet. – prensa cuadrada

quadratone Black and white photo reproduced using four inks— usually two blacks and two grays. – cuadratono

quadrille paper Paper printed with a grid of non-repro blue lines used for pasteup. – papel cuadriculado

quality 1) Subjective term relating to expectations by the customer, printer, and others associated with a printing job, and whether the job meets those expectations.

Quality is a judgment that blends technical and aesthetic consider-ations, communication goals, and the constraints of time, money, materials, and processes. Satis-factory quality is achieved when supplier and customer agree the product is good enough.

Many efforts have been made to develop quality guidelines for features of printing jobs such as gray balance, ink density, and screen ruling. These efforts, made by trade associations and large publishers, are keyed to types of publications such as annual reports, magazines, and inserts. Examples include PGS, SNAP, SWOP, and guidelines for newspapers developed by *USA Today* and the American Newspaper Publishers Association. – calidad

2) British term for *grade.*

quarter bound Book with its spine covered in one material, frequently leather, and its corners and sides covered in another such as cloth, as compared to full bound and half bound. Illustrated on page 23.
– cuarta encuadernación

quarter tones In a photograph or illustration, tones created by dots approximately half way between highlights and midtones. – cuarta tonos

quarto 1) Sheet folded twice, making pages ¼ the size of the original sheet. A quarto makes an 8-page signature. 2) Book made from quarto sheets, traditionally measuring about 9 x 12 inches.

quick printer Printer using duplicator presses to provide fast service. – imprenta rápida

quick printing Printing using small sheetfed presses and cut sizes of bond and offset paper. Paper, plastic, or rubber plates are made directly from camera-ready copy, as compared to metal plates for commercial printing that require making film first.

Quick printing is as much a business point of view as a method of reproduction. Quick printers typically have retail locations in business districts and office buildings as well as in industrial areas. They deal with many customers over-the-counter rather than via sales representatives. They focus on short run jobs such as announcements, booklets, business cards, fliers, newsletters, and stationery.

Many in-plant printers use quick printing equipment and techniques. – impresión rápida

quiet zone Unprinted area just before the start character or just following the stop character of a bar code, where printing might confuse the scanner. – espacio sin imprimir

quire 1) 25 sheets of paper; ½₀ of a ream. 2) British term for *signature.*

quoin Device used to lock metal type in the chase for letterpress printing. – cuña

quotation Price offered by a printer to produce a specific job, thus alternate for *estimate.* The quoted price is the printer's side of the contract based on specifications from the customer. – presupuesto

QWERTY Abbreviation for the keyboard layout standard on typewriters and computers using the English language. The name comes from the arrangement of keys at the left of the upper row.

R

rack brochure Brochure folded to 4 x 9 inches (102 x 229 mm) to fit displays (racks) in locations such as hotel lobbies and travel information centers. – folleto para estante

ragged left type Type whose line beginnings are not aligned vertically. Illustrated on page 270. – texto en bandera izquierda

ragged right type Type whose line endings are not aligned vertically. Illustrated on page 270. – texto en bandera derecha

rag paper Alternate term for *cotton content paper.* – papel de trapos

railroad board Thick, coated, often waterproof stock for products such as signs and cards. – cartulina de ferrocarril

railroad lines One or more parallel lines, on a press sheet from a gravure press, caused by nicks or dirt on the doctor blade. Railroad lines run parallel to the direction of the sheet's movement through the press. – líneas de ferrocarril

rainbow fountain Technique of putting ink colors next to each other in the same ink fountain and oscillating the ink rollers to make the colors merge where they touch, producing a rainbow effect. Rainbow fountains blend ink colors at the edges of colors, as compared to split fountains. – tintero arco iris

raised cap Large capital letter that extends upward above the first line, as compared to dropped cap. Used as a design element. Illustrated on page 263. In Great Britain called cocked-up initial. – mayúscula elevada

raised printing Alternate term for *thermography.* – termografía

RAM Acronym for *random access memory.*

ramped screen Alternate term for *graduated screen tint.* – gradiente

random access memory Computer memory used to hold, manage, and perform functions on files in current use. Abbreviated RAM. – memoria de acceso al azar

random proof Alternate term for *loose proof.* – prueba suelta

range British term for *alignment (1)*. Used as in saying "ranged right" (flush right), "ranged left" (flush left), or "ranged centrally" (centered). – alineación

rangefinder camera Camera whose field of view is seen through a small window located above or to the side of the lens, as compared to single lens reflex camera and view camera.

RA paper sizes One of five categories of ISO paper sizes.

raster image display Image on a computer screen made by a pattern of horizontal and vertical lines.

raster image processor Device that translates page description commands into rasters for an output device such as a laser printer or imagesetter. Because of the abbreviation RIP, converting images to rasters is known as ripping images.

rate card Card or sheet that lists placement costs and gives mechanical specifications for display advertising in a magazine or newspaper. – tarjeta de precios

raw data Data which have been recorded, but not organized or processed. – datos en bruto

raw stock British term for *base stock*.

RC paper Abbreviation for *resin-coated paper*.

readable Characteristic of printed messages that are easy to read and understand, as compared to legible. Readability is determined in part by legibility, but is also affected by typographic decisions such as using serif or sans serif typefaces. (Serif faces are more readable in body copy.) Readability is also affected by writing and editing to ensure clear prose and consistent style. – leíble

reader service card Business reply card bound into a magazine and having numerals printed on it that readers can circle to request information about products advertised. Also called action card and bingo card. – tarjeta de servicio del lector

readership British term for *audience*.

reader spread Mechanicals made in two-page spreads as readers would see the pages, as compared to printer spread. For example, an 11 x 17 mechanical of a reader spread for an eight-page newsletter would have pages 2 and 3 opposite each other. – boceto para el lector

read only memory Computer memory whose contents a user cannot change. Abbreviated ROM. Also called firmware. – memoria solo de lectura

readout Display of information on a computer screen, as compared to printout. – lectura

read rate Speed at which a scanner or other device reads copy. – velocidad de lectura

ream 500 sheets of paper. – resma

ream marked Sheets of paper in a carton or on a skid with markers placed every 500th sheet. – marcado por resma

ream weight Alternate term for *basis weight*. – peso de resma

ream wrapped Paper packaged in bundles containing 500 sheets. Abbreviated RW. – envoltura de resma

recess printing Alternate term for *intaglio printing.* – impresión en hueco

record Unit of related information based on the user's needs, such as names and addresses in a database. – registro

record paper Alternate term for *ledger paper.* – papel ledger

recovered paper British term for *recycled paper.* – papel reciclado

recto Alternate term for right-hand page, as compared to verso. – anverso

recycled paper New paper made entirely or in part from old paper. In Great Britain called recovered paper.

Mills put old paper back into the pulping process and blend it with virgin pulp. Old paper that mills recycle into new paper comes from two sources.

pre-consumer waste Paper that has not been printed. It includes trimmings leftover from converting paper into products such as envelopes, roll ends and damaged paper that printers couldn't use, and waste at the mill itself.

Paper mills have for many years recycled pre-consumer waste as a routine part of doing business.

post-consumer waste Paper that has been printed. It is gathered from end users, sorted, bundled, and returned to a paper mill instead of going into a landfill.

Post-consumer waste costs more to recycle than pre-consumer waste because of the logistics of collection and because mills must remove the ink. Coated papers cost the most to recycle because of the difficulty of removing coatings as well as inks. Color in paper also drives up the cost of recycling because of the expense of removing dyes.

Guidelines, laws, and goals regarding recycled paper deal with two issues: the percentage of recycled fibers in new paper and the source of those fibers. A paper listed as 50% recycled, the current EPA guideline for wood-pulp paper, may use entirely pre-consumer waste and no post-consumer waste. Very few recycled papers include more than 10% post-consumer waste.

The recycling process shortens the fibers of paper and cannot remove 100% of the ink. As a result, recycled papers are slightly more opaque and slightly less bright than comparable grades of virgin paper. Shorter fibers also mean that recycled papers score, fold, die cut, and emboss easily and lie flat, but are not as strong as virgin sheets. – papel reciclado

red patch Window on a mechanical made using red masking material such as Rubylith. – ventana roja

reducer 1) Chemical (potassium ferricyanide) used to remove fine layers of emulsion from film. Using reducers on a negative makes dense areas lighter, thus makes a print darker. Reducers are used on halftones for dot etching. Also called farmer's reducer.

2) Chemical used to make ink thinner, thus reducing its tack and making it flow more easily. – 1 & 2, tiner

reduction Image reproduced smaller than its original. – reducción

reel 1) Roll of paper wound directly off the papermaking machine, thus measuring the full width of the Fourdrinier wire. This becomes the master roll (also called jumbo roll and log) from which smaller rolls are cut. 2) Alternate term for any roll of paper. – 1 & 2, bobina

reel-fed press Alternate term for *web press.* – prensa de bobina

reel paper Alternate term for *continuous paper.*

reel-to-reel press Web press that is set up to rewind the printed roll for later finishing instead of to cut it immediately into sheets.

reference marks Typographic symbols such as the asterisk (*), paragraph (¶) and section (§) used to guide readers. – signos de referencia

reflectance Alternate term for *brightness.* – reflectancia

reflection densitometer Densitometer that measures light reflected from paper and other surfaces. – densitometro

reflective copy Products, such as fabrics, illustrations, and photographic prints, viewed by light reflected from them, as compared to transparent copy. Also called reflex copy. In Great Britain called flat artwork. – copia por reflexión

reflex copy Alternate term for *reflective copy.* – copia reflexión

register To place printing properly with regard to the edges of paper and other printing on the same sheet. Such printing is said to be in register. Illustrated page 67. See also *fit.*

Technically speaking, any images that do not appear precisely where they are intended are out of register. As a practical matter, however, many printing jobs are slightly out of register. Printers and customers approve those jobs because precise register is difficult to achieve and maintain on every sheet.

The definition of register that is close enough depends on factors such as the quality of prepress work, the press and paper being used, and the objectives of the printed piece. For example, art reproductions, sales brochures, and newspapers have totally different requirements for register.

The correct term is 'register,' not 'registration.' Printers plan for register, schools plan for registration. Printed images are in register or out of register. Strippers register film when making flats and press operators adjust presses for register. – registro

register bond Alternate term for *form bond.* – papel bond para formas

register marks Cross-hair lines on mechanicals and film that help keep flats, plates, and printing in register.

dot gain and ink holdout

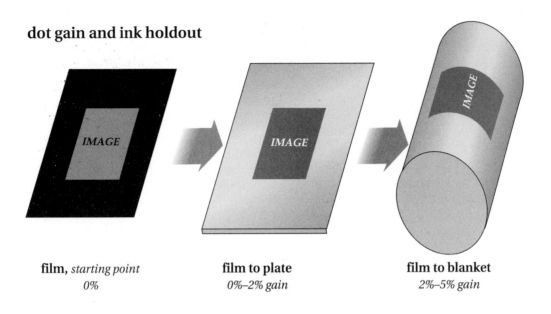

film, *starting point*
0%

film to plate
0%–2% gain

film to blanket
2%–5% gain

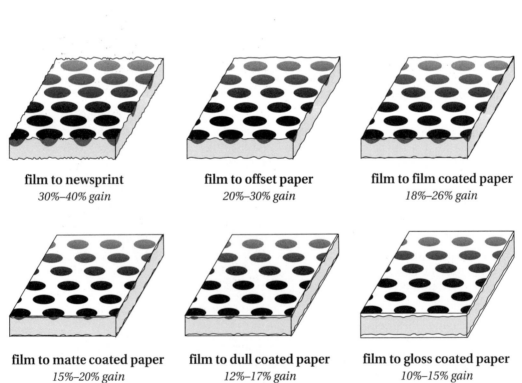

film to newsprint
30%–40% gain

film to offset paper
20%–30% gain

film to film coated paper
18%–26% gain

film to matte coated paper
15%–20% gain

film to dull coated paper
12%–17% gain

film to gloss coated paper
10%–15% gain

Register marks provide common targets which, when perfectly aligned, help ensure register of other images. Also called cross-marks and position marks. – marcas de registro

register unit Mechanism on a sheetfed press, consisting of headstops and sideguides, that positions paper precisely for feeding into the press, thereby ensuring correct register. – unidad de registro

release Alternate term for *model release* or *property release.*

release paper Paper treated with silicone or other coatings to make it useful as backing for self-adhesive labels, bumper stickers, and as packaging for sticky products. Also called backing paper, carrier sheet, and liner. – papel protector

relief printing Printing method whose image carriers are surfaces with two levels having inked areas higher than non-inked areas. Relief printing includes block printing, flexography, and letterpress. – impresión en relieve

remittance envelope Self-addressed envelope from a business making it convenient for a person receiving an invoice to send payment. Remittance envelopes typically have large flaps to allow for printing of advertising or instructions on the flap. Illustrated page 209. – sobre de remesa

repeat length Circumference of the impression cylinder of a web press

that is running reel-to-reel. For example, a flexographic press printing labels that rewind onto a backing sheet might have a repeat length of 15 inches. – límite de cada impresión

repeatability Ability of a device, such as an imagesetter, to produce film or plates which yield images in register. – repetible

reply card Alternate term for *business reply card.*

report cover Lightweight loose-leaf binder using screws or flexible metal strips to bind pages. Also called brief cover and service cover. – cubierta de informe

repp finish Finish on text paper that simulates coarsely-woven fabric.

reprint 1) To repeat the printing of a job. Also called rerun. 2) Portion of a publication produced as a booklet, such as a reprint of an article from a magazine. – 1, reimprimir; 2, reimpresión

repro 1) Abbreviation for reproduction copy, an alternate for *camera-ready copy.* 2) British term for *artwork.*

reproduce To copy or print an original. – reproducir

reproduction copy Alternate term for *camera-ready copy.* – copia para reproducir

repro film Alternate term for *graphic arts film.* – película para artes gráficas

reprographics General term for diazo, xerography, and other methods of copying used by designers, architects, engineers, or for general office use. – reprográficos

repro paper Thick, coated paper used for making proofs of mechanicals. Also called baryta paper.

rerun Alternate term for *reprint.*

rescreen To create a halftone of an image that is already printed as a halftone; for example, rescreening a photo appearing in a magazine for reprinting in a newsletter. When not done properly, rescreening yields a moiré. – retramar

resin-coated paper Paper for photographic prints, typesetting, and PMTs that, when properly processed, will not yellow with age. Also called RC paper. – papel tratado con resina

resist Any material or chemical used to protect a surface from the effects of acid or light.

Resists may protect either printing or non-printing areas. For example, etching an engraving plate may require coating it with a photosensitive resist. The portion of the resist exposed to light can be washed away, leaving the underlying metal unprotected. Acid burns an image into the cylinder without affecting the non-image area that remains covered by the resist.

Resists work similarly to masks in photography and friskets in airbrushing. – protección

resolution Sharpness of an image on film, paper, computer screen, disk, tape, or other medium. Illustrated page 215.

The resolution of an image focused by a lens or captured by a film is measured using a standardized target. A lens that produces a sharp image is said to have good resolution; one that produces a fuzzy image has poor resolving power.

The resolution of a digital image is expressed in dots per inch. Most laser printers have a resolution of 300 dpi. Imagesetters have resolutions from 1,000 to over 3,600 dpi. Higher resolution improves image sharpness, but also requires more powerful machines and longer times for processing and printing. For example, a 300 dpi laser printer draws only 90,000 dots per square inch. An imagesetter, however, may draw anywhere from 1.5 million to 13 million dots, depending on its resolution, to render that image. – resolución

resolution target An image, such as the GATF Star Target, that permits evaluation of resolution on films, proofs, or plates. – blanco de resolución

résumé Printed summary of educational background and work experience. A résumé is only one or two pages long. Called a vita (short for curriculum vitae) by people in academic professions. – resumen

retouch To enhance the appearance of or correct flaws in a negative, print, or film separation. Retouching uses techniques such as spotting, airbrushing, and dot etching, and includes electronically enhancing an image on a computer screen before outputting it for camera work or platemaking. Illustrated on pages 75 and 232. – retocar

retree British term for *job lot paper.*

return envelope Alternate term for *business reply envelope.* – sobre de servicio del lector

reversal film Photographic film for transparencies, as compared to negative film. – película reversál

reverse Type, graphic, or illustration reproduced by printing ink around its outline, thus allowing the underlying color or paper to show through and form the image. Also called knockout and liftout. The image 'reverses out' of the ink color. Illustrated on page 213. – inversa

reverse collate To collate from the last page to the first page, as compared to forward collate. Also called descending collate.

reverse reading Alternate term for *wrong reading.* – lectura invertida

reverse type Type printed as a reverse. Also called cameo, dropout type, and knockout type. – tipo inverso

review copy Free copy of a book sent to a potential reviewer. – copia complementaria

RGB Abbreviation for red, green, blue, the additive color primaries. Illustrated on page 78.

rhodamine red A magenta that is bluer than rubine and which some printers think gives better results with four-color process printing

when red is a dominant color on the sheet. – rojo rodamino

ribbon Alternate term for *web* on a web press. – bobina

right angle fold Alternate term for *French fold.* – doblado de ángulo recto

right angle perf Perforation at a 90° angle to another perforation. – perforación a ángulo recto

right-hand page Page on the right when a publication lies open. Also called recto page. Because it is farthest from the front of a publication, so has the highest page number, the right-hand page is also called the high-folio page. – página derecha

right justified Alternate term for *flush right.* – justificado por la derecha

right reading Copy that reads correctly in the language in which it is written. In English, right reading is left to right, top to bottom. Also describes a photo whose orientation looks like the original scene, as compared to a flopped image.

The term 'right reading' is part of complete specifications for plate-ready film. See *RRED* and *RREU*. – lectura directa

rights Conditions and terms of a licensing agreement between a copyright owner and a publisher. Rights to a creative work could include domestic rights within the country of origin, foreign rights in other countries, movie or TV rights, serial rights for periodicals, and translation rights in specific other languages. – derechos

ring binder Binder with rings that open and close to hold sheets of paper. Illustrated on page 16. Also called binder. – carpeta de anillos

RIP Abbreviation for *raster image processor.*

ripple finish Finish on text paper that looks like small waves in a pool of water. – acabado ondulado

rising cap Oversize capital letter projecting up for the first line of type. Used as a design element. – mayúscula elevada

river Distracting pattern of white space running down through text type because of irregular word spacing. – sendero

roll fold Series of parallel folds into the publication. – doblado de rollo

rollout Direct mailers sent to all of the intended audience, as compared to test run.

roll set Permanent curl in paper that lies closest to the the core (center) of the roll. Also called core curl.

Paper with roll set will not relax to stay flat, thus cannot be cut and used for sheetfed printing. Web-printed products on paper taken too close to the core may suffer from roll set. Because of roll set, web printing cannot use 100% of the paper on a roll. – arrollado permanente

roll-o-tab mailer Printed card, with a rotary file card die cut into it, that fits a #10 envelope.

Rolodex card Brand name for *rotary file card.*

ROM Abbreviation for *read only memory.*

Roman numerals Numerals represented by letters such as I (1), X (10), and C (100).

Roman numerals are used in the graphic arts to designate quantities of paper. Price per M sheets means price per 1,000 sheets; price per CWT means price per 100 (C) weight (WT), meaning the price for 100 pounds.

Publishers use Roman numerals to designate front matter in books. For example, an introduction might begin on page iv. – números romanos

roman type Type with serifs and that is upright, as compared to italic. Illustrated on page 255. Also called plain type.

Roman is the basic typeface in any type family. Other typefaces in the family are based on the roman. For example, light is lighter than roman and bold is darker. – tipo romano

ROP Abbreviation for run of press, a newspaper term referring to images printed throughout the press run, not just for one edition.

rosette Regular pattern created by halftone dots of process colors. Illustrated on page 81. – rosetón

rotary file card Die-cut card ready to insert into a rotary file. Also called by the brand name Rolodex card. – tarjeta para archivo rotativo

rotary press Printing press which passes the substrate between two rotating cylinders when making an impression. Illustrated on page 246. – prensa rotativa

rotation Alternate term for *color sequence.* – rotación

rotogravure Gravure printing using a rotary web press. – rotograbado

rotopaper Supercalendered newsprint made to print gravure. – paper supercalandrado

rough Abbreviation for *rough layout.*

rough draft First version of a manuscript. – manuscrito preliminar

rough layout Sketch giving a general idea of size and placement of text and graphics in the final product. Also called esquisse and rough. In Great Britain called visual. – boceto preliminar

round-back bind To casebind with a rounded (convex) spine, as compared to flat back bind. Rounding the spine makes the face of the book convex, thus protecting it. – encuadernación de lomo redoneado

round dot One of several shapes of dots available in halftone screens. – punto redondo

rounding Giving a curved shape to the spine of a casebound book. – redondeo

row Horizontal arrangement of type on a page or in a table, as compared to a column. – fila

R print Color photographic print made from a transparency using Kodak R Print paper and processing. Often used generically to refer to any color print made from a transparency without using an internegative. In Great Britain called colour comp print, R type.

RRED Abbreviation for right reading emulsion down.

RREU Abbreviation for right reading emulsion up.

RS232 port Standard recepticle used to connect computers and peripherals. – puerta de RS232

rub-down lettering British term for *dry transfer lettering.*

rub fastness Alternate term for *abrasion resistance.* – resistencia a la abrasión

rubine red Red pigment used in magenta that is less blue than rhodamine pigment. Some printers think that rubine gives better results with four-color process printing. – rojo rubino

rub-on lettering Alternate term for *dry transfer lettering.* – letras transferibles

Rubylith. Brand name for red masking film.

ruby window Mask on a mechanical, made with Rubylith, that creates a window on film shot from the mechanical. – ventana rubi

rule 1) Line used as a graphic element to separate or organize copy. The width of rules is measured in points or millimeters. Illustrated on page 163. In Great

Britain called line. 2) Straight metal edge used to score or perforate. – filete

ruleout Alternate term for *ruleup*. – maqueta de imposición

ruleup Map or drawing given by a printer to a stripper showing how a printing job must be imposed using a specific press and sheet size. Also refers to a sheet of the paper to be used for a printing job with trim and folding marks drawn on it to ensure correct imposition. Also called press layout, printer's layout, and ruleout. – maqueta de imposición

ruling Alternate term for *screen ruling*. – lineatura de la trama

run Total number of final pieces ordered or printed. Specifications might call for a run of 10,000, but delivered quantity could mean the run was actually 10,714. – tiraje, tirada

runaround Type set to conform to part or all of the shape of a neighboring photograph or illustration. Illustrated on page 165. Also called wraparound. – arracada

runnability Subjective term referring to how well paper handles on press. Runnability is affected by paper cleanliness, trim, conditioning, and many other factors during printing. – imprimibilidad

running foot/head Alternate term for *footer/header*. – título de pie/cabeza

run-of-paper British term for *run of the book*.

run of the book Refers to a location that could occur at any place (anywhere in the run) of a publication, not limited to one side of a sheet or a specific signature. For example, spot color that will be printed run-of-the-book could be used as a design element on any page within the publication. In Great Britain called run-of-paper. – posición de tirada

run time Time required to complete one sequence, such as a press run or a computer run. – tiempo de pasada o tirada

RW Abbreviation for *ream wrapped*.

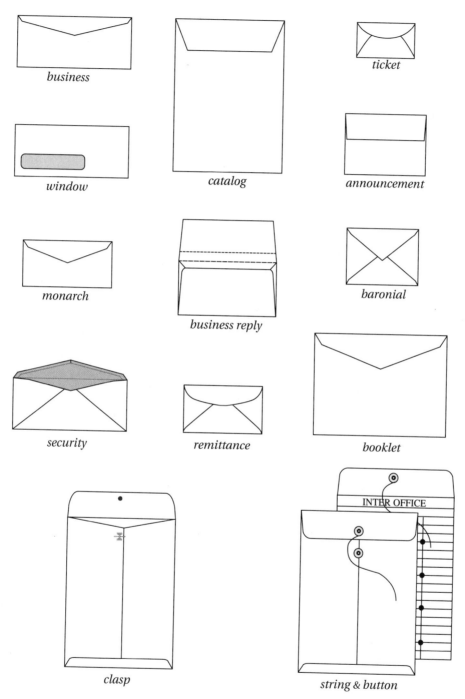

business

window

catalog

ticket

announcement

monarch

business reply

baronial

security

remittance

booklet

clasp

INTER OFFICE

string & button

common envelopes

S

saddle The center fold of a signature where it is bound. – lomo

saddle stitch To bind by stapling sheets together where they fold at the spine, as compared to side stitch. Illustrated on page 16. Also called pamphlet stitch, saddle wire, and stitch bind. – engrapado al lomo

saddle wire Alternate term for *saddle stitch.* – engrapado al lomo

safe area Alternate term for *live area.* – área activa

safelight Colored light, such as red or amber, that does not affect photosensitive emulsions. Safelights are used in photographic darkrooms and stripping areas. – luz de seguridad

safety paper Paper made to show evidence of erasure or prevent duplication or tampering. Printers use safety paper for checks, stamps, stocks, tickets, and other valuable items. Also called check paper, protective paper, and security paper. In Great Britain called cheque paper. – papel de seguridad

safety pattern Alternate term for

blockout pattern. – patrón de seguridad

sales representative Person at a printing company, advertising agency, or other organization who maintains contact with customers and tries to ensure that the organization provides satisfactory products and services. Also called account executive. – representante de ventas

salvage fee Alternate term for *kill fee.*

same size Instructions given to a printer to reproduce a photo at its original size, not to reduce or enlarge the image. – mismo tamaño

sample book Alternate term for *swatch book.* – muestrario

sandwich board Double-faced sign, usually screen printed. Also called A board. – anuncio tipo sandwich

sans-serif type Type without serifs. Also called gothic type. Illustrated on page 259. In Great Britain called lineale. – tipo sans-serif

satin finish Alternate term for *dull finish.* – acabado satinado

saturation Alternate term for *chroma.* – saturación

SAU Abbreviation for *standard advertising units.*

sawtoothing 1) Defect in printing where a ragged pattern appears along the edge of an image. Sawtoothing can occur in screen printing from the pattern of the screen mesh and in lithography from use of coarse screen tints and halftones. 2) Alternate term for *jaggies* in type. – 1, diente de sierra

scale To identify the percent by which photographs or art should be enlarged or reduced to achieve the correct size. An 8 x 10-inch photo for reproduction as a 4 x 5-inch image is scaled to 50%. – cambiar de tamaño

scaling wheel Alternate term for *proportional scale.* – escala proporciónal

scalloped columns Page layout in which columns of unequal length are aligned at the top so their bottoms vary. Also called hanging columns. – columnas salientes

scamp British term for *layout (1).*

scan To read an image using a pinpoint beam of light. The beam of light might be moving or stationary. For example, drum scanners for making color separations move the light across transparencies or prints attached to a spinning drum. On the other hand, scanners that read bar codes on mail keep the light motionless while passing the bar code in front of it. – explorar

scanner Electronic device used to scan an image. Simple scanners read digital images such as bar codes and OCR type. Monotone scanners make halftones and may read typefaces. Color scanners read transparencies and prints to make separations. Scanners on presses help maintain register and ink density. – scanner

scan rate Speed at which a scanner reads and translates data. With color scanners, resolution, scaling, and equipment all affect the scan rate. – velocidad de exploración

scattergram Graph using a pattern of dots to show the relationship between two sets of data. Illustrated on page 129. – disperograma

scatter proof Alternate term for *loose proof.* – prueba suelta

schedule 1) List of events giving times, dates, and locations. Also called calendar. 2) Plan for the sequence and deadlines for a series of related activities, such as a production schedule for a printing job. – 1 & 2, programa

schoolbook perforation Perforation close to and parallel to the spine so that pages in workbooks may be easily torn out. – perforación de cuadernos escolares

Scitex Brand name of color scanners and other machines used for electronic color prepress.

score To compress paper along a straight line so it folds more easily and accurately. Scoring also helps to prevent coatings on coated papers from cracking when the paper is folded. Illustrated on page 247. Also called crease. – rayar

SC paper Abbreviation for *supercalendered paper.*

screen 1) Fabric with relatively coarse mesh used for screen printing. 2) Alternate term for *halftone screen.* 3) (verb) To convert a continuous-tone image into a halftone or a solid into a screen tint.
– 1, pantalla; 3, tramar

screen angles Angles at which screens intersect each other. When overlapped at improper angles, screens produce moiré patterns.
   Screen angles are measured starting with the horizontal line of the press sheet representing 0°. The common screen angles for separations are black 45°, magenta 75°, yellow 90°, and cyan 105°. Halftones are usually printed at 45°.
– ángulos de trama

screen clash British term *moiré (1).*

screen density Refers to the amount of ink that a screen tint allows to print. Illustrated on page 213. Also called screen percentage.
   Screen density is expressed as percent of ink coverage. For example, a 10% screen allows ink to cover 10% of the image area.
   Density, ruling, ink color, and dot gain determine how screen tints look when printed. Hues become lighter tones when screened. For example, black becomes gray, dark blue becomes light blue, and red becomes pink. – densidad de la trama

screen determiner Device used to determine the screen ruling of a printed piece. – determinador de la trama

screen font Type font that a computer screen can show, as compared to a printer font.

screen frequency Alternate term for *screen ruling.* – lineatura de la trama

screening paste Alternate term for *squeegee paste.*

screen percentage Alternate term for *screen density.* – densidad de la trama

screen printing Method of printing by using a squeegee to force ink through an assembly of mesh fabric and a stencil. Illustrated on page 241.
   Screen printing creates vivid colors because it lays down ink films three to five times thicker than possible with lithography. It adapts well to large products, short runs, and substrates with irregular shapes. Screen printing is used to print items such as billboards, wallpaper, bottles, electrical circuits, ring binders, lawn signs, and articles of clothing. – impresión serigráfica

screen ratio In screen printing, the relationship of the area of a screen occupied by dots compared to the area occupied by white space. A ratio of 1:3 means that the dots occupy one third as much space as the open areas between them.
– proporción de la trama

screen ruling Number of rows or lines of dots per inch or centimeter in a screen for making a screen tint

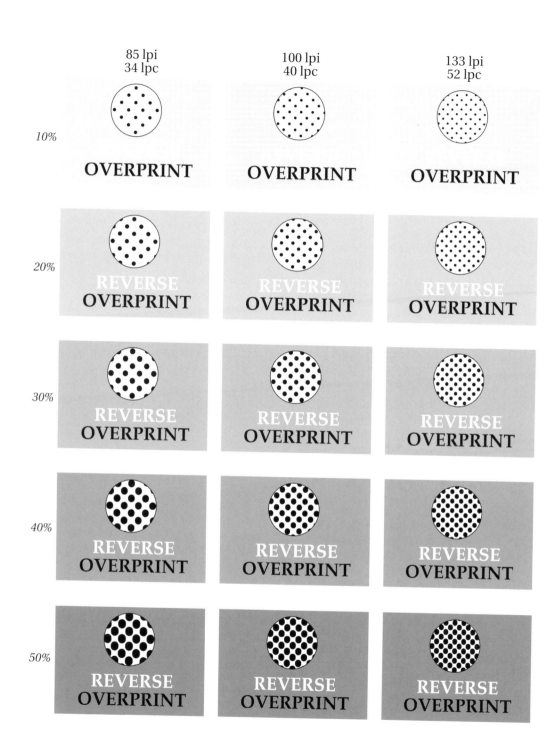

85 lpi
34 lpc

100 lpi
40 lpc

133 lpi
52 lpc

10%

OVERPRINT

OVERPRINT

OVERPRINT

20%

REVERSE
OVERPRINT

REVERSE
OVERPRINT

REVERSE
OVERPRINT

30%

REVERSE
OVERPRINT

REVERSE
OVERPRINT

REVERSE
OVERPRINT

40%

REVERSE
OVERPRINT

REVERSE
OVERPRINT

REVERSE
OVERPRINT

50%

REVERSE
OVERPRINT

REVERSE
OVERPRINT

REVERSE
OVERPRINT

screen rulings and percentages

or halftone. Illustrated on page 213 and 218. Also called line count, ruling, screen frequency, screen size, and screen value.

Common screen rulings are:
- 65 lines per in/25 lines per cm
- 85 lines per in/34 lines per cm
- 100 lines per in/40 lines per cm
- 120 lines per in/47 lines per cm
- 133 lines per in/52 lines per cm
- 150 lines per in/60 lines per cm
- 175 lines per in/70 lines per cm
- 200 lines per in/80 lines per cm
- 300 lines per in/120 lines per cm

Screen ruling affects how screen tints and halftones look when printed. When printed on coated paper, fine screens yield sharper images than coarse screens, but are more difficult to print. A 100-line screen has 10,000 dots per square inch, whereas a 133-line screen has 17,689—almost twice as many.

Lines-per-inch screen rulings and dots-per-inch digital outputs have different meanings. With digital output, each halftone dot consists of several pixels. A halftone dot built from two or three pixels at 300 dpi is much less precise than one built from four or five pixels at 1200 dpi. See also *computer memory, dots-per-inch,* and *halftone dots.*

The best screen ruling for a printing job is determined by the image to be reproduced, technique used to make the screen, and the press and paper used for the job. No job has a 'correct' screen ruling. – lineatura de la trama

screen size Alternate term for *screen ruling.* – lineatura de la trama

screen tint Color created by dots instead of solid ink coverage. Illustrated on page 162. Also called Benday, fill pattern, screen tone, shading, tint, and tone.

Screen tints appear less dense than solid coverage, thus simulate shading and lighter colors. Screen tints of two or more colors may be overlapped to create other colors. See also *build a color, screen density,* and *screen ruling.* – tono tramado

screen tone Alternate term for *screen tint.* – tono tramado

screen value Alternate term for *screen ruling.* – lineatura de la trama

screw and post bind To bind using a bolt that screws into a post. Bolts and matching posts are available in lengths ranging from ¼ inch to 3 inches. Illustrated on page 16. – encuadernación con tornillo

scribe To scratch the emulsion of a negative or plate. When a negative is scribed, light can pass through, as compared to opaquing.

Scribing of negatives is used to correct broken type and make other minor repairs in images before platemaking. Scribing a plate removes part of an image. Press operators sometimes scribe plates to eliminate a spot without having to remove the plate from the press. – rayar

scrim Alternate term for *crash (1).*

script 1) Type that imitates cursive handwriting. 2) Text of a play or movie, complete with stage directions. – 1, letra cursiva; 2, guión

gray levels

133 line halftone screen

scanned at 16 levels of gray

| 100 | 93 | 87 | 80 | 73 | 67 | 60 | 53 | 47 | 40 | 33 | 27 | 20 | 13 | 7 | 0 |

133 line halftone screen

scanned at 256 levels of gray

line reproduction

no screen

no gray scale levels

SCSI Acronym for *small computer system interface*. Pronounced "scuz-zy."

scuff resistance Alternate term for *abrasion resistance*. – resistencia a la abrasión

scum 1) Undesirable thin film of ink in non-image areas. Scumming may appear on portions of a sheet or across the entire sheet and results from poor ink/water balance. Also called blush, catch up, haze, and toning.
    2) Thin crust or film that forms over ink not kept mixed in the can or fountain. – 1, velo; 2, espuma

season Alternate term for *condition*. – curar

secondary colors 1) Additive secondaries are colors made by mixing equal parts of two light primaries: cyan from blue and green; magenta from blue and red; yellow from red and green.
    2) Subtractive secondaries are colors made by printing equal parts of any two pigment primaries: red from magenta and yellow; green from yellow and cyan; blue from magenta and cyan. – colores secundarios

second class mail US Postal Service classification for newspapers, magazines, and other periodicals that meet specific requirements. – correo de segunda clase

seconds merchant Alternate term for *job lot merchant*. – vendedor de papel de segund

section 1) Separate portion of a newspaper, such as the business section or sports section. 2) British term for *signature*. – 1, sección

security envelope Envelope with a screen tint printed on the inside to prevent showthrough. Illustrated on page 209. – sobre seguridad

security paper Alternate term for *safety paper*. – papel de seguridad

selective binding Placing signatures or inserts in magazines or catalogs according to demographic or geographic guidelines.
    Selective binding is done with a computer-controlled combination of binding machines and inkjet printers. One publication may have several versions. For example, a selectively bound catalog might include order forms for previous customers that are different from order forms for new customers. A selectively bound magazine might have an advertising insert from a business serving only one state or region. – encuadernación selectiva

selective key A black printer made to outline or highlight certain areas when using four-color process printing. A selective key would be run as a fifth color—a black in addition to the black printer in the CMYK sequence. – plancha selectiva

self-adhesive label Alternate termfor *peel-off label*. – etiqueta autoadhesiva

self-copy paper Alternate term for *carbonless paper*. – papel autocopiante

self cover Printed product with a cover printed on the same paper as the text, as compared to a plus cover. A newsletter is self cover. Illustrated on page 53. – autocubierta

self ends Outer pages of the first and last signatures in a casebound book that, when glued to the cover, make end papers unnecessary. – auto guardas

self-mailer Printed piece designed to mail without an envelope.

self-published Book or other publication published by the person who is also its author. Also called privately printed. – publicado por el autor

semibold type Type darker than normal but lighter than bold. – tipo seminegro

semicoated carbon paper Carbon paper coated on one side. – papel carbón semitratado

separate 1) (verb) To produce color separations. 2) (noun) Alternate term for *offprint*. – 1, seleccionar

separated art Art with elements that print in the base color on one surface and elements that print in other colors on other surfaces. Also called preseparated art.

Separated art on a mechanical would have some elements on the mounting board and others on acetate overlays. Separated art on film would have different negatives for each color to be printed. – arte preseparado

separation Alternate term for *color separation*. – separacíon de colores

separator Alternate term for *color separation service*. – separador

sepia Light reddish-brown tone on a photograph making it seem old, like an antique. – sepia

serial Alternate term for *periodical*.

serial identification code Alphanumeric set that may follow an ISSN to identify issue date and number of a periodical. Abbreviated SIC. – código de identificación de serie

serial rights Copyrights sold or licensed to a periodical. – derechos de publicación

series Group of articles or books dealing with a single subject or theme. – series

serif Short line crossing the ending strokes of most characters in roman typeface. Illustrated on page 259. – serif

serif type Type with serifs. Illustrated on page 259. – tipo serif

serigraphic printing Printing method whose image carriers are woven fabric, plastic, or metal that allow ink to pass through some portions and block ink from passing through other portions. Serigraphic printing includes screen and mimeograph. – impresión serigráfica

service bureau 1) Business using imagesetters to make high resolution printouts of files prepared on microcomputers. Also called output house and prep service.

elliptical dot, chain dot   continuous tone   square dot

highlight dots   *shadow dots*   *midtone dots*

150 line half tone screen   *65 line* half tone screen

fine mezzotint screen   coarse mezzotint screen

218

mortice

original image　　　flopped

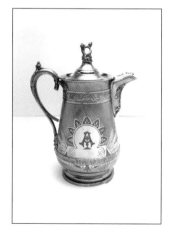

drop out half tone

ghost half tone

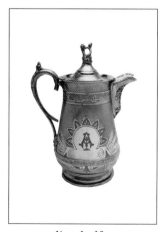

outline half tone

In practice, there is no distinction among typesetting shops, camera services, color separators, and service bureaus. The term 'service bureau' includes a wide variety of businesses that help agencies, publishers, printing buyers, and printers prepare copy for printing.

2) Business that maintains mailing lists and related databases for organizations such as publishers, trade associations, and direct mail companies. – 1, servicio de preimpresión

service cover Alternate term for *report cover*. – cubierta de informe

setoff Undesirable transfer of wet ink from the top of one sheet to the underside of another as they lie in the delivery stack of a press. Also called offset. In Great Britain called ink setoff. – manchado

set size The width of the widest character in a typeface, as compared to the point size. – anchura de composición

set solid Type set with no leading between the lines. 12-point type set solid is specified 12/12. – composición compacta

set up Ink dry enough to resist smearing, but is not yet completely dry. – secado suficiente

setup Alternate term for *makeready*. – preparación

sew To bind using thread to fasten signatures together at the spine of a book, making a stronger binding than one using only glue. Binderies sew signatures using various thread

patterns, such as McCain, Singer, and Smyth, depending on their machinery and on requirements for the job. – coser

shade 1) Hue made darker by the addition of black, as compared to tint. 2) Alternate term for *value* of color. – 1, tono; 2, valor

shaded type Alternate term for *shadow type*. – tipo sombreado

shading Alternate term for *screen tint*. – tono de trama

shading film Dry transfer materials used to make screen tints.

shadow black Black printer made to print primarily in the shadow areas, as compared to full-scale black and half-scale black. Sometimes used in four-color process printing. Also called ghost key and skeleton black. – plancha para sombra

shadow box Box with a screen tint along two sides to create the illusion of a shadow. – caja sombreada

shadows Darkest areas of a photograph or illustration, as compared to midtones and highlights. Illustrated on pages 218 and 233. – sombras

shadow saturation Alternate term for *total area coverage*. – saturación de sombra

shadow type Type with drop shadows. Illustrated on page 255. Also called shaded type. – tipo sombreado

sharpen 1) Alternate term for *dot loss*. 2) To etch separations. – 1, pérdida de puntos; 2, grabar separaciones

sharp Refers to an image in good focus, having good register, or lacking defects such as doubling or slurring. – nítido

sheet 1) One piece of paper. 2) Alternate term for brand of paper, as in "SilkRun is a bright sheet." – hoja, pliego

sheeter Machine that cuts rolls of material, such as paper or cloth, into sheets. – máquina cortadora de hojas o pliegos

sheetfed paper identifiers Bar code specifications for containers of sheets of paper. – identificadores de pliegos

sheetfed press Press that prints sheets of paper, as compared to a web press. – prensa de pliegos

sheet matching Technique of printing and assembling many sheets into a billboard so colors appear consistent and images align. – coordinación de pliegos

sheetwise Technique of printing one side of a sheet with one set of plates, then the other side of the sheet with a set of different plates. Also called work and back. In Great Britain called sheetwork.

sheetwork British term for *sheetwise.*

shell Preprinted product on which imprinting will be done. Also called blank and color blank. – concha

shingling 1) Allowance, made during pasteup or stripping, to compensate for creep. Creep is the problem; shingling is the solution. Also called

stair stepping and progressive margins.

2) Trimming a series of sheets each shorter than the one before to allow readers to see part of each sheet.

3) Press sheets fanned out to permit convenient comparison of images. – 1, proporación de los márgenes

shoot out/shoot in Using a computer to eliminate part of an image, such as a stain on a wall, and replacing it with a satisfactory image.

shopper Newspaper consisting mostly of classified ads and given free to readers. Also called green sheet and pennysaver. In Great Britain called throwaway. – periódico gratuito

short-grain paper Alternate term for *grain short paper.* – papel con fibra a lo corto

short ink Relatively thick ink that doesn't flow easily, as compared to long ink. – tinta densa

short lens Alternate term for *wide angle lens.* – lente corto

short run Relatively small quantity to print in relation to the size and speed of press used.

A short run of fliers at a quick print shop could be any quantity less than 100, whereas a short run of books or magazines could be any quantity less than 5,000. A run of 100,000 booklets could be a short run on a full web press, depending on the trim size and number of pages. – tiraje pequeño

short ton 2,000 pounds, as compared to a long ton of 2,240 pounds.
– tonelada corta

shot One exposure made by a camera. – toma

showcard Alternate term for *poster board.*

show-color proof Alternate term for *loose proof.* – prueba suelta

show through Printing on one side of a sheet that is visible from the other side due to insufficient opacity of the paper, as compared to strike through. – traslucir

shrink Alternate term for *choke.*

shrink wrap Method of wrapping packages or products in clear plastic film then using heat to tighten the film around the item. Shrink wrapping protects the items and keeps them from shifting against each other. – envoltura contraída

shutter Device on a camera that controls exposure time. – obturador

SIC Abbreviation for *serial identification code.*

sidebar Block of information related to and placed near an article, but set off by design and/or typography as a separate unit. Illustrated on page 163. – escritura lateral

side guides Adjustable posts on the register unit of a press that properly position sides of a sheet. In Great Britain called side lays. – guías laterales

side lays British term for *side guides.*

side stitch To bind by stapling through sheets along one edge, as compared to saddle stitch. Illustrated on page 16. Also called cleat stitch and side wire.
– engrapado lateral

side wire Alternate term for *side stitch.* – engrapado lateral

signature Printed sheet folded at least once, possibly many times, to become part of a book, magazine, or other publication. Illustrated on pages 23 and 223. In Great Britian, also called quire or section.

The concept of signature is unrelated to the size of the sheet, but rather to the fact that it is folded to become part of a publication. Signatures always contain pages in increments of four, such as 4, 8, 12, 16, 24 or 32 pages.

Technically speaking, a sheet isn't a signature until it's folded. In practice, however, printers refer to any press sheet that will be folded and bound as a signature. – signatura

signature fold Series of folds needed to turn a press sheet into a signature with the correct sequence of pages.
– doblado de signatura

Signature proof Brand name for integral proof. – prueba Signatura

signatures British term for *collating marks.*

sign paper Rigid, water-resistant paper made for outdoor signs.
– papel para anuncios

silhouette halftone Alternate term for *outline halftone.* – mediotono perfilado

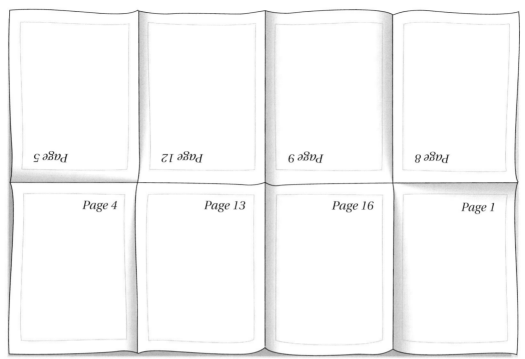

This press sheet with 8 pages printed on each side is a 16-page signature. Other common signature sizes are 4 pages, 8 pages, 12 pages, 24 pages, and 32 pages.

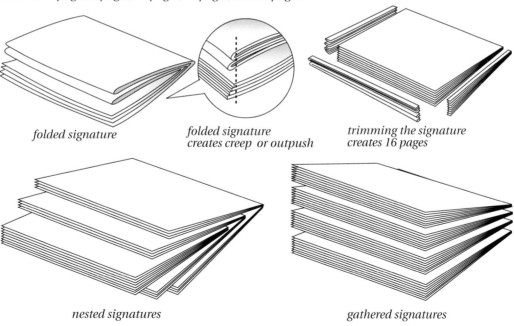

folded signature

folded signature creates creep or outpush

trimming the signature creates 16 pages

nested signatures

gathered signatures

signature

silk screen printing Out-of-date term for *screen printing*. – impresión serigráfica

silurian paper Alternate term for *tinted fiber paper*. – papel de fibra coloreada

silverprint Proof similar to blueline. Also called blackprint. – impresión plateada

simplex decal Decal made to release when soaked in water. – calcomonia simplex

single-face board Alternate term for *single-wall board*. – cartón con una cara plana

single lens reflex camera Camera using a system of mirrors to allow viewing of the subject through the same lens that focuses the image on film, as compared to rangefinder camera and view camera. Abbreviated SLR. – cámara flex de ojetivo simple

single-sheet proof Alternate term for *integral color proof*. – prueba integral

single-wall board Corrugated board with one sheet glued to the corrugation. Also called single-face board. – cartón con una cara plana

sinkage 1) Alternate term for *mottle*. 2) Extra-deep head margin often found on the first page of an article or chapter. – 2, margen superior extraordinario

16-page press Alternate term for full-web press. See *web press*.

size 1) (noun) Compound mixed with paper or fabric to make it stiff and less able to absorb moisture. Size makes a substrate better able to hold its shape and prevents ink from soaking in.
2) (verb) Alternate term for *scale*.

size coated paper British term for *film coated paper*.

skeleton black Alternate term for *shadow black*. – plancha para sombra

sketch Rough drawing. – bosquejo

skid 1) Shipping and selling unit of approximately 2,500 pounds of paper, in sheets. 2) Alternate term for pallet.

skinny 1) Alternate term for *choke*. 2) Characteristic of a photographic negative that has been reduced to drop out details in the background, thus providing space for a title or headline. A negative lacking detail because of overexposure or over-development may also be called skinny.

skin pack Alternate term for *blister card*. – envoltura

slack sized Paper treated with relatively small amount of size because it doesn't need to be especially water resistant, as compared to hard sized. Also called soft sized. – papel ligeramente encolado

sleeve Wrapping placed around a magazine to protect it while in the mail. Sleeves are open at both ends and usually made of brown kraft paper. – banda de papel, funda

slick 1) Magazine printed on glossy paper. 2) Alternate term for *flier* when printed on glossy paper.

3) Reproductions of logos, illustrations, or display ads ready to be added to mechanicals like clip art. – 1, revista; 3, reproducción

slick paper Alternate term for *gloss coated paper*. – papel glaseado

slide Transparency mounted for projection. Slides are most commonly made from 35mm transparencies. – diapositiva

slip case Box open at one end and made to hold a specific book or set of books so the spines show. – estuche para libros

slip proof Alternate term for *galley proof*. – prueba de galera

slip sheet Blank sheet put between newly-printed products to prevent setoff or scuffing. Also called interleaf.

A slip sheet may be put between many different items, such as between flats or pieces of working film to protect them during shipment. – hoja divisoria

slit 1) To cut paper using a disk or wheel. At the mill, reels are slit into smaller rolls. During printing, the web is sometimes slit into narrower ribbons. 2) Straight, die-cut line within a sheet. Slits form openings for insertion of tabs. – 1, cortar; 2, corte

slotted bind Alternate term for *burst perfect bind*. – encuadernación a la americana ranurada

slow film Film that requires a large amount of light (long exposure or large f/stop) to record an image, as compared to fast film. Film rated ISO 64 or under is considered slow. – película lenta

slow lens Lens incapable of being opened to a large aperture, thus preventing photography at short shutter speeds and/or using slow films, as compared to fast lens. – lente lento

SLR Abbreviation for *single lens reflex*.

slug 1) Line of type in address labels that stays constant for all addresses. For example, addresses on direct mail pieces often include the slug line 'or current occupant.' 2) Name of a typesetting job, repeated on all galley proofs. 3) Alternate term for *standing headline*. 4) Strip of metal used to space type set for letterpress printing. Slugs are six, 12, or 18 points thick. 5) Line of type set by a Linotype machine.

slur Defect in printing due to slight movement of the substrate, blanket, or plate at the instant that they contact each other. Slurred dots have slight tails or fuzzy trailing edges that make the overall image seem unsharp. – borrón

slurry Alternate term for *furnish*.

small caps Capital letters approximately the x-height of lower case letters in the same font. Used for logos and nameplates, and to soften the impact of normal caps. THIS LINE USES BOTH REGULAR CAPS AND SMALL CAPS. – versalitas

small computer system interface Connection method allowing a

overexposed   normal exposure, contrast   underexposed

flat, low contrast   high key, diffuse highlights

specular highlights   low key photograph

computer to control up to seven peripherals using a common control cable and command set. Common SCSI devices include hard disks, scanners, CD-ROM drives, and some printers. Abbreviated SCSI. Pronounced "scuz-zy."

small-format camera Camera using film 35mm or smaller. – cámara de formato pequeño

smooth finish The most level finish offered on offset paper. In Great Britain called machine finish. – acabado alisado

Smyth sew One pattern of sewing for casebinding.

SNAP Abbreviation for specifications for non-heatset web advertising printing, specifications recommended for web printing of free standing inserts on uncoated paper.

snappy Characteristic of a photo with strong contrast, as compared to soft. – buen contraste

snap set Multicopy business form with copies bound by a glue strip along one edge, making it easy to snap the set apart into individual copies. – forma separable

soft Characteristic of a photo with weak contrast, as compared to snappy. May also refer to a photo slightly out of focus, especially when lack of sharpness is deliberate. – blando

soft bind Alternate term for *perfect bind*. – encuadernación perfecta

soft copy Copy viewed on a computer screen, as compared

to hard copy. – copia en pantalla

soft cover Alternate term for *perfect bind* or *burst perfect bind.*

soft dots Halftone dots with fringes. Soft dots may be hardened by photographic techniques while duplicating the film or by etching. – puntos débiles

soft key Low-contrast black printer for four-color process printing. – impresora del negrote bajo contraste

soft photo 1) Photograph with slightly less than the desired contrast—not flat or washed out, but not quite satisfactory. 2) Photo deliberately made to suggest a restful or elegant mood. – 1 & 2, fotografía suave

soft proof Proof on a computer screen. – prueba en pantalla

soft sized Alternate term for *slack sized.* – encolado ligero

solid 1) Any area of the sheet receiving 100% ink coverage, as compared to a screen tint. An area of an image on film or a plate that will print as 100% coverage is also called a solid. 2) Type set with no leading. – 1, sólido; 2, compacto

sort 1) One character of metal type. 2) Alternate term for *pi character.* – 1, tipo; 2, carácter pi

soy-based inks Inks using vegetable oil to replace some petroleum products as pigment vehicles. – tintas con base de soya

space advertising Alternate term for *display advertising.* – anuncio con grafico

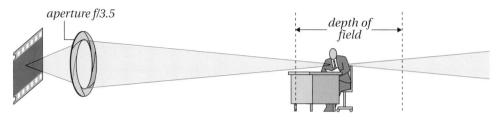

aperture f/3.5

depth of field

wide open aperture f/3.5 creates shorter depth of field

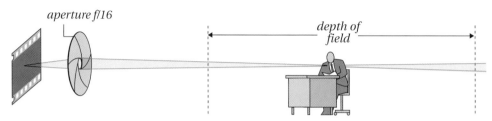

aperture f/16

depth of field

stopped down aperture of f/16 creates greater depth of field

55 mm at f3.5   *55mm at f16*

depth of field

25 ISO film   *3,200 ISO film*

grain

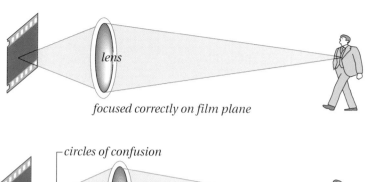

focused correctly on film plane

circles of confusion

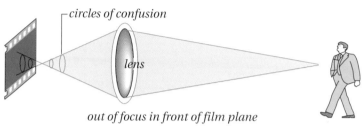

out of focus in front of film plane

focus

24 mm

55 mm

86 mm

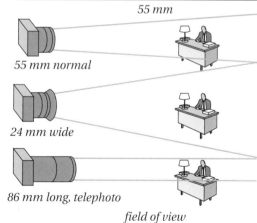

55 mm normal

24 mm wide

86 mm long, telephoto

field of view

lens format

spadia Advertising sheet designed to wrap halfway around another section. Spadias are most commonly seen folded around the comics in Sunday newspapers. – spadia

Spanish grass Alternate term for *esparto.*

SPC Abbreviation for *statistical process control.*

special effects General term for reproduction of photographs using techniques such as line conversion and posterization. – efectos especiales

special fourth class rate US Postal Service mail category giving discounts to published material, such as books and phonograph records. – precio especial de cuarta clase

specialty advertising Printed advertising on products such as coasters, mugs, matchbooks, jewelry, pencils, and playing cards. – publicidad de especialidad

specialty papers Carbonless, pressure-sensitive, synthetic, and other papers made for special applications. – papeles especiales

specialty printer Printer whose equipment, supplies, work flow, and marketing is targeted to a particular category of products. For example, a printer specializing in publications would typically have web presses and be organized to work with the schedules and delivery requirements of the publishing industry.

Specialty printers are known by product specialty, as in 'book printer.' Some common products that printers specialize in include advertising inserts, books, checks, direct mailers, envelopes, financial documents (stocks and bonds), forms, greeting cards, and publications (magazines and catalogs). – imprenta especializada

specifications Complete and precise written description of features of a printing job such as type size and leading, paper grade and quantity, printing quality, or binding method. Abbreviated specs.

Type specs define typeface, size, line measure, indentations, headlines, and other features of typography. Type size and leading are expressed as the upper and lower numerals in a fraction, with the points for leading measured baseline to baseline. Type 10/12 means 10-point type with twelve points of leading. Type 14/14 means 14-point type set solid.

Paper specs describe all paper required. Specifications for paper spell out eight requirements: quantity in number of sheets or by weight; size of sheets or rolls; grain direction; basis weight; color; brand name; finish; grade.

Film specs specify features such as film gauge, screen ruling, right or wrong reading, emulsion up or down, total area coverage, whether film should be loose or stripped, and whether the job prints sheetfed, web, or other printing method such as flexography.

Printing specs concentrate on press work, such as quantities, ink colors, and dot gains, but often include prepress, paper, and finishing. Printing specs might also refer to guidelines such as SNAP or SWOP.

Finishing specs range from very simple, such as telling folding requirements and trim size, to very complicated, such as when describing case binding that might also include a slip case. Finishing specs might also deal with additional printing methods such as die cutting or foil stamping. – especificaciones

specs Abbreviation for *specifications.*

spectrophotometer Instrument used to measure the index of refraction of color. – espectrofotómetro

specular highlight Highlight area with no printable dots, as compared to a diffuse highlight. Glare from chrome on an automobile would create a specular highlight in a photo. Illustrated on page 226. Also called catchlight and dropout highlight. – zona clara especular

SPI Abbreviation for *sheetfed paper identifiers.*

spine Bound edge of a publication. Also called backbone. – lomo

spine marks Alternate term for *collating marks.* – marcas del lomo

spiral bind To bind using a spiral of continuous wire or plastic looped through holes. Illustrated on page 16. Also called coil bind.
– encuadernación con espiral

spirit duplicate Method of printing that dissolves traces of carbon from a master to make each impression. Also called direct process duplicate, ditto, fluid duplicate, and hectography.

Spirit duplicators were popular with schools and other institutions because masters were inexpensive and easy to make and because the process lent itself to making just a few copies. – multicopiar al alcohol, hectografía

splice To join the end of one roll of paper with the beginning of another. In web printing, rolls are spliced without stopping the press. – empalmar

split fountain Technique of putting ink colors next to each other in the same ink fountain and printing them off the same plate to print more than one ink color from the same plate and inking unit. Split fountains keep edges of colors distinct, as compared to rainbow fountains that blend edges. – tintero dividido

split run 1) Different images, such as advertisements, printed in different editions of a publication. A split run of a city magazine might have different ads for urban and suburban editions.

2) Printing of a book that has some copies bound one way and other copies bound another way. A split run of 10,000 books might have 8,000 perfect bound and 2,000 casebound. – 1 & 2, tiraje dividido

unmanipulated image

burn, darken

dodge, lighten, brighten

retouching instructions

dodged and burned, retouched print

background

foreground

horizontal, landscape format

midtones   *highlights*   *shadows*

crop marks

cropped to vertical, portrait format

spoilage Paper which, due to mistakes or accidents, must be thrown away instead of delivered printed to the customer, as compared to waste.

Spoilage could result from poor conditioning, defective plates or blankets, poor presswork, poor operation of bindery equipment, or many other unintentional situations. It is different from waste, which is throwaway that printers anticipate and plan for as part of normal procedures. – estropear

sponsored publication Book, magazine, newsletter, or other publication paid for by the organization whose ideas, products, or services it describes. – publicación patrocinada

spot (verb) Alternate term for *opaque (2)*. – opacar

spot color 1) One ink color applied to portions of a sheet, as compared to flood or painted sheet. A red headline or blue logo is spot color on a page where all other images are black. 2) Alternate term for *flat color*. – 1, color en manchas; 2, color plano

spot glue Glue applied to portions of a sheet. – engomar en manchas

spot varnish Varnish applied to portions of a sheet, as compared to flood varnish. Spot varnishing is done to accent photos or create a pattern by printing a faint image. – barniz en manchas

spray powder Alternate term for *anti-offset powder*. – polvo secador

spread 1) Two pages that face each other and are designed as one visual or production unit. See also *printer spread* and *reader spread*.

2) Layout of several photos, especially on facing pages.

3) Technique of slightly enlarging the size of an image to accomplish a hairline trap with another image. A spread can be created photographically using a contact frame or digitally using image assembly software. Illustrated on page 60. Also called fatty. – 1, doble página; 3, ampliar

sprocket feed paper Alternate term for *pin feed paper*.

square back bind Alternate term for *flat back bind*.

square dot One of several shapes of dots available in halftone screens. Illustrated on page 218.

squeegee Tool used in screen printing to force ink through a screen onto the substrate. Illustrated on page 241. – racleta

squeegee paste Ink made for screen printing on glass. Also called screening paste.

SRA paper sizes One of five categories of ISO paper sizes. – tamaños de papel SRA

stabilization paper Paper for typesetting and contact prints that requires little processing. Output on stabilization paper begins to fade and turn brown in a few weeks. – papel de estabilización

stack advertisements Small display ads organized as a set, such as ads for movie theaters owned by one company. – anuncios en juego

stacked Alternate term for *gathered.*

stacked screen build See *build a color.*

stain To cover the edges of a book with ink to give them a marbled effect. – pintar

stair step Alternate term for *shingling.* – escalón

stamp Alternate term for *foil stamp.*

standard advertising units Pages and fractions of pages that newspapers sell to advertisers. Abbreviated SAU. – unidades estandar de anuncios

standard artwork Alternate term for *clip art.* – arte estandar

standard inspection report Form used by customers and vendors following SWOP guidelines.

standard offset color bar Alternate term for *color control bar.*

standard viewing conditions Background of 60% neutral gray and light that measures 5000 degrees Kelvin — the color of daylight on a bright day. Illustrated on page 79. Also called lighting standards.

Lighting conditions influence how people perceive colors. For that reason, graphic arts professionals use standard viewing conditions when inspecting comps, photos, proofs, and press sheets. Most studios, agencies, and printers have viewing areas that meet these conditions. – condiciones estandarizadas de observación

standing Refers to material or items kept available and ready to use, thereby saving the time and cost of preparing new elements for every job. A printer might keep standing type or film for a regular customer. An engraver might have standing dies available for a variety of common printed products. – pendiente de reimpresión

standing headline Headline whose words and position stay the same issue after issue. Headlines such as 'President's message' and 'This week in the garden' are often standing headlines. Illustrated on page 163. Also called slug. – título pendiente de reimpresión

standing pages Alternate term for *vertical format.* – formato vertical

starch-filled cloth Inexpensive cloth used to cover boards for casebound books. Starch fills the mesh openings to yield a smooth surface for coloring or stamping. – tela rellenada de almidón

star target Image developed by GATF to reveal doubling and slurring. Illustrated on page 62. – diana estrella

start character Character at the beginning of a bar code to signal the beginning and direction of scanning. – carácter inicial

stat Short for photostat, therefore a general term for an inexpensive photographic print of line copy or halftone. – fotoestática

stat camera Small process camera.
– cámara fotoestática

station Alternate term for *printing unit.* – mecanismo impresor

stationery Letterhead, envelopes, business cards, and other printed materials for correspondence. Also called business cabinet. – papelería membretada

statistical process control Method used by printers and other graphic arts professionals to understand and control production processes. Abbreviated SPC.

Statistical process control involves collecting numerical data about each step and all materials in the production sequence, then analysing the data to locate causes for variations. – control del proceso por estatísticas

Status T Response standard developed by ANSI and ISO for wide-band reflection densitometers. Adherence to Status T helps ensure accurate communication among all users.

steel engraving screen One of many special effect screens. – trama de grabado en acero

stencil Mask that blocks ink from getting onto the non-image area. The open area of a stencil forms the image. Stencils used in screen printing may be thought of as screen printing plates. Illustrated on page 241. – esténcil, plantilla

stencil knife Alternate term for *art knife.* – cuchilla de plantilla

stencil printing Method of printing using a plastic stencil wrapped around a rotating drum containing ink. As the drum rotates, centrifugal force pushes the ink to the outside of the drum, through the stencil, and onto the paper. Brand names for stencil printing machines include Gestetner and Mimeograph. – impresión con esténcil

stencil resist Resist created by a piece of film or paper, as compared to a photo resist. – protección del esténcil

step and repeat Prepress technique of exposing an image in a precise, multiple pattern to create a flat or plate. Images are said to be stepped across the film or plate. For example, a printer might plan to print an 8½ x 11-inch flier 4-up on a 17 x 22-inch sheet. One negative could be stepped to create the plate.

step exposure Technique of testing a variety of exposure times to determine the best exposure for a photographic print. Also called test strip. – exposición escalonada

step index Capital letters printed at the face edge of pages and visible when a book is closed because of stairstep cutouts in preceding pages. Illustrated on page 23. – índice escalonado

step wedge Alternate term for *gray scale.* – cuña escalonada

stet Proofreader mark for 'let it stand' instructing a typesetter to ignore an indicated change and keep the original version. – vale lo tachado

sticker Alternate term for *self-adhesive label*. – etiqueta engomada

stipple 1) Pattern of dots of various sizes. An illustration or photograph might be stippled as a special effect. Text or bond paper might have a stipple finish. 2) Technique of repairing portions of images on film by using a pointed instrument to erase (stipple out) unwanted emulsion. – 1, punteado; 2, puntear

stitch bind Alternate term for *saddle stitch*. – engrapado al lomo

stock 1) With regard to printing, alternate term for paper or other substrate. 2) With regard to paper-making, alternate term for *furnish*.

stocking merchant Paper distributor that maintains an inventory of commonly used papers. – distribuidor de papel

stocking papers Popular sizes, weights, and colors of papers available for prompt delivery from a merchant's warehouse. – papeles comunes

stock order Order for paper that a mill or merchant sends to a printer from inventory at a warehouse, as compared to a mill order. – pedido de almacen

stock photo Photograph from a collection available for commercial use, as compared to a photo taken on assignment. – fotografía en archivo

stop character Character at the end of a bar code to signal the computer to stop scanning. – carácter final

stop out British term for *mask*.

straight copy Copy that is all text with no charts, tables, formulas, or other elements that make typesetting complicated. – texto solamente

straight line screen Screen that converts continuous-tone copy to lines, as compared to halftone screen. Illustrated on pages 87. Also called line conversion screen. – trama de conversión a línea

streaking Defect on photographs or in printing that looks like water lines.
   Streaking on photographs may result from uneven application of chemicals or uneven drying. On printed products, streaking may result from uneven ink flow, poor balance between ink and water, uneven squeegee edge (in screen printing), defects in the substrate, and many other causes. – rayas

strength Alternate term for *chroma*.

stretch frame Frame made to pull screen printing fabric uniformly tight after it is secured to the inside. Also called frame. – marco para estirar

stretch ink Ink made to retain its approximate density and shape as it stretches with its substrate, such as a balloon. – tinta elástica

strike off Alternate term for *press proof*. – prueba de prensa

strike-on type Type made when the keys of a typewriter or the pins of a pin printer strike a ribbon to transfer an image to paper. In Great Britain called direct impression. – tipo de golpe

strike through Printing on one side of a sheet that is visible from the other side due to problems with ink, as compared to show through. Also called bleed through. – penetración de la tinta

string and button envelope Envelope designed for frequent use, such as for interoffice mail. Illustrated on page 209.

string score Score created by pressing a string against paper, as compared to scoring using a metal edge. String scoring is relatively gentle, thus less likely to crack coatings or fibers. – rayar con hilo

strip 1) To assemble images on film for platemaking. Stripping involves correcting flaws in film, assembling pieces of film into flats, and ensuring that film and flats register correctly. Also called film assembly and image assembly. In Great Britain called negative assembly. 2) Alternate term for *chrome strip* in gravure printing. – 1, montar

stripper Person who works in a stripping department.
   A stripper not only corrects and assembles negatives, but may also plan impositions, prepare proofs, make plates, and operate highly complex machines such as step-and-repeaters. – montador

stripping proof Alternate term for *composite proof*. – prueba de montaje

stripping table Alternate term for *light table*. – mesa de montaje

strip waste Paper near the outside of a roll that is unusable because of dirt or edge damage, as compared to core waste. – desperdicio de la orilla

strobe Alternate term for *electronic flash*. – flash electrónico

stub roll Alternate term for *butt roll*.

studio camera Alternate term for *view camera*. – cámara de estudio

stuffer Advertisement or bulletin printed on lightweight paper and intended to be enclosed (stuffed) with an invoice, such as a credit card or utility bill, or other regular mailing. – relleno

style Copyediting rules for treatment of such matters as titles, modes of address, and numerals. In Great Britain called style of the house. – estilo

style of the house British term for *style*.

style sheet Document containing rules for copyediting and typography to be used within an organization or for a publication. Style sheets may be printed documents or files within computer programs. – hoja de estilo

stylus Hard, pointed instrument shaped like a pen. Strippers use styluses to scribe on film and plates. – estilete

stylus printer Alternate term for *pin printer*. – impresora por puntos

subhead 1) Secondary headline set below the main headline to supplement its information. Also called deck. When the subhead is two or three sentences, it's a summary deck. **2**) Small heading within a story or chapter. Illustrated on page 164. Also called crosshead. – 1 & 2, subtítulo

subscript Character smaller than the text type in use and set to extend slightly below the baseline. Subscripts are usually numerals, such as the '2' in H_2O. Also called inferior character. – subíndice

substance weight Alternate term for *basis weight,* usually referring to bond papers. Also called sub weight. – peso base

substrate Any surface or material on which printing is done. – base

subtitle Phrase that amplifies or supplements information provided by a title. A book might have a subtitle printed on its cover; a chapter might have a subtitle; a newsletter might have a subtitle describing its goals and audience. Illustrated on page 162. – subtítulo

subtractive color Color produced by light reflected from a surface, as compared to additive color. Subtractive color includes hues in color photos and colors created by inks on paper. – color substractivo

subtractive primary colors Yellow, magenta, and cyan. In the graphic arts, these are known as process colors because, along with black, they are the inks used in four-color process printing. Illustrated on page 78. – colores primarios substractivos

sub weight Abbreviation for *substance weight.*

suede finish Alternate term for *dull finish.* – acabado mate

sulphate paper Paper made from pulp cooked in alkaline chemicals. Also called kraft paper. – papel sulfato

sulphite paper Paper made from pulp cooked in acid chemicals. Most medium quality printing and writing papers are sulphites. – papel sulfito

summary deck Two or three sentences that express the highlights of an article and that appear between the headline and the lead paragraph. Illustrated on pages 160 and 162. – resumen, sumario

supercalendered paper Paper calendered using chrome and fiber rollers to produce a smooth, thin sheet. Usually done to uncoated, groundwood papers for magazines, catalogs, and directories. *The Reader's Digest* is printed on supercalendered paper. Abbreviated SC paper. – papel supercalandrado

superior character Alternate term for *superscript.* – carácter superior

superscript Character smaller than the text type in use and set to start above the baseline. Superscripts are often numerals used for footnotes and in equations, such as the '2' in 10^2. They include symbols such as ™ and ®. Also called superior character. – exponente

supplement Separate section of a newspaper giving background on the news or dealing with special topics such as science or book reviews. – suplemento

supplied insert Insert that an advertiser has printed and sent to a publication rather than having it printed at the publication's facilities. Supplied inserts include order forms, blow-in cards, and bound-in signatures. – inserción surtida

surprint Alternate term for both *imprint (1)* and *overprint*.

swash Curved flourish on selected characters of a typeface. – adorno

swatchbook Book with samples of papers or ink colors. Also called sample book. – muestrario

SWOP Abbreviation for specifications for web offset publications, specifications recommended for film and proofs web offset printing using # 5 coated groundwood.

synthetic paper Plastic made into sheets that simulate paper.

Synthetic paper resists tearing and does not deteriorate when wet. Synthetic paper is used for envelopes, maps, field guides, instructions, and other products used under adverse conditions. It has no grain direction and may require printing with special inks. – papel sintético

system Collection of devices, techniques, and people operating with one goal.

Graphic arts professionals often refer to a system as the assembly of hardware and software used to make, correct, output, and store color separations. A production sequence or organized method, however, such as a pressroom or bindery, can also be thought of as a system. – sistema

System Brunner System of test forms, color control bars, and measuring devices.

system functions British term for *system software.*

system software Software that runs the computer itself, as compared to applications software and utility software. In Great Britain called system functions. – programa del sistema

screen printing

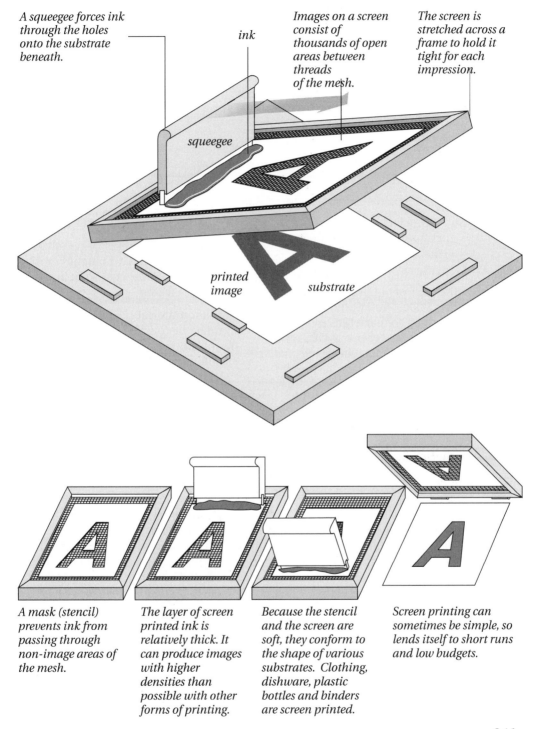

A squeegee forces ink through the holes onto the substrate beneath.

ink

Images on a screen consist of thousands of open areas between threads of the mesh.

The screen is stretched across a frame to hold it tight for each impression.

squeegee

printed image

substrate

A mask (stencil) prevents ink from passing through non-image areas of the mesh.

The layer of screen printed ink is relatively thick. It can produce images with higher densities than possible with other forms of printing.

Because the stencil and the screen are soft, they conform to the shape of various substrates. Clothing, dishware, plastic bottles and binders are screen printed.

Screen printing can sometimes be simple, so lends itself to short runs and low budgets.

T

TA Abbreviation for *typesetter alteration*. Sometimes alternate term for PE.

tab 1) (noun) Small projection along the edge of paper products such as files folders and notebook dividers. 2) (verb) To make tabs by diecutting. 3) (noun) Spot of glue ready to moisten for sealing a self-mailer. – 1, lengüeta

tab index Capital letters printed on tabs protruding from the foredge of a book. Illustrated on page 23. – índice de lengüeta

table Collection of information displayed in columns and rows. Tables are often used to present numerical data. – tabla

table of contents List of sections, such as chapters, and their beginning page numbers, appearing near the front of a book or magazine. – tabla de contenido

tablet Alternate term for *pad (2)*.

table tent Printed piece made of heavy stock , usually C1S cover, and used for displays. Illustrated on page 87. Also called counter card and tent card. – anuncio para mesa

tabloid 1) Newspaper or newsletter with trim size 11 x 17 inches or A3. 2) Newspaper specializing in gossip. – 1 & 2, tabloide

tabular material General term referring to charts, graphs, tables, and similar infographics, as compared to text copy. – material tabular

TAC Abbreviation for *total area coverage*.

tack The stickiness of ink.

Ink that is too tacky does not transfer easily to paper, thus can cause picking and other problems on press. Ink that is not tacky enough may dry too quickly, thus not yield a dense color.

Tack may be expressed as a number, with 9-12 being low tack, 13-17 medium or average, and 18-25 being high tack. – adherencia

tag Grade of dense, strong paper used for products such as badges and file folders. – etiqueta

tagged image file format Computer file format used to store images from scanners and video devices. TIFF files are compact and standard so they read efficiently on different brands of computers. Abbreviated TIFF. – formato de archivo de imagen etiquetada

tagline Slogan or comment that explains a logo. For example, the subtitle of a newsletter is often called a tagline. – subtítulo

tail 1) Alternate term for *trailing edge*. 2) Bottom of the spine of a casebound or perfect bound book. – 1, borde posterior; 2, cola

tailband Alternate term for *footband*.

tailpiece Dingbat or other symbol indicating the end of an article or chapter. – símbolo al final

tails British term for *foot of page*.

tall page Alternate term for *vertical format*. – formato vertical

tare weight Weight of packaging or of an empty container or vehicle. For a roll of paper, tare is the wrapper and core. Gross weight minus net weight equals tare weight. – peso del envase

target ink densities Densities of the four process inks as recommended for various printing processes and grades of paper.

Inks printed at the target densities yield the best gray balance and reproduce images with the greatest fidelity under the specific conditions for each situation.

Target densities for printing on newsprint are lower than for printing on the coated groundwood used by most magazines and catalogs. The highest target densities are for sheetfed printing on premium coated paper used for brochures and annual reports. See also *total area coverage*. – metas en densidades de las tintas

taster British term for *blad*.

TAW Abbreviation for throwaway. See *worstway*.

teacher's manual Guide for teachers using a specific textbook that helps teachers plan lessons and write tests based on that textbook. – manual para maestros

tear sheet Sheet removed or photocopied from a periodical and sent to advertisers, publishers, authors, and artists as notice of publication and evidence of satisfactory printing. – hoja arrancada

technical camera Alternate term for *view camera*. – cámara técnica

technical manual Alternate term for *manual*. – manual técnico

telephoto lens Camera lens that significantly magnifies objects, as compared to portrait lens and wide angle lens. On a 35mm camera, a telephoto lens has a focal length greater than 105mm. Illustrated on page 229. Also called long lens. – lente telefoto

template Pattern used to draw illustrations, make page formats, or lay out press sheets. A template may be a physical object that guides a pencil, an underlay for a light table, or a computer file with preset formats or outlines for the final printed piece. – plantilla

tender Alternate term for *estimate* and *quotation*. – presupuesto

tensile strength Measure of paper's ability to withstand pressure before pulling apart. – resistencia a la tensión

tent card Alternate term for *table tent*. – tarjeta de mostrador

terabyte One billion (1,000,000,000) kilobytes. – terabyte

terms and conditions Specifics of an order for printing that a printer and a customer make part of their contract.

Terms and conditions include requirements for payment and procedures for resolving disputes. Printers often print terms and conditions on the back of quotation forms to ensure that they are part of the agreement when a customer signs a form. See also *trade customs*. – términos y condiciones

testimonial Alternate term for *endorsement (1)*. – testimonio

test run 1) Press run intended to experiment with techniques and materials, as compared to a production run. 2) Direct mailers sent to a sample of the intended audience, as compared to roll out. – 1, tiraje de prueba; 2, entrega de prueba

test strip Alternate term for *step exposure*. – exposición escalonada

text 1) Main portion of type on a page, as opposed to elements such as headlines and captions. 2) Main

body of a book or similar publication, as opposed to supplemental sections such as bibliography and appendix. In Great Britain called body copy, body text. – 1 & 2, texto

text file Computer file consisting only of alphanumeric characters.

textbook Book that students are required to study as the most important reading material for the class. – libro de texto

text paper 1) Designation for printing papers with textured surfaces such as laid or linen. Some mills also use 'text' to refer to any paper they consider top-of-the-line, whether or not its surface has a texture. Illustrated on page 115.

Mills make text papers to ensure rich colors and superior printability. They come in a wide variety of colors and are often used for annual reports, announcements, brochures, and other products that require special attention and appearance. Text papers typically come in basis weights of 70# (104 gsm), 80# (118 gsm), and 100# (143 gsm).

2) Alternate term for *body stock*. – 1, papel texturado; 2, papel texto

text type Type used for text and captions, as compared to display type. Also called body type and composition type.

Text type is often considered any type smaller than 14 points. Authorities disagree about whether 14-point type is text or display size. In practice, it depends on context. Body copy set in 14-point type uses that type as text type. The same type used for subheads could be considered display size. – tipo texto

T4S Abbreviation for trim four sides, meaning to use a guillotine cutter to cut the paper square by trimming each side.

thermal proof Color output from a desktop computer using a thermal printer. – prueba térmica

thermal transfer Image that transfers from its backing to the product, such as a garment, under heat as well as pressure, such as a thermal release decal. Thermal desktop printers assemble four-color process images from dots of very thin film bonded by heat to the base paper. – transferencia térmica

thermography Method of printing using colorless resin powder that takes on the color of underlying ink. The powder is applied to wet ink so it bubbles and bonds to the paper when heated. Illustrated on page 246. Also called raised printing.

Thermography was developed to imitate engraving and is very popular for use on business cards and letterhead. The process can reproduce screen tints as well as line art. – termografía

thermoplastic binding British term for *perfect binding*.

thesaurus Alphabetical list of synonyms. – tesoro

thesis paper Alternate term for *acid-free paper*. – papel sin ácido

thick negative Photographic negative that appears dark (too dense) due to over exposure, over development, or both. Thick negatives produce washed out prints with poor highlights. – negativo oscuro

thin negative Photographic negative that appears pale (not dense enough) due to underexposure, underdevelopment, or both. Thin negatives produce dark prints with little shadow detail. – negativo pálido

third class mail US Postal Service classification for catalogs, brochures, and other advertisements that meet specific requirements. Also called bulk mail. – correo de tercera clase

threadless binding British term for *perfect binding*.

three-knife trimmer Machine that trims three sides of a printed piece in one operation. Binderies use three-knife trimmers to trim flush cover products such as magazines, catalogs, and perfect bound books. – guillotina trilateral

three-point register Register method on feeding unit of most sheetfed presses consisting of two headstops and one side guide. – registro de tres puntos

three-quarter web press See *web press*. – prensa de tres cuartos bobina

three-quarter tones In a photograph or illustration, tones created by dots approximately half way between shadows and midtones. – tres cuartos tonos

throwaway 1) Alternate term for *worstway*. 2) British term for *shopper*.

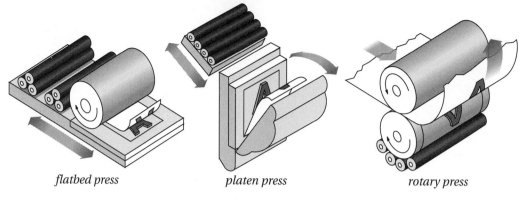

flatbed press *platen press* *rotary press*

letterpress

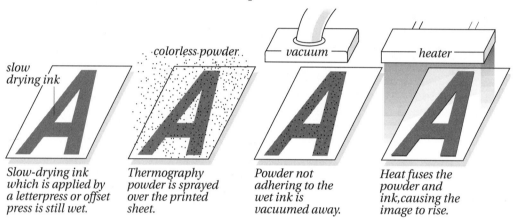

slow drying ink

colorless powder

vacuum

heater

Slow-drying ink which is applied by a letterpress or offset press is still wet.

Thermography powder is sprayed over the printed sheet.

Powder not adhering to the wet ink is vacuumed away.

Heat fuses the powder and ink, causing the image to rise.

thermography

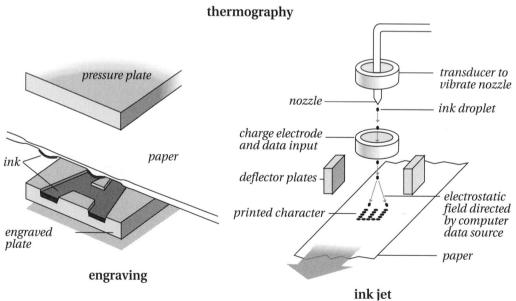

pressure plate

ink

paper

engraved plate

engraving

transducer to vibrate nozzle

nozzle

ink droplet

charge electrode and data input

deflector plates

printed character

electrostatic field directed by computer data source

paper

ink jet

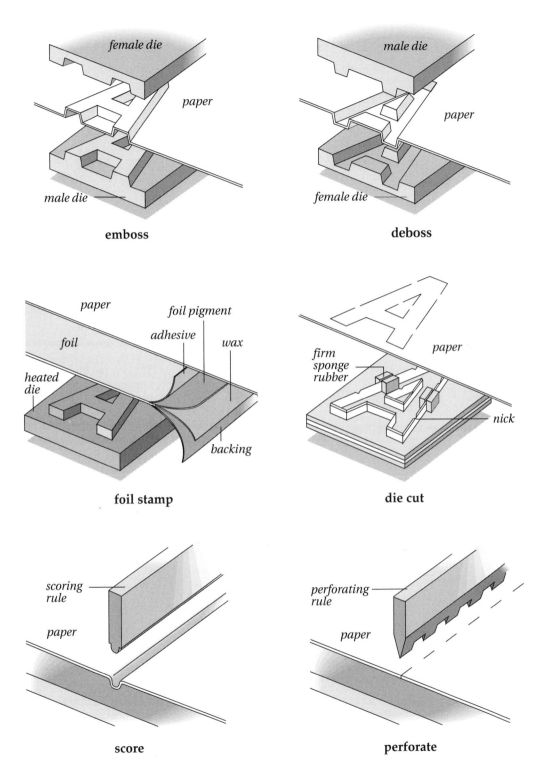

emboss

female die
paper
male die

deboss

male die
paper
female die

foil stamp

paper
foil pigment
foil
adhesive
wax
heated die
backing

die cut

paper
firm sponge rubber
nick

score

scoring rule
paper

perforate

perforating rule
paper

247

throwout British term for *foldout.*

thrust Alternate term for *creep.*
– deslizarse

thumb index Capital letters printed at the face edge of pages and visible when a book is closed because of cut-outs in preceding pages. Illustrated on page 23. Also called cut-in index. – índice recortado

thumbnail sketch Small rough sketch of a design. – dibujo en miniatura

ticket Small printed product showing price, schedule, and seating and used as proof of payment. – boleto

ticket envelope Long, thin envelope specifically for tickets. Illustrated on page 209. – sobre para boletos

tic marks Alternate term for *crop marks.* – contraseñas

TIFF Abbreviation for *tagged image file format.*

tight register Subjective term referring to nearly exact register. May mean register within half a row of dots, depending on the size of the dots and person using the term. For some printers, 'tight register' is not quite so demanding as 'hairline register.' For others, the terms are the same. Also called close register. See also *register.* – registro casi exacto

tin To bind by crimping a metal strip along one edge of the sheets. Tinning is commonly used to bind calendars. – estañar

tint 1) Alternate term for *screen tint.* 2) Hue made lighter by the addition of white, as compared to shade.
– 1, tono de la trama; 2, diluir

tint build See *build a color.*

tinted fiber paper Paper containing thousands of fibers dyed a variety of colors to contrast with the color of the base stock. Also called silurian paper. – papel de fibra coloreada

tip in To glue one edge of a sheet to a signature or another sheet. A coupon might be tipped into the cover of a brochure. A supplied insert might be tipped into a magazine. Also called on lay and tip on.
– engomar una orilla

tip on Alternate term for *tip in.*

tissue Thin, translucent paper used for overlays and slip sheets. Also called tracing paper. – papel mantequilla

title page Page at the beginning of a book bearing the full title, author's or editor's name, and the name of the publisher. – página de título

tombstone 1) Two headlines next to each other so that, at first glance, they appear to be one. 2) Advertisements with black borders, typically announcing mergers and other business transactions.

ton Measure of weight that can have one of three meanings: 2,000 pounds (short ton, used within the US), 2,240 pounds (long or Imperial ton, used within Canada and the United Kingdom), and 1,000 kilos (2,200 pounds, the metric ton used elsewhere in the world). Cargo travelling between countries is usually measured in metric tons, even if originating in a nation using another system. Also spelled *tonne*. – tonelada

tonal range Alternate term for *density range*. – gama tonal

tone 1) Alternate for *value* of a color. 2) Alternate for *screen tint*. – tono

tone break Defect in a graduated screen or a halftone. Tone breaks show as visible steps from one value to another where the value change should appear continuous. The problem is similar to fadeout, but can occur in shadows and midtones as well as in extreme highlights.

Tone breaks may appear when the wrong shape of halftone dots have been used or when an output device, such as an ink jet printer, has insufficient resolution to reproduce an image. When breaking occurs with non-impact printing, it may be called contouring. – cambio de tono

tone compression Reduction in the density range (tonal range) from original scene to printed reproduction.

Tone compression is unavoidable in the transition from original scene to photograph to printed product. It can, however, be taken into account to ensure the most satisfactory reproduction of the original scene.

Everyday scenes may have density ratios up to 1000:1, the difference between the lightest whites and the darkest blacks. The human eye can perceive this difference.

Photographs are limited to a ratio of approximately 100:1 and halftones to a ratio of approximately 20:1. The darkest blacks on press sheets are much lighter than on photographs or than in nature; the lightest whites on press sheets are much darker than in photos or nature.

Viewers notice loss of details in highlights more easily than in shadows. Tones in photos may be deliberately compressed to ensure faithful reproduction on press by reducing densities in shadows and holding densities in highlights.

Photographers wishing to compress tones take into account the paper on which the photo will be reproduced. As a rule of thumb, coated paper can reproduce photos having a four f/stop tonal range and uncoated paper can reproduce three f/stops. A four f/stop tonal range is approximately the same as a density range of 1.90; a three f/stop tonal range is about the same as a 1.20 density range. See also *density range* and *measured photography*. – compresión del tono

tone line Halftone special effect made using positive and negative films of the same image. – línea de tono

toner 1) Powder forming the images in photocopy and laser printing. 2) Powder or liquid forming the images in some color proofing systems. 3) Pigment or dye used to darken the value of an ink color. – 1 & 2, toner; 3, virador

toning Undesirable film of ink covering a printed sheet. Also called blush. When the thin ink coverage is intentional, it's an effect called an accent tone. – virado

tonne Alternate spelling for *ton.*

tool Alternate term for both *emboss* and *deboss.* – estampar

tooth Rough surface of paper finishes such as antique or vellum and of papers made for drawing. Such surfaces are called 'toothy,' as in "this vellum paper seems especially toothy." Also called bite. – dentado

total area coverage Total of the dot percentages of the process colors in the final film. Abbreviated TAC. Also called density of tone, maximum density, shadow saturation, total dot area, total dot density, and total ink coverage.

Color separators and printers compute total area coverage by adding CMYK dot percentages in areas of dark shadow. For example, if CMYK each equal 75%, total area coverage equals 300%. If all four process colors were printed solid, total area coverage would be 400%.

Many publications, especially those printed on relatively porous paper such as newsprint, specify a total area coverage of approximately 250%. This maximum helps ensure that shadow areas hold detail. Coverage specifications for coated paper are typically 300% to 325%. – área total cubierta

total dot density Alternate term for *total area coverage.* – área total cubierta

total ink coverage Alternate term for *total area coverage.* – área total cubierta

touch plate Plate that accents or prints a color that four-color process printing cannot reproduce well enough or at all. Touch plates are usually on the fifth inking unit. For example, a touch plate might carry red to make apples seem more real. Also called kiss plate. – plancha de toque

tough check paper Strong paperboard made for products such as tickets and tags. – papel fuerte

tower Alternate term for *printing unit.* – mecanismo impresor

tracing paper Alternate term for *tissue.* – papel para dibujar

track To increase or decrease space between all characters in a line, paragraph, or document. Also called character compensation and, incorrectly, track kerning.

Tracking adjusts the space between characters according to rules that take into account the size of the type and the optical traits of each character. It is different from both letterspacing and kerning.

Tracking improves legibility by increasing space between small characters and decreasing space between large characters. It may also be used to copyfit. – proporcionar

track ball Ball that, when rotated, controls the cursor on a computer screen. Also called control ball. In Great Britain called trackerball. – bola de control

tracker ball British term for *track ball.*

tracking Printing flaw caused by guide wheels on presses that pick up ink from wet sheets and leave traces on sheets that follow. Also called marking. – manchar

track kerning British term for *track*.

trade book Book sold to the general public in bookstores, as compared to more specialized books such as textbooks. – libro comercial

trade camera service Alternate term for *camera service*.

trade customs Business terms and policies codified by trade associations such as Printing Industries of America. There are trade customs in the graphic arts for color separators, printers, and typesetters.

  Trade customs have no legal standing. They are industry guidelines, thus are starting points for information appearing on quotations and contracts. Many customers and their vendors negotiate slight changes to suit specific business needs. See also *terms and conditions*. – normas

trade journal Magazine published for people in a specific business or profession, as compared to a consumer magazine. – revista para un oficio

trademark Word, mark, symbol, figure, or name used to distinguish products of one manufacturer or merchant from those of others. A trademark is designated by the symbol ™.

  Trademarks may be registered with the government in the country where the product will be distributed in order to ensure exclusive use of the trademark by its owner. Registered trademarks are designated by the symbol ®. – marca registrada

trade paperback Paperback book manufactured using better paper and printing than a mass market book. Quality paperbacks are usually sold only in bookstores, as compared to newsstands and supermarkets. – libro en rústica comercial

trade shop Service bureau, printer, or bindery working primarily for other graphic arts professionals, not for the general public. – taller para un oficio

trade tolerance Percent of overs or unders considered acceptable by both customer and vendor when ordering paper or printing.

  The tolerance depends on the size and complexity of the job. With press runs shorter than 10,000 copies, trade customs suggest that a 10% variation is acceptable. With longer press runs, 5% or even 3% may be a more appropriate tolerance. – tolerancias

trailing edge Edge of a sheet opposite the gripper edge, thus passing through the press last. Also called leave edge and tail. – borde posterior

train Series of mechanisms that perform a task in sequence. For example, printers call the series of rollers that deliver ink to the blanket the ink train. – tren

tranny Alternate term for *transparency*. – transparencia

transfer lettering Alternate term for *dry transfer lettering.*

transfer screens Screen tints made of the same materials as dry transfer lettering and applied to mechanicals using the same techniques. – tramas transferibles

transfer type Alternate term for *dry transfer lettering.* – letras transferibles

translite Transparent film, glass, or plastic that is lit from behind and used for signs and displays. Translites may be painted, screen printed, or made photographically. Also called transparency. – transparencia

translucent Able to allow light through but not allowing clear images or sharp edges to be seen, as compared to transparent. – translúcido

transmission densitometer Densitometer that measures the amount of light transmitted through film and other materials. – densitometro de transmisión

transparency 1) Positive photographic image on film allowing light to pass through. A 35mm slide is a transparency mounted for projection. Also called chrome, color transparency, and tranny. Often abbreviated TX. Illustrated on pages 72 and 75. 2) Alternate term for *translite.* – 1, transparencia

transparency film Photographic film made to produce transparencies, as compared to print film. Films whose brand names end in 'chrome,' such as Ektachrome and Fujichrome, are transparency films. – película para transparencias

transparent Easily seen through, such that images on the far side are clear and distinct, as compared to translucent. – transparente

transparent copy Products, such as transparencies, viewed by light passing through them, as compared to reflective copy. – copia transparente

transparent ink Inks using a transparent base that allows other colors to show through. Most printing inks are opaque. Process inks must be transparent for the CMYK halftone dot patterns to simulate colors. – tinta transparente

trap 1) To print one ink over another or to print a coating, such as varnish, over an ink. The first liquid traps the second liquid. A second ink that covers a first ink without bleeding is considered properly trapped. This form of trapping is often called ink trapping. See also *dry trap* and *wet trap.* 2) To create hairline overlaps to ensure that colors trap, so appear registered. Hairline traps can be created using chokes or spreads. This form of trapping is often called image trapping. Illustrated on page 60. – 1 & 2, atrapar

T Ref Control image used to verify that a wide-band densitometer is calibrated to Status T values.

trial proof Alternate term for *press proof.* – prueba de prensa

triangle Tool used with a t-square for drawing angles accurately. These tools typically have one 90-degree angle and either two 45-degree angles or one 30-degree and one 60-degree angle. – triangulo

trichromatic British term *tritone (2)*.

trim To cut blank paper, press sheets, folded products, or bound products to the required size. – cortar

trim marks Lines on mechanicals, films, plates, or press sheets to show where to cut edges off paper or where to cut pieces apart after printing. – marcas de corte

trim size Alternate term for *finished size*. – tamaño final

tritone 1) Black and white photo reproduced using three ink colors, usually two blacks and a gray. 2) Pastel color reproduced using magenta, cyan, and yellow, but no black. In Great Britain called trichromatic. 3) Any image reproduced using three ink colors. – 1-3, tritono

TRUMATCH Swatching System Color specifying system using the four process colors to create 2,000 colors arranged according to hue, saturation, and brightness.

T square T-shaped tool with a long blade and head perpendicular to the blade. Used for drawing straight and parallel lines. – regla T

tungsten light Alternate term for *incandescent light*.

turnaround time Amount of time needed to complete a job or one stage of a job. – tiempo de vuelta,

turnkey system Computer system consisting of hardware, software, training, and support, thus ready at the time of installation to begin working for its owner. – sistema llave de mano

turning bar Roller or bar set to turn paper over as it goes through a web press. – barra de inversión

tusche Black, waxy liquid used to create a stencil on a printing screen or to add small amounts of image on a lithographic plate. – retoque

two-color printing Printing with two different colors of ink. Black is considered a color, so two-color printing could use black and brown inks, or blue and red, or any other two colors. – impresión bicolor

two-point perspective Three-dimensional objects illustrated so that opposite lines seem to end at two spots in the distance. Illustrated on page 195. – perspectiva de dos puntos

two-tone paper Alternate term for *duplex paper*. – papel de doble tono

two up See *up (1)*.

TX Abbreviation for *transparency*.

type Letters, numerals, punctuation marks, and other symbols produced by a machine and which will be reproduced by printing. – carácter tipográfico

type area British term for *live area*.

typeface Set of characters with similar design features and weight. Garamond Light is a typeface. Illustrated on page 255. Also called face. – ojo del tipo

type family Group of typefaces with similar letter forms and a unique name. Garamond, including all weights and styles such as light, semibold, and bold italic, is a type family. Illustrated on page 255. Also called family of type. – familia de tipos

type gauge British term for *line gauge.*

type overlay Overlay on a mechanical or film separation that carries some or all of the type.

A type overlay is used to change text while keeping the rest of the image the same. For example, catalog prices that are expected to change might be on an overlay so that they can be easily changed without having to produce an entirely new mechanical.
– superpuesta de texto

type series Complete range of sizes of one typeface. – serie de tipos

typesetter 1) Machine that sets photo type or hot type. 2) Person who operates a typesetting machine. Also called compositor.
– 1, componedora; 2, compositor

type shop Typesetting business.
– taller de composición

type size Height of a typeface measured from the top of its ascenders to the bottom of its descenders, expressed in points. Illustrated on page 259. In Great Britain called body. – medida de tipo

type specimen book Book of printed samples of type families and typefaces offered by a type shop or a type font company. – muestrario de tipos

type style Characteristic of a typeface such as bold, italic, or light. Illustrated on page 255. – estilo de tipos

type weight Boldness of a typeface, such as light, book, or ultrabold. Illustrated on page 255. – peso de tipos

typewriter Machine that produces type on paper when a keystroke makes a relief character strike an inked ribbon. – máquina de escribir

typo Abbreviation for *typographical error.*

typographical error Error attributed to a mistake while keystroking instead of to poor spelling or grammar. Also called misprint after being printed. In Great Britain called literal. – error tipográfico

typography 1) The art and science of composing type to make it legible, readable, and pleasing. 2) The arrangement of type on a page.
– 1 & 2, tipografía

Tyvek Brand name of synthetic paper used for envelopes.

Roman *Italic* Book

Outline **Shadowed**

style

Light Regular

Bold **Ultrabold**

weight

Condensed Expanded

width

Avant Garde Bodoni Futura Helvetica Palatino
Berkeley Courier **Garamond** **Melior** **Times**

typeface

abcdefghijklmnopqrstuvwxyz
ABCDEFGHIJKLMNOPQRSTUVWXYZ 123456789)(*&^%$#@!?><.,'"'";:

type font

Bodoni Book Bodoni Regular **Bodoni Bold**
Bodoni Book Italic *Bodoni Italic* **Bodoni Ultra Bold**

type family

U

UC Abbreviation for upper case, used as a proofreader's instruction to capitalize a character.

UCA Abbreviation for *undercolor addition.*

UCR Abbreviation for *undercolor removal.*

ultrabold type Type that is heavier than bold. Illustrated on page 255. Also called black type. – letra ultranegra

Ultrakote Brand name for UV coating.

ultraviolet coating Liquid applied to a printed sheet, then cured with ultraviolet light. UV inks and coatings have a high gloss. UV coatings are thicker and more durable than varnish or aqueous coatings. Ink jet printing does not adhere well to UV coating and UV coating must be applied over inks designed to trap the coating. In Great Britain called uv varnish. – baño ultravioleta

uncalendered paper Paper not smoothed by calendering. – papel no calandrado

uncoated paper Paper that has not been coated with clay. Illustrated on page 202. Also called offset paper.

Mills produce uncoated paper with a variety of surfaces. Vellum and antique are rough; English and smooth are level. They also rate uncoated paper as #1, #2, #3, and commodity. Higher rated stock has better ink holdout, more brightness, and better opacity than stock with a lower rating.

Uncoated paper comes in a wide range of basis weights, from 26# (40 gsm) for reference books and statement stuffers to 80# (120 gsm) for cookbooks and calendars. Many printers use #2 offset in 60# (90gsm) as a house sheet for products such as bulletins and newsletters. Uncoated paper comes in a wide variety of colors. – papel no estucado

uncompensated stack Bundles or stacks on a pallet that are stacked uniformly, as compared to brick packed. – montón no compensado

undercolor addition Technique of making color separations that increases the amount of cyan, magenta, or yellow ink in shadow areas. Usually done to make blacks look darker, thus increasing tonal range. Abbreviated UCA. – adición del color de fondo

undercolor removal Technique of making color separations such that the amount of cyan, magenta, and yellow ink is reduced in midtone and shadow areas while the amount of black is increased. Abbreviated UCR.

UCR reduces problems with wet trapping and increases control over shadow areas. – reducción del color de fondo

underdevelop To leave film, photo paper, or a printing plate in developing chemicals for too little time or to develop in weak chemicals. – revelar insuficiente

underexpose To prevent enough light from reaching film, photo paper, or a printing plate. Illustrated on pages 82 and 226. – exposición insuficiente

underline 1) Rule placed under a line of type: this line is underlined. Also called underscore. 2) Alternate term for *caption*. – 1, subrayar; 2, leyenda

underlying page Alternate term for *master page*. – página patrón

underrun Quantity of paper or printing delivered that is less than the quantity ordered. If a mill order called for 100,000 pounds of paper and only 95,000 pounds were delivered, the buyer received a 5% underrun. See *trade tolerance* for guidelines for underruns and overruns on printing jobs. – tiraje corto

underscore Alternate term for *underline*. – subrayar

underside British term for *wire side*.

Uniform Product Code 12-digit bar code printed on retail products to enable scanners to read prices and keep inventory records. Abbreviated UPC and available from the Uniform Code Council in Dayton, Ohio.

union bug Nickname for the logo of the labor union whose members printed a specific product. – logotipo del sindicato

unit cost The cost of one piece produced during a print run.

Unit cost is computed by dividing the total cost of the job — variable costs plus fixed costs — by the quantity of products delivered. For example, if the fixed costs for 10,000 posters were $2,400 and the variable costs were $5,300, the total costs were $7,700. The unit cost for the 10,000 posters is 77¢. – costo unitario

unit spacing Alternate term for *equal spacing*. – espaciacado equitativo

universal film Separations that printers can use to make plates for more than one method of printing, such as offset or gravure.

unsharp masking Technique of making a halftone or separation appear sharper (in better focus) than the original photo or the first proof. Also called edge enhancement and peaking.

Unsharp masking adjusts dot size along edges where one tone changes to another, making some dots larger and some smaller. The result is edges with increased contrast between their light and dark sides, improving the sharpness of the overall image.

Scanner operators achieve unsharp masking while making color corrections and other improvements to scanned images. They may also use the technique to eliminate harsh lines that define the inset image when assembling images on a computer screen. – enmascar para mejorar la nitidez

up 1) Term to indicate multiple copies of one image printed in one impression on a single sheet. 'Two up' or 'three up' means imposing the identical piece twice or three times on the same flat.

2) Functioning, as compared to down. A press working properly is up; a broken press is down. – 1, a la vez, 2, en función

UPC Abbreviation for Uniform Product Code.

uplink To send information from an earth station up to a satellite, as compared to downlink. – trasmisión vía satélite (tierra a satélite)

upload To receive data at a host computer from a client computer or peripheral, as compared to download. – cargar

uppercase letters Alternate term for *capital letters*. Called uppercase because of the way that metal type was arranged in cases (trays). The upper case contained capital letters, while the lower case contained small letters. Illustrated on page 259. – letras mayúsculas

upstairs 1) Upper half of a newspaper page, as compared to downstairs. 2) Alternate term for *vertical format*. – 1, mitad superior; 2, formato vertical

up style Typographic format for headlines using capitals to start each word, thus ignoring rules of grammar, as compared to down style. – estilo de mayúsculas

up time Time that a machine or system is working properly, as compared to down time. – tiempo productivo

user guide Alternate term for *manual*. – manual

UV coating Abbreviation for ultraviolet coating.

uv varnish British term for *uv coating*.

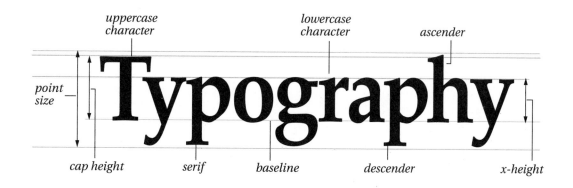

uppercase character · lowercase character · ascender

point size

cap height · serif · baseline · descender · x-height

serif type · san serif type

28 points baseline to baseline

Leading is the space between lines of type

26-point type set with 2 points leading

leading

points · picas · ciceros

47 pt. type picas · 47 pt. type ciceros

type measurement

36 points

36 points

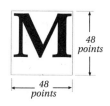

48 points

48 points

an em is used to measure individual type characters. A 36-point em is a 36-point square

V

vacuum frame Device that uses a vacuum to draw materials, such as film and plates, tightly against each other. Used for making contact prints, duplicate film, proofs, and plates. Also called platemaker.
– prensa de vacío

value The shade (darkness) or tint (lightness) of a color. Also called brightness, lightness, shade, and tone. Illustrated on page 79. – valor

Vandyke Alternate term for *blueline*.

vanity press Book publisher that requires authors to pay the costs of publishing. – publicación por vanidad

variable contrast paper Photographic print paper whose contrast changes depending upon filters used when printing. – papel de contraste variable

variable costs Costs of a printing job that change depending on how many pieces are produced, as compared to fixed costs. Costs for paper, printing, and binding are examples of variable costs. – costos variables

variable information printing Reproduction using a laser printer, commercial laser copier, ink jet system, or other device imaged by a computer.

Variable information printing allows instant changes in content. For example, individualized messages, such as advertising targeted at special audiences, might be printed using ink jet while the machine also prints addresses.
– impresión de información variable

varnish Liquid applied as a coating for protection and appearance. In Great Britain called lacquer.

Varnish is applied by a press, either in line with printing inks or on a separate pass to allow for dry trapping. It comes in dull and gloss finishes and is usually clear. See also *flood varnish* and *spot varnish*.

Printers may add varnish to ink to increase or reduce tack and reduce chalking. These substances are sometimes called additive varnishes to distinguish them from over-printing varnishes. – barniz

Velo Bind Brand name for binding that passes plastic prongs through holes in a stack of paper and fuses them to plastic strips on both sides of the stack.

vellum bind To bind using soft leather or vellum paper.
– encuadernación en vitela

vellum bristol Bristol paper with a vellum finish. – papel Bristol avitelado

vellum finish Somewhat rough, toothy finish; smoother than antique, rougher than English.
– acabado avitelado

vellum paper 1) Paper made to resemble the feel and color of leather. 2) Translucent paper used for tracing. – 1 & 2, papel vitela

velour finish Alternate term for *dull finish.* – acabado terciopelado

Velox Brand name for high-contrast photographic paper. Halftones on Velox paper are made by contact printing halftone negatives. The word 'Velox,' however, is often used referring to PMTs and Photostats as well as true Velox prints.

velvet finish Alternate term for *dull finish.* – acabado terciopelado

verso Alternate term for *left-hand page*, as compared to recto.
– página izquierda

vertical bar code Bar code aligned parallel to height. Also called ladder code. – código de barras vertical

vertical format Upright format on a computer screen, page, or printed product, as compared to horizontal format. Also called magazine format, portrait format, standing page, tall page, and upstairs. Most publications are printed in vertical format. Illustrated on page 233.
– formato vertical

VGA Abbreviation for *video graphics array.*

vibration Unpleasant visual effect caused when two colors that are next to each other on the color wheel, such as red and purple, appear next to each other on a printed piece. The colors are said to vibrate. Also called pop.
– vibración

video graphics array Computer board supporting a monitor that displays up to 256 colors or 64 shades of gray at 800 x 600 resolution, as compared to lower resolution CGAs and EGAs.

view camera Camera that allows the photographer to focus the scene on ground glass mounted in the camera, as compared to rangefinder camera and single lens reflex camera. Also called studio camera and technical camera.

View cameras use medium or large format film. They are used in studios and other settings where photographers carefully compose scenes and plan exposures. – cámara de vista

viewing booth Small area or room that is set up for proper viewing of transparencies, color separations, or press sheets. Also called color booth. See also *standard viewing conditions.*

Viewing booths may be found at most agencies, publishers, service bureaus, and printers that deal with color. At some printers, the viewing area for press sheets may be a properly lighted table near a press instead of an actual booth or room. – cabina de inspección

viewing conditions See *standard viewing conditions.*

vignette 1) Ornamental border on part of a title page. 2) Alternate term for *graduated screen tint.*
– 1 & 2, viñeta

vignette halftone Halftone whose background gradually and smoothly fades away. Also called dégradé.
– mediotono viñeteado

virgin paper Paper made exclusively of pulp from trees or cotton, as compared to recycled paper. – papel virgen

visible spectrum Range of light, from red to violet, that humans can see.

The visible spectrum does not include infrared or ultraviolet light.
– espectro visible

visiting card Alternate term for *business card.* – tarjeta de presentación

visual British term for *rough layout.*

visual editor Person who checks and corrects photographs, illustrations, graphics, and color for inconsistencies, inaccuracies, and conformity to style requirements, as compared to a copy editor. – editor visual

vita Alternate term for *résumé* used by people in academic professions.
– curriculum vitae

VOC Abbreviation for volatile organic compounds, petroleum substances used as the vehicles for many printing inks.

voucher Free copy of a magazine given to an advertiser as evidence that ads were printed correctly.
– copia complementaria

fi

fl

ligatures

We slept most all day, and started out
at night, a little ways behind a monstrous
long raft that was as long as going by a
procession. She had four long sweeps at
each end, so we judged she carried as
many as thirty men, likely. She had five
big wigwams aboard, wide apart, and an
open campfire in the middle, and a tall
flagpole at each end.

    There was a raftsman on a craft such
as that. Near the wheel house we could
see hammocks strung out for taking the
night air. From time to time some one
would venture out to see what they were
passing by on the river bank, but
otherwise, she was just gliding by.

2 em indent

We slept most all day, and started out at
night, a little ways behind a monstrous
long raft that was as long as going by a
procession. She had four long sweeps at
each end, so we judged she carried as
many as thirty men, likely. She had five
big wigwams aboard, wide apart, and an
open campfire in the middle, and a tall
flagpole at each end.

    There was a raftsman on a craft
such as that. Near the wheel house we
could see hammocks strung out for
taking the night air. From time to time
some one would venture out to see what
they were passing by on the river bank,
but otherwise, she was just gliding by.

no initial paragraph indent

Wa

not kerned

Wa

kerned

We slept most all day, and started out at
night, a little ways behind a monstrous
long raft that was as long as going by a
procession. She had four long sweeps at
each end, so we judged she carried as
many as thirty men, likely. She had five
big wigwams aboard, wide apart, and an
open campfire in the middle, and a tall
flagpole at each end.

There was a raftsman on a craft such as
that. Near the wheel house we could see
hammocks strung out for taking the
night air. From time to time some one
would venture out to see what they were
passing by on the river bank, but
otherwise, she was just gliding by.

no indent, additional space

We slept most all day, and started out at
   night, a little ways behind a
   monstrous long raft that was as long
   as going by a procession. She had four
   long sweeps at each end, so we judged
   she carried as many as thirty men,
   likely. She had five big wigwams
   aboard, wide apart, and an open
   campfire in the middle, and a tall
   flagpole at each end.
There was a raftsman on a craft such as
   that. Near the wheel house we could
   see hammocks strung out for taking
   the night air. From time to time some
   one would venture out to see what
   they were passing by on the river
   bank, but otherwise, she was just
   gliding by.

hanging indent

T ommy Barnes was asleep
now, and when they waked
him up he was scared, and
cried, and said he wanted to
go home to his ma and didn't
want to be a robber.

raised cap

T ommy Barnes was
asleep now, and when
they waked him up he
was scared, and cried,
and said he wanted to
go home to his ma and
didn't want to be a
robber.

hanging character

T ommy Barnes was
asleep now, and when
they waked him up he was
scared, and cried, and said
he wanted to go home to his
ma and didn't want to be a
robber.

dropped cap

W

wall Side of an engraved image or cell on a gravure cylinder. – pared

wallet envelope Envelope shaped like a business envelope, but made with a larger flap and from heavier paper. – sobre cartera

warm colors Yellows, oranges, and reds that suggest warm places or scenes, as compared to cool colors. Warm colors have higher color temperatures than cool colors. – colores cálidos

washed out Characteristic of printing or a photograph whose images appear faded. Washed out printing results from poor ink coverage. Washed out photos result from overexposure or overdevelopment. – decoloración

wash up To clean ink and fountain solutions from rollers, fountains, and other press components. – lavar

waste Unusable paper or paper damaged during normal make-ready, printing, or bindery operations, as compared to spoilage.

Waste is expressed as a percent of the paper needed to produce the quantity specified. If a job calls for 10,000 sheets and the printer anticipates 4% waste, the order is placed for 10,400 sheets.

The amount of waste anticipated for a specific job depends on many factors. Some general expectations are: shorter press runs produce a higher percentage of waste than longer ones; web printing yields more waste than sheetfed printing; waste increases with number of colors printed, complexity of bindery operations, and quality expectations.

The terms 'spoilage' and 'waste' are often used as synonyms, but they mean different things. Printers anticipate waste and plan for it when buying paper. They do not anticipate spoilage, which results from defects, mistakes, alterations, or other circumstances that might have been prevented. – desperdicio

WatchPrint Brand name for integral proofing system for printing on newsprint.

water balance See *ink/water balance.*

water-base inks Inks that may

264

be washed up using water, as compared to oil-based inks.
– tintas con base de agua

water fountain Reservoir that holds fountain solution on a lithographic press. Also called dampener fountain. In Great Britain called damper. – mecanismo mojador

watermark Translucent logo in paper created during manufacture by slight embossing from a dandy roll while paper is still approximately 90% water. – marca de agua

waterproof ink Ink that will not run or smear when wet. – tinta resistente al agua

waterproof paper Paper containing relatively high quantity of sizing to resist wrinkling when moist. – papel resistente al agua

water rollers Rollers, on an offset press, that control the flow of fountain solution to the printing plate. Also called dampening rolls. Illustrated on page 167. – rodillos mojadores

water spot Printing defect caused when water falls onto the blanket or plate, causing weak ink coverage. – mancha por agua

wavy edges Edges of sheets of paper in a stack or bound into a book that are not straight because the paper absorbed moisture. – bordes ondulados

wax 1) Sticky substance used to stick type and other elements to mounting boards during pasteup.
Graphic arts wax melts at a low temperature and spreads evenly. It remains pliable when cool so that elements easily lift from the mounting board for repositioning.
2) Substance added to ink and varnish to aid scuff resistance and add tack. Wax turns varnish from clear to slightly yellow and can cause bubbles under film lamination and foil stamping.
– 1 & 2, cera

waxer Device for melting and spreading wax used for pasteup.
– encerador

web Printing paper threaded from a roll through a web press. Also called ribbon. – banda

web break Tearing of the paper as it travels through a web press, causing operators to rethread the press.
– ruptura de la banda

web gain Unacceptable stretching of paper as it passes through the press.
– estirones de la banda

web press Press that prints from rolls of paper, usually cutting it into sheets after printing. Illustrated on page 179. Also called reel-fed press.
Web presses come in many sizes. Some common categories are:
form webs For printing business forms, direct mailers, catalog sheets, stationery, and other products whose flat trim size is typically 8½ x 11 inches. Form webs use rolls 8½-10 inches wide.
mini webs For printing brochures, newsletters, and other products whose flat trim size is typically 11 x 17 inches. Mini webs use rolls 11-14 inches wide.

half webs For printing 8-page signatures whose flat trim size is typically 17 x 22 inches. Half webs use rolls 17-20 inches wide and are also called mid-sized webs.

three quarter webs For printing 8-page signatures whose flat trim size is typically 17 x 22 inches. Three-quarter webs use rolls 22 -27 inches wide. Also called 8-page webs.

full webs For printing 16-page signatures whose flat trim size is typically 23 x 35 inches. Full webs use rolls 35-40 inches wide. Also called 16-page webs.

Web presses may use any of the common methods of printing with ink, such as flexography, gravure, letterpress, lithography, and screen. – prensa de bobina

wedding paper Thick, soft, glare-free paper that is easy to emboss. – papel para bodas

weight, of paper See *basis weight.*

weight, of tint Relative lightness or darkness of a screen tint as affected by dot loss or gain.

weight, of type Relative lightness or darkness of characters. The weight of type typically ranges from light through medium, semibold, bold, and ultrabold. Medium weight, sometimes called book weight, is the standard darkness to which other weights are compared. – negrura del tipo

well 1) Tiny cavity to hold ink in a gravure cylinder. Also called cell and cup. Illustrated on page 117.

2) Portion of a magazine containing its primary editorial matter. – 1, hueco

well post Point at which the walls of more than two wells on a gravure cylinder meet.

wet-on-wet British term for *wet trap.*

wet trap To print ink or varnish over wet ink, as compared to dry trap. Wet trapping allows printing of two or more inks on just one pass through a press instead of using additional passes after ink has dried. In Great Britain called wet-on-wet. – atrapar con tinta fresca

white light Light used in standard viewing conditions; 5,000 degrees Kelvin in North America, 6,500 degrees Kelvin elsewhere. – luz blanca

white out British term for *copyfit (2).*

whiteprint Proof that is a paper print of an image on film, such as a PMT or Velox. – prueba de papel impreso

white space Area of a printed piece that does not contain images or type. Also called negative space. – espacio en blanco

wholesaler Alternate term for *distributor.* – mayorista

wide angle lens Camera lens whose field of view is wider than the eye can normally see, as compared to telephoto lens. On a 35mm camera, a wide angle lens has a focal length less than 40mm. Illustrated on page 229. Also called short lens. – lente granangular

wide page Alternate term for *horizontal format.* – página ancha

wide web paper Alternate term for *grain short paper*, referring to a sheet cut from the web against the grain. – papel con fibra a lo corto

widow See *orphan.*

wild art Photograph, graphic, or other visual element standing alone, not accompanied by text other than a caption. – arte sin texto

wild formation Relatively irregular, clumped distribution of fibers in paper. – formación irregular

window 1) In an envelope, a clear section through which material inside the envelope can be seen. Used with business forms designed so that the shipping address shows through.

2) In a printed product, a die-cut hole revealing an image on the sheet behind it.

3) On a mechanical, an area that has been marked for placement of a piece of artwork. The area might be designated by keylines or with masking material, such as Rubylith. When photographed using graphic arts film, a window made using masking material (dark area) creates a window on the film (transparent area). Halftones or other visuals are stripped into windows on film.

4) On a computer screen, a rectangular area in which information appears or in which a photograph or illustration will be placed. – 1-4, ventana

Wire-O binding Brand name for method of mechanical binding using double loops of wire.

wire printer Alternate term for *pin printer.* – impresora por puntos

wire side Side of the paper that rests against the Fourdrinier wire during papermaking, as compared to felt side. In Great Britain called underside.

Watermarks are wrong reading when viewed from the wire side. Paper packaged in sheets has the wire side down. When using bond papers, writing and printing should be done on the felt side, opposite the wire side. – lado del alambre

with the grain Parallel to the grain direction of the paper being used, as compared to against the grain. See also *grain direction.* – al sentido de la fibra

woodfree paper Alternate term for *free sheet.* – papel sin madera

word processing To create and edit documents using a computer word processing program or system. – procesamiento de palabras

word processor Computer program specifically for writing and editing documents. – procesador de palabras

word spacing Spacing between words. Normal word spacing is ⅓ em. Illustrated on page 270. In Great Britain called interword spacing. – espaciado entre palabras

work and back Alternate term for *sheetwise.*

work and flop Alternate term for *work and tumble.* – imprimir y voltear a lo largo

work and roll Alternate term for *work and tumble.* – imprimir y voltear a lo largo

work and tumble To print a sheet so that the same combination of images is printed on both front and back using the same set of plates. The sheet is tumbled end over end for the second pass. Also called print and tumble, work and flop, and work and roll.

Work and tumble uses opposite gripper edges.

Both work and turn and work and tumble, as compared to sheetwise, save time and money by reducing makeready and materials. – imprimir y voltear a lo largo

work and turn To print a sheet so that the same combination of images is printed on both front and back using the same set of plates. The sheet is flipped side to side for the second pass. Also called print and turn. In Great Britain called half-sheet work. Work and turn uses the same gripper edges. – imprimir y voltear a lo ancho

work and twist To print a sheet so that half of one side of the sheet is printed, then the other half of the same side. – imprimir y girar

workbook A book or booklet that contains both lessons and exercises for use in a class. – cuaderno de trabajo

work for hire Writing, illustration, photography, or other creative work for which the creator agrees that the client owns the copyright to the finished product. – trabajo para alquilar

working Alternate term for *pass*. For example, "Print varnish on a second working" is the same as saying "Print varnish on a second pass." – pasada

working film Intermediate film that will be copied to make final film after all corrections are made. The copying is done to place as many images as possible on just one composite film. Also called buildups. In Great Britain called intermediates. – película de trabajo

working proof Any proof marked up for changes. – prueba marcada

work order Alternate term for *job ticket.* – pedido de trabajo

work print Low quality photograph marked for cropping and other changes before the final product is produced. Work prints are also used to indicate the position of images on mechanicals. – fotografía usada para marcar

WORM Acronym for write once read many times. WORMs are optical discs that permanently store information.

worstway Loose halftones or proofs made without attention to quality and used for position only. Worstways from separators are similar to outtakes from photographers. Also called throwaway. – worstway

wove finish Somewhat smooth, slightly patterned finish on bond paper. – acabado tejido

wraparound 1) Four pages with a signature nested into it, as compared to an insert. Also called outsert and, when covering a publication in the mail, cover wrap. 2) Alternate term for *runaround*. – 1, funda; 2, arracada

wrap around fold Alternate term for *letter fold*. – doblado carta

wrapping paper Paper printed with festive designs and used to wrap gifts. – papel para envolver

write to fit Writing and editing so the resulting words fit the space available. – escribir consciente del espacio

writing paper Alternate term for *bond paper*. – papel bond

wrong reading An image that is backwards when compared to the original. Also called flopped and reverse reading. – lectura invertida

WYSIWYG Acronym for what you see is what you get, the ability of a computer screen to reproduce closely what appears on the output device. Pronounced "wiz-e-wig."

We slept most all day, and started out at
night, a little ways behind a monstrous long
raft that was as long as going by a
procession. She had four long sweeps at
each end, so we judged she carried as many
as thirty men, likely. She had five big
wigwams aboard, wide apart, and an open
campfire in the middle, and a tall flagpole at
each end. There was a raftsman on a craft
such as that. Near the wheel house we could
see hammocks strung out for taking the
night air. From time to time some one would
venture out to see what they were passing by
on the river bank, but otherwise, she was just
gliding by.

centered

We slept most all day, and started out at
night, a little ways behind a monstrous long
raft that was as long as going by a
procession. She had four long sweeps at
each end, so we judged she carried as many
as thirty men, likely. She had five big
wigwams aboard, wide apart, and an open
campfire in the middle, and a tall flagpole at
each end. There was a raftsman on a craft
such as that. Near the wheel house we could
see hammocks strung out for taking the
night air. From time to time some one would
venture out to see what they were passing by
on the river bank, but otherwise, she was just
gliding by.

**flush left,
ragged right**

We slept most all day, and started out at
night, a little ways behind a monstrous long
raft that was as long as going by a
procession. She had four long sweeps at
each end, so we judged she carried as many
as thirty men, likely. She had five big
wigwams aboard, wide apart, and an open
campfire in the middle, and a tall flagpole at
each end. There was a raftsman on a craft
such as that. Near the wheel house we could
see hammocks strung out for taking the
night air. From time to time some one would
venture out to see what they were passing by
on the river bank, but otherwise, she was just
gliding by.

justified

We slept most all day, and started out at
night, a little ways behind a monstrous long
raft that was as long as going by a
procession. She had four long sweeps at
each end, so we judged she carried as many
as thirty men, likely. She had five big
wigwams aboard, wide apart, and an open
campfire in the middle, and a tall flagpole at
each end. There was a raftsman on a craft
such as that. Near the wheel house we could
see hammocks strung out for taking the
night air. From time to time some one would
venture out to see what they were passing by
on the river bank, but otherwise, she was just
gliding by.

**flush right,
ragged left**

letterspacing can be adjusted
normal letterspacing

wordspacing can be adjusted
normal wordspacing

letterspacing can be adjusted
increased letterspacing

wordspacing can be adjusted
increased wordspacing

letterspacing

wordspacing

X-Y-Z

X-ACTO knife Brand name of art knife.

xerocopy paper Alternate term for *copier paper.* – papel para copias

xerography Technical name for *photocopy.* – xerografía

x height Vertical height of a lower-case x in a typeface. X height varies from one typeface to another. Illustrated on page 259. Also called body height. – altura x

yapp bind To bind using a soft material so that rounded corners may hang over edges of a book. Yapp binding is used to protect gilded edges on products such as bibles and dictionaries. – encuadernación yapp

yearbook Book with photos of students and their activities during a school year. Also called annual. – anuario

yellowing Slow change in color of white paper caused by the environ-ment or age. Groundwood papers yellow much faster than free sheets. Also called color reversion. – amarilleo

yellow pages Classified directories published for telephone customers that are printed on yellow, light-weight, groundwood paper. – páginas amarillas

yellow printer Flat, plate, or ink station that controls the yellow ink in four-color process printing. Illustrated on pages 72. – plancha amarilla

z-fold Alternate term for *accordion fold.* – doblado en z

zig zag fold Alternate term for *accordion fold.* – doblado en zigzag

ZIP code Acronym for *Zone Improve-ment Plan code,* five numerals that identify every post office and substation in the US. – código postal

ZIP plus four Five-digit ZIP code plus four additional numerals giving carrier route information. – código postal más cuatro dígitos

zoom lens Lens in a camera or copy machine that can be adjusted to various focal lengths along a continuum, thus can enlarge or reduce images. – lente zoom

Spanish index

Spanish to English index

a la vez
up (copias)

abarquillamiento
curl

abarquillamiento del núcleo
core curl

abrir
open up

absorción
absorption

acabado alisado
smooth finish

acabado avitelado
vellum finish

acabado cáscara de huevo
eggshell antique
eggshell finish

acabado de alto brillo
high finish

acabado de fieltro
felt finish

acabado de máquina
machine finish

acabado de plato
plate finish

acabado estampado
embossed finish

acabado imitación cabritilla
kid finish

acabado inglés
English finish

acabado lino
linen finish

acabado martelé
cockle finish

acabado mate
dull finish
flat finish
low finish
matte finish
suede finish

acabado mármol
marble finish

acabado ondulado
ripple finish

acabado satinado
satin finish

acabado tejido
wove finish

acabado terciopelado
velour finish
velvet finish

acabado verjurado
laid finish

acentos
accent marks

acercamiento proporcional
character compensation

acercamiento
close up

acetato
acetate

acomodar
fit

acoplar
kern

adaptador gráfico a color
color graphics adapter

adaptador para gráficos mejorados
enhanced graphics
adapter

adherencia
tack

adición del color de fondo
undercolor addition

adorno
swash

aerógrafo
aerograph
airbrush

ágata
agate

agenda
agenda

agente
agent

agrupar piezas para correo
co mail

al sentido de la fibra
with the grain

alambre Fourdrinier
Fourdrinier wire

albertipia
albertype
collotype

álbum
album

alimentador
feeder

alimentador de hojas
feeding unit

alineación
alignment (texto)
jog
range

alineación de caracteres
character alignment

alineado a la derecha
flush right
quad right

alineado a la izquierda
flush left
quad left

alineado centrado
quad centre

almacenar en paletas
palletization

almacenes de memoria
media (computadora)

almanaque
almanac

alteración
alteration

alteración del autor
author alteration

alteración del cliente
customer alteration

alto contraste
high contrast

altura de mayúscula
cap height

altura x
body height
x height

alzado
gathered
stacked

amarillento
color reversion

amarilleo
yellowing

amarillo de proceso
process yellow

amarrar
counter stack

ambas caras
double faced

amolado
grindoff

ampliación
enlargement

ampliadora
camera lucida
enlarger

ampliar
blow up
spread (imagen)

análisis de preexploración
prescan analysis

anchura de composición
set size

anchura total
full measure

anexo
addendum

anexo publicitario
back-of-the-book

ángulos de trama
screen angles

anillo de Newton
Newton ring

anillo suelto
loose ring

anteportada
bastard title
half title

antiperfil dentado
anti-alaising

antología
anthology
omnibus

anuario
annual
yearbook

anuncio clasificado
classified advertising

anuncio con gráfico
display advertising
space advertising

anuncio para mesa
table tent

anuncio para puerta
door hanger

anuncio tipo sandwich
sandwich board

anuncios en juego
stack advertisements

anverso
recto

apaisado
broadside

apéndice
appendix
back matter
end matter

apilamiento
piling

apilar como ladrillos
brick pack

aplicación
application

arcillas
fillers (en papel)

archivo
archive
file
morgue

archivo EPS
EPS file

archivo PostScript encapsulado
encapsulated
PostScript file

área abierta
open area (fotografía)

área activa
live area
safe area

área de la copia
copy area

área de la imagen
image area

área de puntos
dot area

área de tipo
type area

área sin imagen
non-image area

área total cubierta
density of tone
total area coverage
total dot density
total ink coverage

arracada
runaround
wraparound (texto)

arreglar
assemble
make up (acción)

arreglos
makeready
setup

arrollado permanente
roll set

arte compuesto
composite art

arte de líneas
line art

arte escogida
pickup art

arte estandar
standard artwork

arte final
art
artwork

arte listo para cámara
finished art

arte original
original art

arte preseparado

preseparated art
separated art

arte sin texto
wild art

artes gráficas
graphic arts

artículo
column

artículos publicitarios
advertising specialties

artista de arte final
production artist

artista de bocetos finales
mechanical artist
pasteup artist

asignación
allocation

asociar
associate
marry

atascarse
clogging

atlas
atlas

atrapar
trap

atrapar con tinta fresca
wet trap

atrapar con tinta seca
dry trap

atrapar la tinta
ink trap

aumento de precio
markup

auto guardas
self ends

autobiografía
autobiography
memoirs

autocubierta
self cover

autor
author

autorización
model release
property release
release

avería
crash (evento)
scrim

aviso del copyright
copyright notice

azul no reproducible
dropout blue
fade-out blue
non-reducing blue
non-repo blue

balance de la tinta
ink balance

balance del agua
water balance

balance del color
color balance

balance entre tinta y agua
ink/water balance

banda
ribbon
web

banda al pie
tailband

banda de papel
sleeve

banda de pie
footband

bandas laterales de apoyo
bearer bars (en la prensa)

bandera
banner (anuncio)
flag (tela)

banderola
pennant

baño acuoso
aqueous coating

baño infrarojo
infrared coating
IR coating

baño ultravioleta
ultraviolet coating
UV coating

barata
close out

barba del papel
deckle edge

barniz
varnish

barniz brillante
gloss varnish

barniz en manchas
spot varnish

barniz mate
dull varnish
matte varnish

barniz ultravioleta
UV varnish

barra de colores
color bar
color control bar
color guide

barra de inversión
turning bar

barras guías
bearer bars (código de barras)

base
substrate

base de datos
database

bastidor de cierre
chase (marco)

bastidor de contacto
contact frame

baudio
baud

bibliografía
bibliography

bisagra
hinge

bisel
bevel

bit
bit

bitono
duotone

bitono de dos negros
double black duotone

bitono falso
dummy duotone
duograph
fake duotone
false duotone

blanco de impresión
impression target

blanco de resolución
resolution target

blando
soft

bloc de hojas
pad

bloqueado
blocked up (productos)
blocking

bobina
reel

boceto
artwork
mechanical

boceto base
base
base art
base mechanical

boceto de impresor
printer's layout
ruleout

boceto de página
page layout

boceto definitivo
comprehensive layout

boceto final
artboard
pasteup (producto)

boceto final de línea
line mechanical

boceto final duro
hard mechanical

boceto final electrónico
electronic mechanical

boceto preliminar
rough
rough layout

bola de control
track ball
tracker ball

boletín
bulletin
newsletter

boletín interno
house organ

boleto
ticket

bolsa
bag

bolsa del supermercado
shopping bag

bolsa para etiqueta
label holder

bolsa plástica
plastic wrap

bolsa plástica transparente
polybag
polywrap

bolsillo
pocket

bond para mimeógrafo
Mimeograph bond

bono
bond (certificado)

borde adelgazado
feather edge

borde de avance
pitch edge

borde de contacto
butt fit

borde de corte
butt line

borde de encuadernación
grind edge

borde de pinzas
bite
gripper edge

borde frontal
leading edge

borde posterior
tail
trailing edge

bordes dorados
gilding

bordes ondulados
wavy edges

borrador
draft

borrón
slur

borroso
halation (imagen)

bosquejo
esquisse
layout sheet
sketch

bosquejo suelto
loose sketch

brillantez
brightness

brillo
brightness
gloss

brillo de la tinta
ink gloss

bristol marfil
ivory bristol

bromuro
brom
bromide

bruñir
burnish

buen contraste
snappy

buffer
buffer

bulto
bundle

burbuja
bubble

byte
byte

cabecera
flag (de periódico)
headband
header
nameplate

cabeza
head

cabeza de clavo
nailhead

cabezada
headband

cabina de inspección
color booth
viewing booth

caja
box (contenedor)
carton
frame (gráficos)

caja California
California job case

caja incompleta
broken carton

caja para observación
light box (viewing)

caja sombreada
shadow box

caja tipográfica
case (para tipos)

calandrar
calender

calcomanía
bumper sticker
decal

calcomanía simplex
simplex decal

calcular
copyfit

calendario
calendar

calibración del texto
cast off

calibre
caliper

calidad
quality

caligrafía
calligraphy

callejón
alley

cámara de estudio
studio camera

cámara de formato grande
large-format camera

cámara de formato mediano
medium format camera

cámara de formato pequeño
small-format camera

cámara de fotoreproducción
copy camera
graphic arts camera
process camera

cámara de vista
view camera

cámara digital
digital camera

cámara electrónica
electronic camera

cámara flex de objetivo simple
single lens reflex camera

cámara fotoestática
stat camera

cámara lucida
lucy

cámara técnica
technical camera

cambiar de tamaño
scale (verbo)

cambio de color
color shift

cambio de orden
change order

cambio de tono
tone break

campo
field

campo visual
field of view

canto
face (libro)

capa
layer
ply

capa de fondo
prime coat

capacidad de cubrir
coverage

capítulo
chapter

carácter
character

carácter de control
control character

carácter final
stop character

carácter inicial
start character

carácter pi
sort

carácter saliente
hanging character

carácter superior
superior character

carácter tipográfico
type

caracteres pi
pi characters

caracteres por pulgada/pica
characters per inch/pica

caracteres por segundo
characters per second

carga total de un furgón
carload

cargar
upload

caricatura
cartoon

carpeta
binder (cubierta)
folder (producto)
job jacket
memo book

carpeta de anillos
ring binder

carpeta de hojas sueltas
loose-leaf binder

carpeta de presentación
presentation folder

carta
letter

carta de recibido
acknowledgement

carta informativa
announcement

cartel
bill
poster

cartel de mostrador
counter display

cartel para autobuses
car sign

cartel publicitario
billboard

cartera de presentación
presentation wallet

cartilla
primer

cartografía
cartography

cartón
box
corrugated board
paperboard

cartón con dos caras planas
double-faced board
double-walled board

cartón con una cara plana
single-faced board

cartón de yute
jute board

cartón incompleto
less carton

cartón ondulado sencillo
single-wall board

cartón tamaño mediano
junior carton

cartoncillo
chipboard

cartucho tratado
coated cartridge

cartulina
blank
board paper
card stock
cardboard
case board
packaging paper (board)
paperboard

cartulina ahulada
car sign board

cartulina de alineación
lineup board

cartulina de combinación
combination board

cartulina de ferrocarril
railroad board

cartulina índice
index board

cartulina para boceto final
pasteup board

cartulina para carteles
poster board

cartulina para cubiertas
cover board

cartulina para encuadernación
binder's board

cartulina para montaje
mounting board

cartulina pegada
pasteboard

cáscara de naranja
orange peel

casi calidad de carta
near-letter-quality

cassette
cassette

catágolo
catalog

caucho
blanket (mantilla)

cavidad
cell

cegado
blinding

celda
cell

celofán
cellophane

centrado
center spread
center truck

centro óptico
optical center

cera
wax

certificado
certificate

cian
cyan

cianotipo
blueprint

cicero
cicero

cien libras
hundredweight

cilindro
cylinder

cilindro de mantilla
blanket cylinder

cilindro de plancha
plate cylinder

cilindro impresor
impression cylinder

circuito impreso
printed circuit

circular
bill (cartel)
circular
flier
handbill
leaflet

circular volante
flyer

circulo
balloon

cita
pull quote

clave
key (guía)

clisé
cut (ilustración)

CMYK
CMYK

código de barras
bar code

código de barras avanzado
advanced bar code

código de barras horizontal
horizontal bar code

código de barras vertical
ladder code
vertical bar code

código de identificación de serie
serial identification code

código postal
postal code
ZIP code

código postal mas cuatro dígitos
ZIP plus four

cojinete para el ratón
mouse pad

cola
tail (de un libro)

colateral
collateral

colilla del rollo
butt roll
stub roll

colofón
colophon

color aditivo
additive color

color base
base color

color de alta fidelidad
high fidelity color

color del texto
color, typographic

color en manchas
spot color

color fijo
color fast

color natural
natural color

color opaco
flat color (mate)

color plano
block color
flat color (una tinta)

color satisfactorio
pleasing color

color substractivo
subtractive color

coloración del borde
edge coloring
edge enhancement

colores cálidos
warm colors

colores complementarios
complementary colors

colores de cuatricromía
process colors

colores de la tierra
earth colors

colores fríos
cold colors
cool colors

colores independientes de aparatos
device independent colors

colores no reproducibles
non-reproducible colors

colores Pantone
Pantone Colors

colores pasteles
pastel colors

colores primarios
primary colors

colores primarios aditivos
additive primary colors

colores primarios substractivos
subtractive primary colores

colores secundarios
secondary colors

columna
column (texto)

columnas salientes
hanging columns
scalloped columns

collage
collage

combinar
merge

combinar/depurar
merge/purge

compacto
solid (texto)

compaginación
page makeup

compendio
abridgement
compendium

componedora
typesetter (máquina)

componer
compose (texto)

composición
composition (de texto)

composición compacta
set solid

composición electrónica de imagen
electronic image assembly

composición electrónica de página
electronic page assembly

composición en frío
cold type

composición no útil
dead matter

composición válida
live matter

compositor
typesetter (persona)

compositor tipográfico
compositor

compresión de datos
data compression

compresión del tono
tone compression

computadora personal
personal computer

común
commodity

concordancia
concordance

concha
shell

condiciones de observación
lighting standards
standard viewing conditions
viewing conditions

conjunto de tarjetas
card deck

consolidar
amalgamate
consolidate

construcción del color
build a color
color build
stacked screen build
tint build

constructura de planchas
platemaker (máquina)

contador
counter

contaminación de color
color cast

contenedor
container

contenido de humedad
moisture content

contra la fibra
across the grain
against the grain
cross direction
cross fold
cross grain

contraer
choke
shrink
skinny

contramatriz
male die

contramatriz acuñadora
force card

contraseñas
tic marks

contraste
contrast

contraste de impresión
print contrast

contraste mate
flat contrast

control del proceso por estadísticas
statistical process control

conversión de datos
data conversion

convertidor
converter

coordinación de pliegos
sheet matching

copia
copy (duplicado)
print

copia complementaria
review copy
voucher

copia de producción
production copy

copia de seguridad
backup copy

copia de tonos continuos
continuous-tone copy
contone

copia directa positiva
direct positive copy

copia en pantalla
soft copy

copia fotográfica R
R print

copia impresa
hard copy

copia limpia
clean copy
fair copy

copia lista para cámara
camera-ready copy

copia para inspección
inspection copy

copia para reproducir
repro
reproduction copy

copia por contacto
contact print

copia reflexión
reflective copy
reflex copy

copia sobrecompuesta
overset copy

copia sucia
dirty copy

copia transparente
transparent copy

copia verde
green copy

copiadora
copier

copiar
cloning
copy

copias por adelantado
advance copies

corrección con parche
patch correction

corrección del color
color correct

correcciones del editor
blue pencil

corrector del texto
copy editor

corregir
clean up
proofread

correo de cuarta clase
fourth class mail

correo de primera clase
first class mail

correo de segunda clase
second class mail

correo de tercera clase
third class mail

correo directo
direct mail

correo en bulto
bulk mail

cortado al ras
cut flush

cortar
slit
trim

corte
slit

corte de canto
  face cut

corte del color
  break for color
  color break

corte irregular
  bastard cut

coser
  sew

cosido Smyth
  Smyth sew

costo unitario
  unit cost

costos fijos
  fixed costs

costos variables
  variable costs

costura de estremo
  cleat bind
  cleat sew

cromado
  chrome plating

cromo
  chrome

crónica
  feature

croquis
  comprehensive dummy
  layout sheet

cruces de registro
  cross marks

cruzado
  crossover

cuaderno de trabajo
  workbook

cuadrado
  quad

cuadratono
  quadratone

cuadrícula
  grid

cuarta encuadernación
  quarter bound

cuarto
  quarto

cuarto oscuro
  darkroom

cuartos tonos
  quarter tones

cuatricomía
  color process printing
  process printing

cubierta
  brief cover
  cover

cubierta blanda
  soft cover

cubierta de bisagra
  hinged cover

cubierta de cerillos
  matchbook cover

cubierta de informe
  report cover
  service cover

cubierta de un álbum
  album cover

cubierta exacta
  flush cover

cubierta plus
  plus cover

cubierta rígida
  hard cover

cubierta sobresaliente
  overhang cover

cuchilla
  scalpel
  stencil knife

cuchilla para frasqueta
  frisket knife

cuchilla para montaje
  art knife
  pasteup knife

cuchilla tangente
  doctor blade
  flood bar

cuchilla X-ACTO
  X-ACTO knife

cuenta
  count

cuentahilos
  linen tester

cuento
  comic book

cuerpo tipográfico
  point size

cumplimiento
  fulfillment

cuña
  quoin

cuña escalonada
  step wedge

cupón
  coupon

curado
  season

curar
  condition
  cure
  mature

curriculum vitae
  vita

cursiva
cursive

cursor
cursor

chapa
plate (libro)

chorro
blast

datos en bruto
raw data

de cabeza a cabeza
head-to-head

de cabeza a pie
head-to-tail

decoloración
washed out

dedicado
dedicated

dedicatoria
dedication

default
default

deficiencia de tinta
ink starvation

definición
definition

delimitador
delimiter
precedence code

densidad
density

densidad al secar
dryback

densidad de la trama
screen density
screen percentage

densidad del código de barras
density, of bar code

densidad máxima
maximum density

densitómetro
densitometer

densitómetro de reflexión
reflection densitometer

densitómetro de transmisión
transmission densitometer

dentado
bite (papel)
tooth

derechos
rights

derechos de autor
copyright

derechos de publicación
serial rights

descargar
download

descripción resumen
design brief

descromar
dechrome

descuento en volumen
price break

deslizarse
creep
feathering
thrust

desperdicio
waste

desperdicio de la orilla
strip waste

desperdicio del centro del rollo
core waste

desvanecer
dodge

desvanecerse
fadeout

determinador de la trama
screen determiner

diafragma
aperture

diagrama de flujo
flow chart

diana estrella
star target

diapositiva
slide

diazo
diazo

dibujo con medidas
dimension drawing

dibujo en miniatura
thumbnail sketch

dibujo para inspección
inspection drawing

dibujos recortados
clip art

diccionario
dictionary

diccionario geográfico
gazetteer

diente de sierra
sawtoothing

digitalizar
digitize

diluir
tint

dimensión x
x dimension

diploma
diploma

dirección de la fibra
grain direction

dirección de máquina
machine direction

director de arte gráfico
art director

directorio
blue book
directory

disco compacto interactivo
CD-I

disco duro
hard disk

disco flexible
floppy disk

disco magnético
magnetic disk

disco óptico
optical disk

disco rígido
rigid disk

diseñador gráfico
graphic designer

diseño gráfico
graphic design

diseño modificado
makeover

diseño modular
modular design

disparador de cable
cable release

dispersograma
scattergram

dispositivo de salida
output device

disquete
diskette

distancia focal
focal length

distribuidor
distributor
jobber

distribuidor de papel
paper distributor
stocking merchant

divisor
divider

dígito
digit

doblado carta
letter fold
wraparound fold

doblado continuo
barrel fold

doblado de ángulo recto
right angle fold

doblado de cuatro paneles
four-panel fold

doblado de imagen
doubling

doblado de puerta
gate fold

doblado de puerta doble
closed gate fold
double gate fold

doblado de rollo
roll fold

doblado de signatura
signature fold

doblado doble paralelo
double parallel fold

doblado en z
z-fold

doblado en zig zag
zig zag fold

doblado francés
French fold

doblado mapa
map fold

doblado paralelo
parallel fold

doblado tipo acordeón
accordion fold
concertina fold
fan fold

dobladora
folder (máquina)

doble cara
double faced

doble exposición
double exposure

doble página
spread (diseño)

doble página central
natural spread

documento
document

dos a la vez
two up

duplicado
dupe
duplicate

duplicado directo
direct process duplicate

edición
edition
issue
press run (tiraje)

edición demográfica
demographic edition

edición electrónica
desktop publishing

edición limitada
limited edition

editado de pixel
pixel editing

editor
editor
publisher

editor visual
visual editor

editorial
editorial
lead (en un artículo)

efecto halo
halation
halo effect

efectos especiales
special effects

ejemplar de cortesía
desk copy
examination copy

ejemplar gratuito
comp
complementary copy

ejemplo global de los colores
color comprehensive

elemento
element

eliminación de color acromático
achromatic color removal

emblema
emblem

eme
em

empacar flojo
bulk pack

empalmar
splice

empaquetar
package

empiezo de la impresión
press time (la hora)

empujar
push

empujar hacia afuera
pushout

emulsificación
emulsification

emulsión
emulsion

emulsión abajo
face down
ED/E down

emulsión abajo/ emulsión arriba
emulsion down/ emulsion up

emulsión arriba
EU/E up
face up

en función
up (máquina)

en línea
in line
on line

en serie
serial

encajado
nested

encerador
waxer

encerrado
blocked up (mediotono)

enciclopedia
encyclopedia

encolado
size (papel)

encolado ligero
soft sized

encuadernación a la americana ranurada
burst perfect bind
slotted bind

encuadernación con espiral
coil bind
spiral bind

encuadernación con manga plástica
plastic grip bind

encuadernación con peine
comb bind

encuadernación con tapas rígidas
case bind
hard bind

encuadernación con tornillo
Chicago screw post
post bind
screw and post bind

encuadernación de biblioteca
library binding

encuadernación de doble argolla
double wire bind

encuadernación de edición
edition bind

encuadernación de lomo plano
flat-back bind

encuadernación de lomo redondeado
round-back bind

encuadernación en rústica
book block

encuadernación en tela
cloth bind

encuadernación en vitela
vellum bind

encuadernación engomada
glue bind
paste bind

encuadernación GBC
GBC bind

encuadernación mecánica
mechanical bind

encuadernación perfecta
adhesive bind
cut-back bind
paper bind
patent bind
perfect bind
soft bind

encuadernación plástica
plastic bind

encuadernación selectiva
selective binding

encuadernación sin hilo
threadless binding

encuadernación tendida
lie flat bind

encuadernación termoplástica
thermoplastic binding

encuadernación yapp
yapp bind

encuadernado a media piel
half bound

encuadernado total
full bound

encuadernador
bookbinder

encuadernadora
binder (máquina)

encuadernar
bind

endoso
endorsement (anuncio)
testimonial

ene
en

enfajillar
banding (flejar)

enfocar
focus

engomar en manchas
spot glue

engomar una orilla
tip in
tip on

engrapado al lomo
pamphlet stitch
saddle stitch
saddle wire
stitch bind

engrapado en esquina
corner stitch

engrapado lateral
side stitch
side wire

enlace dinámico
dynamic link

enmascar para mejorar la nitidez
peaking
unsharp masking

ensamblar
compose (película)

ensayo
essay

entrada
input

entrega de prueba
test run (correo)

enviar sin sobre
self-mailer

envoltura
blister card
blister pack
skin pack

envoltura contraida
shrink wrap

envoltura de cubierta
cover wrap

envoltura de resma
ream wrapped

epílogo
epilogue

equilibrio del gris
gray balance

error
bug

error de imprenta
misprint

error de impresor
printer error

error tipográfico
literal
typo
typographical error

escala de caracteres E
E scale

escala del gris
gray scale

escala Kelvin
Kelvin scale

escala proporcional
percentage wheel
proportion dial
proportion scale
proportion wheel
scaling wheel

escalón
stair step

escoger
pick up

escribir consciente del espacio
write to fit

escritor fantasma
ghost writer

escritura lateral
sidebar

espaciado entre caracteres
character spacing
letter-fit
letter spacing

espaciado entre líneas
carding
interline spacing
line spacing

espaciado entre palabras
interword spacing
word spacing

espaciado equitativo
equal spacing
unit spacing

espaciado fijo
monospacing

espaciado óptico de caracteres
optical character spacing

espaciado proporcional
proportional spacing

espacio de capítulo
chapter drop

espacio en blanco
white space

espacio en blanco activo
active white space

espacio en blanco pasivo
passive white space

espacio negativo
negative space

espacio sin imprimir
quiet zone

esparto
esparto
Spanish grass

espatula para tintas
pallet knife

especificaciones
specifications
specs

espectro visible
visible spectrum

espectrofotómetro
spectrophotometer

espesor
mic

espesor de película
film gauge

espolvoreado
dusting

espuma
scum (en una lata)

esquema de montaje
flat plan

estabilidad dimensional
dimensional stability

estampado al caliente
heat stamp
hot foil stamp

estampar
tool

estampar bajo relieve
deboss

estampar bajo relieve sin tinta
blind deboss

estampar con láminas
block
foil emboss
foil stamp

estampar con troquel
die stamp

estampar en relieve
cameo
emboss

estampar en relieve sin tinta
blind emboss

estampar sin tinta
blind stamp

estante de isla
island stand

estañar
tin

esténcil
stencil
chase

estilete
stylus

estilo
style

estilo de la casa
house style
style of the house

estilo de mayúsculas
up style

estilo de minúsculas
down style

estilo de tipos
type style

estirones de la banda
web gain

estrella
burst

estría
flute

estropeaje
spoilage

estucado
coating (papel)

estucado de cuchilla
blade coating
knife coating

estuche de promoción
promotional kit

estuche para libros
slip case

etiqueta
label
nametag
tag

etiqueta autoadhesiva
peel-off label
self-adhesive label

etiqueta de aprobación
approval slip

etiqueta de dirección postal
address label

etiqueta engomada
sticker

etiquetas Cheshire
Cheshire labels

exhibición en el lugar de compra
point of purchase
display

expansión de la tinta
feathering

explorar
scan

exponente
superscript

exponer
expose

exposición auxiliar
flash exposure

exposición de la plancha
burn

exposición doble
double burn

exposición escalonada
step exposure
test strip

exposición insuficiente
underexpose

exposición principal
main exposure

exposición sin plantalla
no-screen exposure

exposición suplementaria
booster (luz)
bump exposure

extracto
excerpt

facsimil
facsimile

factor de distorción
distortion factor

factura
invoice
bill (recibo)

factura de envio
bill of lading

familia de tipos
family of type
type family

fantasma
ghosting (imagen débil)

fecha de cierre
closing date
copy date

fecha de distribución
insertion date

fecha de edición
cover date

fecha de entrega
delivery date

fecha de publicación
issue date
publication date

fecha límite
deadline
due date

fibra
grain (papel)

fidelidad
fidelity

fieltro
felt

figura
figure

fijador
hypo
fixative
fixer

fijar
lock up

fila
row

filete
rule (línea)

filtro
filter

filtro polarizador
polarizing filter

filtros correctores de color
color compensating filters

firma de autorización
proof OK

flash
flash

flash electrónico
strobe

flechas del cursor
cursor arrows

flejar
banding (enfajillar)
counter stack

flexografía
aniline printing
flexo
flexography

flotar
float

fluorescente
fluorescent

folio
folio

folio al pie
drop folio

folio alto
high folio

folio sin tinta
blind folio

folleto
booklet
brochure
slick (hoja)

folleto para estante
rack brochure

folleto promocional
blad
taster

fondo
background

fondo de fuelle
gusset

forma
form
forme

forma comercial
business form

forma exterior
outer form

forma interior
inner form

forma para pedido
order form

forma separable
snap set

formación
formation

formación compacta
close formation

formación irregular
wild formation

formato
format

formato apaisado
broadside format
landscape format

formato de archivo de imagen etiquetada
tagged image file format

formato de revista
magazine format

formato horizontal
downstairs (página)
horizontal format
oblong format

formato tipo álbum
album format

formato vertical
portrait format
standing pages
tall page
upstairs (página)
vertical format

forro
liner

fotocopia
photocopy

fotocopiador
photocopier

fotoestática
stat

fotoestática para posición
position stat

fotogelatinografía
artotype
collotype
heliotype

fotograbado
photoengraving

fotografía brillante
glossy print

fotografía clara
high key photo

fotografía compuesta
composite photo

fotografía de cabeza
mug shot

fotografía de color
color photo

fotografía de cuatro pasos
four-stop photography

fotografía digital
digital photography

fotografía en archivo
stock photo

fotografía en blanco y negro
black-and-white photo

fotografía medida
measured photography

fotografía oscura
low key photo

fotografía para marcar
work print

fotografía suave
soft photo

fotogramo
photogram

fotoresistente
photo resist

fotosensible
photosensitive

fototipia
phototype

fotómetro
exposure meter
light meter

franja del color
color fringe

frasqueta
frisket

fuelle
bellows

fuente
font
fount

fuente de impresora
printer font

fuente de pantalla
screen font

fuera de funcionamiento
down

fuera de línea
off line

fuera de registro
misregister
out of register

fuera del color
off-color

funda
sleeve
wraparound (papel)

gaceta
gazette

galera
galley

gama de colores
color gamut

gama tonal
tonal range

ganancia de puntos
dot gain
dot growth
dot spread
press gain

ganancia mecánica de puntos
mechanical dot gain

ganancia óptica de puntos
optical dot gain

gasa
back lining
book cloth
crash (tela)
gauze

generación
generation

genero
genre

gerente de producción
production manager

gigabyte
gigabyte

glosario
glossary
lexicon

grabado a láser
laser engraving

grabado de puntos
dot etch

grabado doble
double etch

grabado electrónico
electronic engraving

grabador
engraver

grabar
engrave
engraving
etch

grabar separaciones
sharpen

gradiente
gradient
graduated screen tint
ramped screen
vignette (trama)

grado
grade

grado de contraste
contrast grade

gráfica circular
circle chart
pie chart

gráficas de los colores
color curves

gráficas financieras
business graphics

gráfico de barras
bar chart

gráfico de líneas
line chart

gráficos
graphics

gráficos de computador
computer graphics

gráficos para presentaciones
presentation graphics

gramaje
grammage

granear
grain

grano
grain (fotografía)

granulado
grainy

gris neutro
neutral gray

gruesor
bulk (papel)

guarda
flyleaf

guía
guide (publicación)
handbook

guía de los colores
color guide (muestra)

guías laterales
side guides
side lays

guillotina
guillotine cutter

guillotina trilateral
three-knife trimmer

guión
dash
hyphen
script (texto)

guión/espacio de eme
em dash/space

guión/espacio de ene
en dash/space

hacer de nuevo
makeover (impresión)

hardware
hardware

hectografía
spirit duplicate

hectografo
hectograph

heliograbadora
helio

helioklishografía
helioklishography

hidrótipo
hydrotype

historieta
comic book

hoja
leaf
sheet

hoja arrancada
tear sheet

hoja de catálogo
catalog sheet

hoja de contacto
contact sheet

hoja de estilo
style sheet

hoja de la casa
floor sheet
house sheet

hoja de prueba
proof sheet

hoja divisora
slip sheet

hoja final
end sheet

hoja informativa
handout

hoja intercalada
interleaf

hoja libre
free sheet

hoja madre
parent sheet

hoja no cuadrada
off-square sheet

hoja pintada
painted sheet

hoja plegada encuadernada
foldout
pullout
throwout

hojas ilustradas sin texto
color blanks

hojuela
foil (plástico)

horno secador
dryer
drying oven

hoyuelo
dimple

hueco
cup
gap
well

huecograbado
gravure

huérfano
orphan

identidad corporativa
corporate identity

identificadores de pliegos
sheetfed paper identifiers

identificar
key

igualación aproximada
commercial match

igualación de producto
product match

igualación del color
match color

iluminación disponible
available light

iluminar
lighten

ilustración
graphics
illustration

imagen
image

imagen latente
latent image

imagen negativa
negative image

imagen original
master art

imagen positiva
positive image

imagen sin tinta
blind image

imposición
imposition

imposicionadora
imposetter

imposiciones para el impresor
printer spreads

imposiciones para el lector
reader spreads

imprenta
printer (compañía)

imprenta comercial
commercial printer
job printer

imprenta de la casa
in-plant printer

imprenta de publicaciones
publication printer

imprenta especializada
specialty printer

imprenta exclusiva
captive printer

imprenta rápida
quick printer

impresión
impression
printing (proceso)

impresión a chorro de tinta
ink jet printing
jet printing

impresión a todo color
full-color printing

impresión apaisada
landscape printing

impresión bajo demanda
on-demand printing

impresión bicolor
two-color printing

impresión C
C print

impresión con dos negros
double black printing

impresión con esténcil
stencil printing

impresión cuatricolor
four-color process printing

impresión de colores falsos
fake color printing

impresión de información variable
variable information printing

impresión de novedades
novelty printing

impresión de salida
printout

impresión del anverso
face printing

impresión directa
direct impression

impresión doble
double bump
double printing

impresión electrostática
electrostatic printing

impresión en el dorso
back printing

impresión en hojas
sheetwork

impresión en hueco
intaglio printing
recess printing

impresión en relieve
relief printing

impresión geométrica
geometric printing

impresión grabado de mediotono
halftone gravure

impresión kiss
kiss impression

impresión offset
offset printing

impresión offset seco
dry offset printing

impresión planográfica
planographic printing

impresión plateada
silverprint

impresión policroma
multicolor printing
polychrome printing

impresión privada
privately printed

impresión rápida
quick printing

impresión serigráfica
screen printing
seriographic printing
silk screen printing

impresión serigráfica industrial
industrial screen printing

impresión sin impacto
non-impact printing

impresión tipográfica
block printing

impresiones por hora
impressions per hour

impresor
printer (persona)

impresor de anuncios
advertising printer

impresora
printer (máquina)

impresora de agujas
needle printer

impresora de impacto
impact printer

impresora de matrix de puntos
dot matrix printer

impresora láser
laser printer

impresora por puntos
pin printer
stylus printer
wire printer

impresora tipográfica
letterpress

imprimátur
imprimatur

imprimibilidad
printability
runnability

imprimir
print (verbo)

imprimir en el reverso
back up

imprimir y girar
print and twist
work and twist

imprimir y voltear a lo ancho
print and turn
work and turn

imprimir y voltear a lo largo
print and tumble
work and flop
work and tumble

incandescente
incandescent

inclinación hacia atrás
backslant

independiente
freelancer

índice
index

índice de aspecto
aspect ratio

índice de lengüeta
tab index

índice escalonado
step index

índice recortado
thumb index

información gráfica
infographics

informe
briefing book

inserción
insert
inset

inserción suelta
free-standing insert

inserción surtida
supplied insert

inspección de los pliegos
press check

instrucciones
endorsement

instructivo
documentation

intensidad
chroma
intensity

intenso
hot

intercalar
collate

intercalar al revés
reverse collate

interface
interface

interface a base de caracteres
character user interface

interface abierto de preimpresión
open prepress interface

interface gráfica con el usario
graphical user interface

interlineado
carding
interline spacing

leading
line spacing

interlinear
lead (espaciado)

intermediario
broker

internegativo
internegative

interpolación
dither

interruptor interior
dual in-line package switch

introducción
introduction
preface

inundar
flood

invasión del color
bleed

inversa
reverse

inversión lateral
flop
lateral reverse

juego alfanumérico
alphanumeric set

juego de caracteres
character set

juego de signaturas
check copy

justificado por la derecha
right justified

justificado por la izquierda
left justified

kenaf
kenaf

labio
binding lap
feed lap
lip

laca
lacquer

lado base
base side

lado de emulsión
emulsion side

lado de fieltro
felt side

lado del alambre
underside
wire side

lámina
foil (metal)

laminante líquido
liquid laminate

laminar
laminate

lapiz azul
blue pencil
non-repo pencil

láser
laser

latón
brass

lavar
wash up

lectura
readout

lectura directa
right reading

lectura invertida
reverse reading
wrong reading

legible
legible

leible
readable

lenguaje de descripción de la página
page description language

lenguaje del color
color, language of

lengüeta
tab

lente
lens

lente corto
short lens

lente granangular
short lens
wide angle lens

lente lento
slow lens

lente macro
close-up lens
macro lens

lente para retratos
portrait lens

lente rápido
fast lens

lente telefoto
long lens
telephoto lens

lente zoom
zoom lens

letra cursiva
script

letra gótica
black type
gothic type

letra ultranegra
ultrabold type
black type

letras anchas
expanded type
extended type

letras condensadas
condensed type

letras finas
light type

letras grandes
large print

letras mayúsculas
capital letters
majuscule letters
uppercase letters

letras minúsculas
lowercase letters
minuscule letters

letras transferibles
alphabet sheet
dry transfer lettering
instant lettering
press-on type
rub-down lettering
rub-on lettering
transfer lettering
transfer type

levantamiento de la fibra
fiber puff

leyenda
caption
cutline
key
keyline
legend
underline

libreta azul
blue book

libro
book

libro comercial
trade book

libro de arte
art book

libro de bolsillo
chapbook

libro de cupones
coupon book

libro de notas
memo book

libro de tamaño excesivo
oversize book

libro de texto
textbook

libro en rústica
bulk (papel)

libro en rústica comercial
trade paperback

libro en rústica
paperback

libro grande ilustrado
coffee table book

libro instructivo
how-to book

libro para el mercado en general
mass market book

ligadura
ligature

lignina
lignin

límite de cada impresión
cutoff
repeat length

línea
line

línea aumentada
line feed

línea base
baseline

línea central
centerline

línea de columna
column rule

línea de contacto
nip (de cilindro)

línea de fecha
dateline

línea de pie
footer

línea de reconocimiento
credit line

línea de superposición
lap line

línea de tono
tone line

línea del nombre
byline

línea flotante
floating rule

línea titular
headline

línea truncada
club line

líneas de cadena
chain lines (papel)

líneas de doblado
fold marks

líneas de ferrocarril
railroad lines

líneas guías
holding lines
keylines

líneas por centímetro

lines per centimeter

líneas por minuto
lines per minute

líneas por pulgada
lines per inch

líneas verjuradas
laid lines (papel)

lineatura de la trama
line count
ruling
screen frequency
screen ruling
screen size
screen value

lineómetro
line gauge
pica pole

lingote
slug

lista de erratos
erratum

lista de hechos
outline

lista de publicaciones
list

lista de publicaciones recientes
front list

lista de publicaciones viejas
back list

litografía
lithography

litografía offset
offset lithography

logotipo
letterhead (diseño)
logo

logotipo del sindicato
union bug

lomo
backbone
saddle
spine

longitude de alfabeto
alphabet length

lugar de la prueba beta
beta site

lugar del cambio
break point

lupa
glass
loupe

luz ambiental
ambient light

luz blanca
white light

luz de fondo
back light

luz de seguridad
safelight

luz incidente
incident light

maculado de tinta
ink set-off

madurar
cure
mature

magenta
magenta

malla
mesh

mancha de reflexión
flare

mancha defectuosa
hot spot

mancha por agua
water spot

manchado
setoff

manchar
marking
tracking

manchas de cadena
chain lines (impresión)

manchas de moho
foxing

manchas de toner
overspray

mano
quire

mantilla
blanket (cuacho)

manual
handbook
manual
user guide

manual de datos
data manual

manual para maestros
teacher's manual

manual técnico
technical manual

manuscrito
manuscript

manuscrito preliminar
rough draft

mapa
map

maqueta
mockup (muestra)

maqueta de imposición
press layout
ruleup

máquina cortadora de
pliegos
sheeter

máquina de escribir
typewriter

máquina Fourdrinier
Fourdrinier machine

marca de agua
watermark

marca de imprenta
imprint (nombre)

marca de la papelera
mill brand

marca de superposición
lap mark

marca de vendedor
merchant brand

marca particular
private brand

marca registrada
trademark

marcado
composition (de una
fotografía)

marcado por resma
ream marked

marcas correctivas
correction marks

marcas de corrección
proofreader marks

marcas de corte
crop marks
cut marks
dimension marks
trim marks

marcas de esquina
corner marks

marcas de identificación
Facing Identification
Marks (correo)

marcas de la malla
mesh marks

marcas de ojos
eye markers

marcas de posición
position marks

marcas de registro
register marks

marcas del centro
center marks

marcas del lomo
spine marks

marcas guías
backstep marks
blackstep marks
collating marks

marcas para el impresor
printer marks

marco
box
frame (fotografía)

marco completo
full frame

marco para estirar
stretch frame

margarita
daisy wheel
print wheel

margen
border
margin

margen del canto
face margin

margen del lomo
bind margin

margen encuadernado
binding edge

margen exterior
fore edge

margen inferior
foot margin

margen superior extraordinario
sinkage (diseño)

margen superiór
head margin

margenes progresivos
progressive margins

máscara
mask
stop out

mate
dull

material atrazado
on extension

material del canto
face material

material especial
penalty stock

material fechado
dated material

material para enmascarar
masking material

material tabular
tabular material

matiz
hue

matriz
counter (troquel)
female die
mat
matrice
matrix

mayorista
wholesaler

mayúscula bajada
dropped cap

mayúscula elevada
raised cap

mayúscula inicial
drop initial

mecanismo entintador
ink station

mecanismo impresor
color station
station
tower

mecanismo mojador
dampener fountain
damper
water fountain

media
media (publicaciones)

media página
junior page

medianil
back margin
gutter

medida
measure

medida de tipo
type size

medida tipográfica
line measure

medios tonos
midtones

mediotono
halftone

medios tonos perdidos
deep-etch halftone
dropout halftone

mediotono de doble punto
double dot halftone

mediotono de escala completa
full-range halftone

mediotono perfilado
knockout halftone
outline halftone
silhouette halftone

mediotono traspintado
ghost halftone

mediotono viñeteado
vignette halftone

megabyte
megabyte

membrete
letterhead (hoja)

memorándum de entrega
delivery memo

memoria
memoirs
memory

memoria de acceso al azar
random access memory

memoria de computador
computer memory

memoria solo de lectura
read only memory

menú
menu

mesa de alineación
lineup table

mesa de montaje
stripping table

mesa luminosa
light table

mesa proyectora
light box

metamérico
metameric

metas en densidades de las tintas
target ink densities

metros por segundo
meters per second

microficha
microfiche

microfilm
microfilm

microlínea
microline

micrómetro
mic
micrometer

micrón
micron

micropelícula
microfilm

microprocesador
microprocessor

mil
mil

minúsculas
lower case

mismo tamaño
same size

mitad inferior
downstairs (ubicación)

mitad superior
upstairs (ubicación)

modelo de colores
color model

modem
modem

modo para borrador
draft mode

monarca
monarch

monitor
monitor

monocromo
monochrome

monografía
monograph

montador
stripper

montaje
flat (película)
montage

montaje de imagenes
image assembly

montaje de películas
film assembly

montaje en papel
board

montajes complementarios
complementary flats

montar
assemble
make up (arreglar)
strip

montar con aceite
oil mount

montar en papel
paste up

montón compensado
compensated stack

montón no compensado
uncompensated stack

mortaja
mortice

mota
doughnut
hickey

moteado
mealy
mottle
sinkage

móvil
mobile

muaré
moiré
screen clash

muestra
comp
dummy (maqueta)

muestra de color
color swatch

muestra de la papelera
mill swatch

muestra de papel
paper dummy

muestra de plegados
folding dummy

muestra definitiva
comprehensive dummy

muestra del gruesor
bulking dummy

muestrario
sample book
swatch book

muestrario circular de colores
color wheel

muestrario de tipos
type specimen book

multicopiar al alcohol
spirit duplicate

multicopista
duplicator

música
music

neblina
haze

negativo base
base negative

negativo clave
key negative

negativo de línea
line negative

negativo en medios tonos
halftone negative

negativo oscuro
thick negative

negativo pálido
thin negative

negocio de reprografía
camera service

negrillas
bold type

negro de escala completa
full-range black
full-scale black

negro de escala media
half-scale black

negro de proceso
process black

negrura del tipo
weight, of type

niveles del gris
gray levels

nítido
sharp

normas de la industria impresora
customs, printing trade
printing trade customs
trade customs

nota al pie
footnote

notas del forro
liner notes

noticia para la prensa
press release

nube de tinta
misting

número clave
key number

número de gruesor
bulking number

número de mallas
mesh count
mesh number

número de páginas
extent
page count

número de servicio del lector
reader service number

número total de lectores
readership

números arábigos
arabic numerals

números romanos
Roman numerals

oblicuo
oblique

obturador
shutter

octavo
octavo

octeto
byte

offset
offset

offset seco
letterset

ojal
grommet

ojete
eyelet

ojo de buey
bull's eye

ojo de pescado
fish eye (lente)
hickey

ojo de tipo
face
typeface

olografía
holography

ondulado
cockling

opacar
block out
opaque
spot

opacidad
covering power
opacity

opaco
flat (fotografía)
opaque

operaciones finales
finish

orden a la papelera
mill order

orden de trabajo
docket
job ticket

orden directa
direct order

orden para hacer
making order

organigrama
organization chart

orientación
orientation

original
copy (para imprimir)

original de línea
line copy
line work

original limpio
fair copy

orilla
binding lap
border

orilla alimentadora
feeding edge

orilla doblada
lap

orilla ondulada
baggy edge

orilla para coger
pickup lap

ortocromático
orthochromatic

oscurecer
darken

ozalid
ozalid

página
page

página ancha
wide page

página central doble
double truck

página de cupones
coupon page

página de derechos
biblio page

página de derechos de autor
copyright page

página de título
title page

página derecha
right-hand page

página doble
double page spread

página izquierda
left-hand page
low folio page
verso

página patrón
master page
underlying page

paginación
pagination

páginas amarillas
yellow pages

páginas para observar
pages to view

páginas por minuto
pages per minute

páginas por pulgada
pages per inch

páginas posteriores
end matter

páginas preliminares
front matter
preliminaries

palanca de apertura
booster

paleta
palette
pallet
skid

paleta pequeña
mini skid

pancarta
banner (anuncio)

pancromático
panchromatic

panel
panel

panel para la dirección postal
address panel

panfleto
pamphlet

pantalla
display
screen (objeto)

pantalla de contacto
contact screen

papel
paper
stock

papel A4
A4 paper

papel aéreo
airmail paper

papel alcalino
alkaline paper

papel altamente encolado
hard sized paper

papel archivo
archival paper

papel atlas
atlas paper

papel autocopiante
action paper
carbonless paper
impact paper
self-copy paper

papel baritado
baryta paper
repro paper

papel base
base stock

papel basto
high-bulk paper

papel biblia
bible paper

papel bond
bond paper
business paper
communication paper
register bond
writing paper

papel bond borrable
erasable bond

papel bond de doble uso
DP bond paper
dual-purpose bond paper

papel bond legal
legal paper

papel bond para formas
form bond

papel bond para láser
laser bond

papel bristol
bristol paper
index bristol

papel bristol avitelado
vellum bristol

papel carbón
carbon paper

papel carbón semitratado
semicoated carbon paper

papel carbón tratado por ambos lados
full-coated carbon paper

papel carta
letter paper

papel cebolla
bank paper
manifold bond
onionskin

papel con algodón
cotton content paper

papel con fibra a lo corto
grain short paper
short-grain paper
wide-web paper

papel con fibra a lo largo
grain long paper
long-grain paper

papel con goma seca
dry gum paper

papel continuo
continuous paper

papel correspondencia
correspondence paper

papel cristal
glassine

papel cromo
chromo paper
enamel paper

papel cuadriculado
graph paper
quadrille paper

papel cuche
art paper

papel cuche estucado
enamel paper

papel cuero
calf paper

papel de arrastre por espigas
pin feed paper

papel de bobina
reel paper

papel de bobina ancha
wide-web paper (prensa)

papel de bobina angosta
narrow web paper

papel de contraste variable
variable contrast paper

papel de doble tono
two-tone paper

papel de estabilización
stabilization paper

papel de fibra coloreada
silurian paper
tinted fiber paper

papel de lujo
premium paper

papel de marca mayor
chart paper

papel de pasta mecánica
groundwood paper

papel de periódico
newsprint

papel de segunda
job lot paper

papel de seguridad
safety paper

papel de trapos
all-rag paper
rag paper

papel duplex
double-faced paper
duplex paper

papel empañado
film coated paper

papel en zigzag
fan fold paper

papel engomado
gummed paper

papel equivalente
comparable stock
equivalent paper

papel estucado
coated paper

papel estucado de lujo
cast-coated paper

papel fuerte
tough check paper

papel glaseado
gloss art paper
gloss paper
gloss-coated paper
slick paper

papel granulado
grained paper

papel grueso
bulking book paper
novel paper

papel guarro
cartridge paper

papel importado
off-shore sheet

papel india
bible paper
india paper

papel kraft
kraft paper

papel ledger
ledger paper
record paper

papel libro
book paper

papel ligeramente encolado
slack sized

papel ligero
lightweight paper

papel lustre
gloss art paper
gloss paper
gloss-coated paper

papel manila
manila paper

papel mantequilla
tissue

papel metático
metallic paper

papel moneda
bank note paper
currency paper

papel NCR
NCR paper

papel no calandrado
uncalendered paper

papel no estucado
uncoated paper

papel offset
offset paper

papel para anuncios
sign paper

papel para bodas
wedding paper

papel para calcomanías
decal paper

papel para carteles
poster paper

papel para catálogos
catalog paper

papel para colgar
hanging paper

papel para copiadora
copier paper

papel para copias
xerocopy paper

papel para cubiertas
cover paper
cover stock

papel para cheques
check paper

papel para dibujar
tracing paper

papel para directorios
directory paper

papel para empaquetar
packaging paper
wrapping paper

papel para etiquetas
label paper

papel para mapas
map paper

papel para prueba
proofing paper

papel para publicaciones
publishing paper

papel para texto
text paper

papel pergamino
diploma paper
parchment paper

papel permanente
permanent paper

papel protector
backing paper
protective paper
release paper

papel RC
RC paper

papel reciclado
recovered paper
recycled paper

papel resistente al agua
waterproof paper

papel rugoso
antique paper

papel SC
SC paper

papel sensible a la presión
pressure sensitive paper

papel sin ácido
acid-free paper
neutral pH paper
permanent paper
thesis paper

papel sin madera
woodfree paper

papel sintético
synthetic paper

papel sucio
dirty paper

papel sulfato
sulphate paper

papel sulfito
sulphite paper

papel supercalandrado
rotopaper
supercalendered paper

papel texto
body stock

papel texturado
text paper

papel tratado
coated paper

papel tratado con resina
resin-coated paper

papel tratado encolado
size-coated paper

papel tratado por ambos lados

coated front and back
paper (CFB)

papel tratado por el frente
coated front paper (CF)

papel tratado por un lado
one-sided art paper

papel virgen
virgin paper

papel vitela
vellum paper

papel xerográfico
copier paper

papel, unidades de venta
paper, selling units

papelera
paper mill

papelería
business cabinet
papeterie

papelería membretada
stationery

papeles burdos
coarse papers

papeles comunes
stocking papers

papeles culturales
cultural papers

papeles especiales
specialty papers

papeles finos
cultural papers
fine papers
graphic papers

papeles industriales
industrial papers

papeles metalizados
foil papers

papiro
papyrus

paquete
package (caja)

paquete para la prensa
media kit
press kit

para posición solamente
for position only

pared
wall

párrafos comunes
boilerplate
canned text

pasada
hit
pass
working

pasador de planchas de contacto
contact platemaker

paso
pitch

paso de diafragma
f/stop

paso y repetición
step and repeat

pasta
furnish
pulp
slurry

pasta mecánica
groundwood pulp
mechanical pulp

pasta para racleta
screening paste
squeegee paste

patrón
master (guía)

patrón de seguridad
blockout pattern
safety pattern

pedido de almacen
stock order

pedido de producción
production order

pedido de trabajo
work order

pegar
paste (acción)

película comercial
commercial film

película compuesta
composite film

película de trabajo
working film

película final
final film

película fotográfica
photographic film

película lenta
slow film

película lista para plancha
plate-ready film

película litho
litho film

película para artes gráficas
graphic arts film
repro film

película para tonos de trama
shading film

película para transparencias
transparency film

película patrón
master film

película plástica en envolturas
film laminate

película positiva
positive film

película rápida
fast film

pelusa del papel
lint

pendiente de reimpresión
standing

penetración de la tinta
strike through

perder
drop out

perfil dentado
aliasing
jaggies

perfilar
outline (texto)

perforación
perf
perforation

perforación a ángulo recto
right angle perforation

perforación de cuadernos escolares
schoolbook perforation

perforar
drill
perforate
punch

pergamino
pergamyn

periféricos
peripherals

periódico
newspaper
periodical

periódico gratuito
shopper
throwaway

período de paro
down time

permiso postal
indicia

perspectiva de dos puntos
two-point perspective

perspectiva de un punto
one-point perspective

perspectiva paralela
parallel perspective

peso base
basis weight
sub weight
substance weight

peso base real
actual basis weight

peso base nominal
nominal basis weight

peso de resma
ream weight

peso del envase
tare weight

peso del papel
weight, of paper

peso M
M weight

peso neto
net weight

peso total
gross weight

pesos equivalentes
equivalent weights

pérdida de puntos
dot loss
sharpen

pica
pica

pictografía
pictograph

pie
foot

pie de página
tails

pies por minuto
feet per minute

pigmento
pigment

pintar
stain

pintura para opacar
opaquing paint

pinzas
grippers

piroxilina
pyroxylin

pixel
pel
pixel

plancha
master (patrón)
plate (impresión)
printer (película)

plancha amarilla
yellow printer

plancha blanda
soft key

plancha cian
cyan printer

plancha clara
light printer

plancha clave
key plate
key printer

plancha de impresión
printing plate

plancha de metal
metal plate

plancha de toque
touch plate

plancha kiss
kiss plate

plancha magenta
magenta printer

plancha mixta
combination plate

plancha negativa
negative working plate

plancha negra
black printer

plancha oscura
dark printer

plancha para sombra
shadow black
skeleton black

plancha selectiva
selective key

plancha traspintada
ghost key

planchista
platemaker (persona)

plano
flat (correo)

plano focal
focal plane

plantilla
guide
stencil
template

platina
platen

plegado a embudo
former fold

plegadora
folder (máquina)

pliego
sheet

pliego autorizado
OK sheet

pliego de prensa
press sheet

pliego por adelantado
advance sheet

pliegos cortados
cut sizes

polvo
dust

polvo offset
offset powder

polvo secador
anti-offset powder
powder
spray powder

porcelana
clay

porcelana china
China clay

porcentaje de abertura
aperture percentage
open area (pantalla)

porcentaje de puntos
dot area
dot percent

porosidad
porosity

portada
frontispiece

portada falsa
half title

portafolio
portfolio

portaimagen
image carrier

portaoriginales
copyboard

posición de tirada
run of the book

positivo en medios tonos
halftone positive

poster
poster
showcard

precio de portada
cover price

precio especial de cuarta clase
special fourth class rate

precios bases
formula pricing

preimpresión
origination
prepress

preimprimir
preprint

premios
premiums

prensa computarizada
computer controlled press

prensa convertible
convertable press

prensa cuadrada
quad press

prensa de 16 páginas
16-page press

prensa de bobina
reel-fed press
web press

prensa de bobina a bobina
reel-to-reel press

prensa de bobina con horno
heat-set web

prensa de bobina máxima
full-web press

prensa de bobina para formas
form web press

prensa de bobina sin horno
cold-set web
non-heat-set web
open web

prensa de caucho contra caucho
blanket-to-blanket press

prensa de correa
belt press

prensa de media bobina
half web press

prensa de minibobina
miniweb press

prensa de ocho páginas
eight-page press

prensa de pliegos
sheetfed press

prensa de retiración
duplex press

perfecting press
perfector

prensa de tres quartos bobina
three-quarter web press

prensa de vacio
vacuum frame

prensa para impresión
printing press

prensa plana
flat-bed press

prensa platina
platen press

prensa rotativa
rotary press

preparación
preparation

preparación del original
copy preparation

preparación tipográfica
mark up

preseparar
presort

presupuesto
bid
estimate
quotation
tender

primer color de impresión
first color down

primer plano
foreground

primer tiraje
first run (edición)

primera impresión
first run (pliego)

primera página
low folio page (signatura)

primera prueba
first proof

procesador de palabras
word processor

procesamiento de imagenes
image processing

procesamiento de palabras
word processing

producto final
end product

productora de imagenes
imagesetter

profundidad
depth

profundidad de campo
depth of field

programa
program
schedule

programa de computador
computer program

programa de diagnóstico
diagnostic program

programa de operación del disco
disk operating system

programa del sistema
system software

progresivos irregulares
bastard progressives

prólogo
foreword

proporción
alignment (diseño)

proporción de contraste
contrast ratio

proporción de la trama
screen ratio

proporción de los margenes
shingling

proporcionar
track
track kerning

prospecto
prospectus

protección
resist

protección del esténcil
stencil resist

protocolo
protocol

prueba
proof
pull

prueba alfa
alpha test

prueba antes de imprimir
off-press proof

prueba azul
blue
blueline
dyeline

prueba beta
beta test

prueba compuesta
composite proof

prueba de acetato
acetate proof

prueba de campo
field test

prueba de cancelación
cancellation proof

prueba de celuloide
celluloid proof

prueba de color
composition proof

prueba de color impuesto
imposed color proof

prueba de galera
checker
galley proof
slip proof

prueba de imposición
imposition proof

prueba de máquina
machine proof

prueba de montaje
stripping proof

prueba de página
page proof

prueba de pliego
out-turn sheet

prueba de posición
position proof

prueba de preimpresión
dry proof
prepress proof

prueba de prensa
press proof
strike off
trial proof

prueba de superpuestas
layered proof
overlay proof

prueba de verificación
contract proof

prueba definitiva
check copy (publicación)
final proof

prueba del libro
book proof

prueba directa de color digital
direct digial color proof

prueba dura
hard proof

prueba en pantalla
soft proof

prueba final
confirming proof

prueba integral
integral proof
laminate proof
plastic proof
single-sheet proof

prueba marcada
working proof

prueba Mullen
Mullen test
pop test

prueba progresiva
prog
progressive proof

prueba Signatura
Signature proof

prueba suelta
loose proof
random proof
scatter proof
show-color proof

prueba térmica
thermal proof

publicación
publication

publicación agotada
out of print

publicación de base de datos
database publishing

publicación disponible
in print

publicación electrónica
electronic publishing

publicación patrocinada
sponsored publication

publicación por vanidad
vanity press

publicado por el autor
self-published

publicar
publish

publicidad de especialidad
specialty advertising

publicista
copywriter

puente
bridge

puerta
port

puerta de RS232
RS232 port

pulgada de columna
column inch

pulpa
pulp

pulpa química
chemical pulp

punteado
stipple (diseño)

puntear
stipple

punto
point

punto cuadrado
square dot

punto digital
digital dot

punto elíptico
elliptical dot

punto en cadena
chain dot

punto redondo
round dot

punto señalizador
bullet
dingbat

puntos conductores
leaders

puntos de aguja
pinholes

puntos de medios tonos
halftone dots

puntos débiles
soft dots

puntos duros
hard dots

puntos por pulgada
dot pitch
dots-per-inch

puntos suspensivos
ellipsis

puntuación saliente
hanging punctuation

pureza
purity

quintal
CWT - C

quinto color
fifth color

quiosco
kiosk

racleta
squeegee

rango de densidad
copy range
density range

rango dinámico
dynamic range

ranura del cilindro
cylinder gap

rasgo ascendente
ascender

rasgo descendente
descender

ratón
mouse

rayado cruzado
crosshatching

rayar
score
scribe

rayar con hilo
string score

rayar con troquel
die score

rayas
banding (defecto)
streaking

rayita
hairline

reborde del doblez
crease

reconocimiento magnético de caracteres
magnetic ink character recognition

reconocimiento óptico de caracteres
optical character recognition

recortar
crop

recortar para registrar
cut to register

recorte de cabeza
head trim

recorte del canto
face trim

recortes de cartón en "L"
cropping angles
cropping Ls

recuadro tipo antiguo
cartouche

recuento
final count
finished count

recuento de caracteres
character count

recuento de líneas
line count (texto)

red
network

redondeo
rounding

reducción
reduction

reducción del color de fondo
undercolor removal

reducir
cut

reemplazar el gris
gray component replacement

referencia
callout

reflectancia
reflectance

registro
record
register

registro casi exacto
tight register

registro de contacto
butt register

registro de superposición
lap register

registro de tres puntos
three-point register

registro exacto
hairline register
close register

registro kiss
kiss register

registro por clavija
pin register

registro satisfactorio
commercial register

regla T
T square

reimpresión
reprint (producto)

reimprimir
reprint (proceso)

relleno
stuffer

remover el cromo
chrome stripping

remover errores
debug

repelado
picking

repetible
repeatability

reporte anual
annual report

representante de ventas
account executive
sales representative

representante para servicio de los clientes
customer service representative

reproducción
slick (hoja)

reproducir
reproduce

reproducir en combinación
gang

reprográficos
reprographics

resistencia
holdout

resistencia a la abrasión
abrasion resistance
rub fastness
scuff resistance

resistencia a la luz
light fast

resistencia a la ruptura
bursting strength
pop strength

resistencia a la tensión
tensile strength

resistencia a la tinta
ink holdout

resma
ream

resolución
resolution

resumen
abridgement
abstract
digest
precis
resume
summary deck

resumen en la solapa
blurb

retícula fina
fine mesh

retiraje
rerun

retiraje exacto
exact rerun

retocado electrónico
electronic retouching

retocar
retouch

retoque
tusche

retramar
rescreen

revelar
develop

revelar insuficiente
underdevelop

reverso
liftout

revestimiento
packing

revisar y corregir
edit

revista
journal
magazine
slick (publicación)

revista en papel de pulpa
pulp magazine

revista para aficionados
fanzine
zine

revista para consumidores
consumer magazine

revista para un oficio
trade journal

revista publicitaria
pennysaver
shopper
throwaway

RGB
RGB

rodillo anilino
anilox roll

rodillo del tintero
fountain roller

rodillo escuridor
dandy roll

rodillo impresor
impression roller

rodillos de plancha
form rollers

rodillos distribuidores
distributing rollers

rodillos entintadores
ink rollers

rodillos mojadores
dampening rolls
water rollers

rojo rodamino
rhodamine red

rojo rubino
rubine red

rollo jumbo
jumbo roll
master roll

rosetón
rosette

rotación
rotation

rotograbado
rotogravur

RRED
RRED

RREU
RREU

ruptura de la banda
web break

salida
output

saltar
jump

sangrado
bleed

sangrado sobre el medianil
gutter bleed/gutter jump

sangria
indent

sangria saliente
hanging indent

saturación
saturation

saturación de sombra
shadow saturation

scanner
scanner

scanner de colores
color scanner

scanner láser
laser scanner

scanner plano
flat-bed scanner

scanner tipo pluma
pen scanner

secado suficiente
set up (tinta)

sección
section (publicación)

sección amplificada
exploded view

sección inferior
basement

secuencia de colores
color sequence

secuencia de impresión
laydown sequence
printing sequence

seleccionar
separate

sello
stamp

semblanza del autor
blurb (biografía)

sendero
river

separación de colores
color separation
separaton

separación de colores en superpuestas
mechanical separation

separación incorrecta
bad break

separación por cámara
camera separation

separaciones universales
universal film

separador
separator

separadores encuadernados
bind-in tabs

sepia
sepia

serie de tipos
type series

series
series

serif
serif

servicio de cámara
trade camera service

servicio de conversión
conversion service

servicio de correo
lettershop
mailing service

servicio de fotocopias
copy shop

servicio de listas
list house

servicio de preimpresión
service bureau

servicio de preparación
preparation service

servicio de separación de colores
color separation service

servidor de archivos
file server

sigla
acronym

signatura
section
signature

signo &
ampersand

signo diacrítico
diacritic

signos comerciales
commercial signs

signos de puntuación
punctuation marks

signos de referencia
reference marks

símbolo al final
tailpiece

símbolos matemáticos
mathematical signs

sistema
system

sistema Brunner
System Brunner

sistema de color Munsell
Munsell color system

sistema de igualación de colores
color matching system

sistema de igualación Pantone
Pantone Matching System

sistema Didot
Didot type sysytem

sistema electrónico de entrada
electronic front end

sistema electrónico de preimpresión a color
color electronic prepress system

sistema llave de mano
turnkey system

sistema operativo
operating system

sistema operativo de disco
DOS

sistema tipográfico angloamericano
Anglo-American type system

sobre
envelope

sobre baronial
baronial envelope

sobre cartera
wallet envelope

sobre coin
coin envelope

sobre con broche
clasp envelope

sobre de remesa
remittance envelope

sobre de servicio del lector
business reply envelope
return envelope

sobre el canal
across the gutter

sobre expandible
expansion envelope

sobre oficio
banker envelope
business envelope
commercial envelope
offical envelope

sobre para boletos
ticket envelope

sobre para carta informativa
announcement envelope

sobre para catálogo
catalog envelope

sobre para folleto
booklet envelope

sobre para pólizas
policy envelope

sobre para servicio del lector
courtesy reply envolope

sobre tipo acordeón
accordion envelope

sobrecubierta
jacket (para un libro)
dust cover

sobreexponer
overexpose

sobreimprimir
imprint
overprint
surprint

sobrerevelar
overdevelop

sobres
overs

sobretiraje
overrun

sobretiraje separado
offprint
separate

sobretrabajo
jacket (para un trabajo)

software de sistema
system functions

solapa
flap

solapa de folio
folio lap

sólido
solid (tinta)

solución mojadora
dampener solution
fountain solution

sombra bajada
drop shadow
flat shadow

sombra del corte
cutline (defecto)

sombras
shadows

sonriendo y dandose la mano
grip and grin

soporte dorsal
easel back

sorteadora de códigos de barras
bar code sorter

spadia
spadia

subcontratar
buy out
farm out
outsource

subíndice
subscript

subindices
inferior character

subrayar
underline
underscore

subtítulo
caption
crosshead
kicker
legend
subhead

subtitle
tagline

sumario
abstract
summary deck

superficie quemada
blister

superpuesta
overlay

superpuesta de acetato
overlay

superpuesta de papel mantequilla
overlay

superpuesta de texto
type overlay

suplemento
supplement

suporte
hanger

tabla
table

tabla de contenido
table of contents

tabla del empaquetado
packing schedule

tableta
tablet

tabloide
tabloid

taller de composición
type shop

taller de encuadernación
bindery

taller para un oficio
trade shop

tamaño básico
basic size

tamaño carta
letter size

tamaño de hoja
flat size

tamaño de puntos
dot size

tamaño final
finished size
trim size

tamaño folio
folio size

tamaño irregular
bastard size

tamaño libro
book size

tamaño madre
parent size

tamaño resumen
digest size

tamaños de papeles A, B, C, RA & SRA
A, B, C, RA & SRA paper sizes

tamaños de papeles internacionales
international paper sizes

tamaños de papeles ISO
ISO paper sizes

tamaños de papeles norteamericanos
North-American paper sizes

tamaños de sobres ISO
ISO envolope sizes

tamaños de sobres norteamericanos
North-American envelope sizes

tapa
case (libro)
hard cover

tapado
filled in
plugged up

tarjeta de archivo
media data form

tarjeta de burbuja
bubble card

tarjeta de datos
data card

tarjeta de felicitaciones
greeting card

tarjeta de mostrador
counter card
tent card

tarjeta de pedido
action card

tarjeta de precios
rate card

tarjeta de presentación
visiting card
business card

tarjeta de Rolodex
Rolodex card

tarjeta de servicio
bingo card

tarjeta de servicio del lector
business reply card
reader service card
reply card

tarjeta de suscripción
bounceback

tarjeta de visita
calling card

tarjeta del cassette
cassette cover
J card

tarjeta encuadernada
bind-in card

tarjeta insertada por aire
blow-in card

tarjeta para archivo rotativo
rotary file card

tarjeta postal
postcard

tarjeta postal doble
double postcard

tecla
key (de una prensa)

teclado
keyboard (objeto)

teclado Dvorak
Dvorak keyboard

teclar
keyboard (acción)

tela rellenada de almidón
starch-filled cloth

temperatura del color
color temperature

terabyte
terabyte

terminación de hoja
pastedown

terminal
station

términos y condiciones
terms and conditions

termografía
raised printing
thermography

tesoro
thesaurus

testimonio
testimonial

texto
body text
text

texto ágata
agate copy

texto centrado
centered type

texto del editorial
editorial matter

texto en bandera derecha
ragged right type

texto en bandera izquierda
ragged left type

texto justificado
justified type

texto simulado
greeking

texto solamente
straight copy

textos de relleno
fillers

tiempo de exposición
exposure time

tiempo de impresión
press time (duración)

tiempo de inversión
turnaround time

tiempo de pasada
run time

tiempo de secado
drying time

tiempo de vuelta
turnaround time

tiempo productivo
up time

tiner
reducer

tinta
ink

tinta brillante
gloss ink

tinta de anilina
aniline ink

tinta de fondo
background tint
base color

tinta de secado en frío
cold-set ink

tinta de secado por calor
heat-set ink

tinta densa
short ink

tinta elástica
stretch ink

tinta fluida
long ink

tinta imprimible por láser
laser-imprintable ink

tinta indeleble
indelible ink

tinta magnética
magnetic ink

tinta mate
dull ink
matte ink

tinta metálica
metallic ink

tinta opaca
opaque ink

tinta para fotocopiadoras
presystem ink

tinta para prensa de bobina sin horno
non-heat-set ink

tinta resistente al agua
waterproof ink

tinta sin plomo
lead-free ink

tinta transparente
transparent ink

tintas con base de aceite
oil-based inks

tintas con base de agua
water-based inks

tintas con base de soya
soy-based inks

tintas de colores incostantes
fugitive color inks

tintas indecoloras
fade-resistant inks

tintas indecoloras y lavables
fast color inks

tintas permanentes
permanent inks

tintero
duct
fountain
ink fountain
pocket

tintero acro iris
rainbow fountain

tintero dividido
split fountain

tipo
sort (letra)

tipo C
C type

tipo de golpe
strike-on type

tipo de metal
hot type

tipo de texto
composition type

tipo digital
digital type

tipo elite
elite type

tipo flotante
floating type

tipo invertido
cameo type
dropout type
reverse type

tipo itálico
italic type

tipo láser
laser type

tipo microelite
microelite type

tipo para títulos
display type
headline type

tipo perfilado
outline type

tipo pica
pica type

tipo por fundición
foundry type

tipo romano
roman type

tipo sans-serif
lineale
san-serif type

tipo seminegro
semibold type

tipo sencillo
plain type

tipo serif
serif type

tipo sombreado
shaded type
shadow type

tipo texto
body copy
body type
text type

tipografía
typography

tipógrafo
composer

tipómetro
type gauge

tira cómica
comic strip

tira divisora
flag (hoja)

tirada
run

tiraje
press run (cantidad)
printing (edición)
run

tiraje corto
underrun

tiraje de combinación
combination run

tiraje de producción
production run

tiraje de prueba
test run (impresión)

tiraje dividido
split run

tiraje grande
long run

tiraje pequeño
short run

título
banner (periódico)

título de capítulo
chapter head

título de pie/cabeza
running foot/head

título marginal intercalado
cut-in headline

título pendiente de reimpresión
standing headline

título provisional
catch line

tolerancias
trade tolerance

tolerancias de cortes
cutting tolerances

toma
shot

tonelada
long ton
ton
tonne

tonelada corta
short ton

toner
toner (polvo)

tono
shade
tone

tono tramado
screen tint
screen tone
shading

tope
masthead

trabajo a mano
hand work

trabajo de media hoja
half sheet work

trabajo para alquilar
work for hire

trama ancha
coarse mesh
coarse screen

trama de círculos concéntricos
concentric circle screen

trama de conversión a línea
line conversion screen

trama de grabado en acero
steel engraving screen

trama de lino
linen screen

trama de líneas cruzadas
crossline screen

trama fina
fine mesh
fine screen

trama mediana
medium screen

trama mezzotinto
mezzotint screen

trama muselina
muslin screen

trama para medios tonos
halftone screen

tramar
screen

tramas transferibles
transfer screens

transferencia fotomecánica
Photomechanical
transfer

transferencia por difusión
diffusion transfer

transferencia térmica
thermal transfer

transformación de bits
bit map

translúcido
translucent

transparencia
tranny
translite
transparency

transparencia de color
color transparency

transparentar
bleedthrough

transparente
transparent

traslucir
show through

traspintarse
ghosting (image débil)

tratado
coating (papel)

tratado por el reverso
coated back (CB)

tratado por un lado
coated one side (C1S)

tratamiento del papel
film coating

trazado
layout

tren
train

tres cuartos tonos
three-quarter tones

triángulo
triangle

tricromático
trichromatic

tritono
tritone

troquel
die

troquelar
die cut

troquelar kiss
kiss die cut

tubo de rayos catodicos
cathode ray tube

último color a imprimir
last color down

unidad central de proceso
central processing unit

unidad de registro
register unit

unidad impresora
deck
printing unit

unidades de anuncios
advertising units

unir
merge

uso propio
in house

usuario final
end user

vale lo tachado
stet

valor
value

velado
burned out

velo
blush
catch up
fog
scum (en papel)

velocidad de exploración
scan rate

velocidad de lectura
read rate

velocidad de película
film speed

velocidad de película ASA
ASA film speed

velocidad de película ISO
ISO film speed

velocidad del lente
lens speed

**vendedor de papel de
segunda**
job lot merchant
seconds merchant

ventana
black patch
window

ventana de diálogo
dialog box

ventana roja
red patch

ventana ruby
ruby window

versalitas
small caps

vibración
vibration

vibrar
pop (diseño)

viñeta
dégradé
vignette (filete)

virado
toning

virador
toner (tinta)

viscocidad
body (tinta)

visual
visual

vitrina
cabinet

viuda
widow

volante
flyer
handbill

worstway
worstway

xerografía
xerography

zona clara difusa
diffuse highlight

zona clara especular
catchlight
specular highlight

zonas claras
highlights

zonas claras perdidas
dropout highlight

Please send _____ Graphically Speaking book(s) at $29.50 each.

name _____

address_____

city, state _____

zip _____ phone _____

shipping within the USA
   ❑ First class mail ❑ UPS ground $5.00 first book, $1.00 each additional book
shipping outside of USA
   Please call 503 368 5584 for rates.   subtotal $ _____

MasterCard or VISA expires_____		shipping $ _____
card # _____		total $ _____
signature _____		

Elk Ridge Publishing
P O Box 633
Manzanita OR 97130
503 368 5584   FAX 503 368 5929

**Prompt service
money back guarantee**

- -

Please send _____ Graphically Speaking book(s) at $29.50 each.

name _____

address_____

city, state _____

zip _____ phone _____

shipping within the USA
   ❑ First class mail ❑ UPS ground $5.00 first book, $1.00 each additional book
shipping outside of USA
   Please call 503 368 5584 for rates.   subtotal $ _____

MasterCard or VISA expires _____		shipping $ _____
card # _____		total $ _____
signature _____		

Elk Ridge Publishing
PO Box 633
Manzanita OR 97130
503 368 5584   FAX 503 368-5929

**Prompt service
money back guarantee**

Please send _____ **Graphically Speaking** book(s) at $29.50 each.

name _____

address _____

city, state _____

zip _____ phone _____

shipping within the USA
   ❏ First class mail ❏ UPS ground $5.00 first book, $1.00 each additional book
shipping outside of USA
   Please call 503 368 5584 for rates.

		subtotal	$ _____

MasterCard or VISA   expires _____   shipping $ _____

card # _____   total $ _____

signature _____

Elk Ridge Publishing
P O Box 633
Manzanita OR 97130   **Prompt service**
503 368 5584 FAX 503 368 5929   **money back guarantee**

Please send _____ **Graphically Speaking** book(s) at $29.50 each.

name _____

address _____

city, state _____

zip _____ phone _____

shipping within the USA
   ❏ First class mail ❏ UPS ground $5.00 first book, $1.00 each additional book
shipping outside of USA
   Please call 503 368 5584 for rates.

subtotal $ _____

MasterCard or VISA   expires _____   shipping $ _____

card # _____   total $ _____

signature _____

Elk Ridge Publishing
PO Box 633
Manzanita OR 97130   **Prompt service**
503 368 5584 FAX 503 368-5929   **money back guarantee**